Client Accounting
for the
Law Office

Paralegal Titles from Delmar Publishers

Legal Research, Steve Barber, Mark A. McCormick, 1996
Wills, Estates, and Trusts, Jay H. Gingrich, 1996
Criminal Law and Procedure, 2E, Daniel E. Hall, 1996
Introduction to Environmental Law, Harold Hickock, 1996
Civil Litigation, 2E, Peggy N. Kerley, Joanne Banker Hames, Paul A. Sukys, 1996
Client Accounting for the Law Office, Elaine M. Langston, 1996
Law Office Management, 2E, Jonathan S. Lynton, Terri Mick Lyndall, Donna Masinter, 1996
Foundations of Law: Cases, Commentary, and Ethics, 2E, Ransford C. Pyle, 1996
Administrative Law and Procedure, Elizabeth C. Richardson, 1996
Legal Research and Writing, David J. Smith, 1996

Legal Research and Writing, Carol M. Bast, 1995
Federal Taxation, Susan G. Covins, 1995
Everything You Need to Know About Being a Legal Assistant, Chere B. Estrin, 1995
Paralegals in New York Law, Eric M. Gansberg, 1995
Ballentine's Legal Dictionary and Thesaurus, Jonathan S. Lynton, 1995
Legal Terminology with Flashcards, Cathy J. Okrent, 1995
Wills, Trusts, and Estate Administration for Paralegals, Mark A. Stewart, 1995
The Law of Contracts and the Uniform Commercial Code, Pamela R. Tepper, 1995
Life Outside the Law Firm: Non-Traditional Careers for Paralegals, Karen Treffinger, 1995

An Introduction to Paralegal Studies, David G. Cooper, Michael J. Gibson, 1994
Administrative Law, Daniel E. Hall, 1994
Ballentine's Law Dictionary: Legal Assistant Edition, Jack G. Handler, 1994
The Law of Real Property, Michael P. Kearns, 1994
Ballentine's Thesaurus for Legal Research and Writing, Jonathan S. Lynton, 1994
Legal Ethics and Professional Responsibility, Jonathan S. Lynton, Terri Mick Lyndall, 1994
Criminal Law for Paralegals, Daniel J. Markey, Jr., Mary Queen Donnelly, 1994
Family Law, Ransford C. Pyle, 1994
Paralegals in American Law: Introduction to Paralegalism, Angela Schneeman, 1994
Intellectual Property, Richard Stim, 1994

Legal Writing for Paralegals, Steve Barber, 1993
Administration of Wills, Trusts, and Estates, Gordon W. Brown, 1993
Torts and Personal Injury Laws, William R. Buckley, 1993
Survey of Criminal Law, Daniel E. Hall, 1993
The Law of Corporations, Partnerships, and Sole Proprietorships, Angela Schneeman, 1993

Client Accounting
for the
Law Office

Elaine M. Langston

Delmar Publishers

I**T**P An International Thomson Publishing Company

Albany • Bonn • Boston • Cincinnati • Detroit • London • Madrid • Melbourne
Mexico City • New York • Pacific Grove • Paris • San Francisco • Singapore • Tokyo
Toronto • Washington

NOTICE TO THE READER

Background by Jennifer McGlaughlin
Design by Douglas J. Hyldelund

Delmar Staff

Acquisitions Editor: Christopher Anzalone
Developmental Editor: Jeffrey D. Litton
Project Editor: Eugenia L. Orlandi

Production Coordinator: Jennifer Gaines
Art & Design Coordinator: Douglas J. Hyldelund

Copyright © 1996
By Delmar Publishers
divisions of International Thompson Publishing Inc.

The ITP logo is a trademark under license.

Printed in the United States of America

For more information, contact:

Delmar Publishers
3 Columbia Circle
Box 15015
Albany, New York 12212-5015

International Thomson Editores
Campos Eliseos 385, Piso 7
Col Polanco
11560 Mexico D F Mexico

International Thomson Publishing Europe
Berkshire House 168 - 173
High Holborn
London WC1V 7AA
England

International Thomson Publishing GmbH
Königswinterer Strasse 418
53227 Bonn
Germany

Thomas Nelson Australia
102 Dodds Street
South Melbourne, 3205
Victoria, Australia

International Thomson Publishing Asia
221 Henderson Road
#05 - 10 Henderson Building
Sinapore 0315

Nelson Canada
1120 Birchmount Road
Scarborough, Ontario
Canada M1K 5G4

International Thomson Publishing - Japan
Hirakawacho Kyowa Building, 3F
2-2-1 Hirakawacho
Chiyoda-ku, Tokyo 102
Japan

1 2 3 4 5 6 7 8 9 10 xxx 01 00 99 98 97 96

Library of Congress Cataloging-in-Publication Data

Langston, Elaine M.
    Client accounting for the law office / Elaine M. Langston.
        p. cm.
    Includes bibliographical references and index.
    ISBN 0-8273-7443-7
    1. Practice of law—United States—Accounting. 2. Lawyers—United States—Fees—Accounting. I. Title
KF315.L35 1996
340'.068—dc20

95-24137
CIP

Delmar Publishers' Online Services

To access Delmar on the World Wide Web, point your browser to:
http://www.delmar.com/delmar.html
To access through Gopher: gopher://gopher.delmar.com
(Delmar Online is part of "thomson.com", an Internet site with information on
more than 30 publishers of the International Thomson Publishing organization.)
For more information on our products and services:
email: info@delmar.com
or call 800-347-7707

CONTENTS

▌▌▌▌ CHAPTER 3   Time Records   86

▌▌▌▌ CHAPTER 4   Disbursement Records   111

IIII APPENDICES   A-1

IIII Glossary   G-1

IIII Additional Materials and Resources   M-1

IIII Index   I-1

DELMAR PUBLISHERS INC.

 AND

LAWYERS COOPERATIVE PUBLISHING

ARE PLEASED TO ANNOUNCE THEIR PARTNERSHIP TO CO-PUBLISH COLLEGE TEXTBOOKS FOR PARALEGAL EDUCATION.

DELMAR, WITH OFFICES AT ALBANY, NEW YORK, IS A PROFESSIONAL EDUCATION PUBLISHER. DELMAR PUBLISHES QUALITY EDUCATIONAL TEXTBOOKS TO PREPARE AND SUPPORT INDIVIDUALS FOR LIFE SKILLS AND SPECIFIC OCCUPATIONS.

LAWYERS COOPERATIVE PUBLISHING (LCP), WITH OFFICES AT ROCHESTER, NEW YORK, HAS BEEN THE LEADING PUBLISHER OF ANALYTICAL LEGAL INFORMATION FOR OVER 100 YEARS. IT IS THE PUBLISHER OF SUCH RENOWNED LEGAL ENCYCLOPEDIAS AS **AMERICAN LAW REPORTS, AMERICAN JURISPRUDENCE, UNITED STATES CODE SERVICE, LAWYERS EDITION,** AS WELL AS OTHER MATERIAL, AND FEDERAL- AND STATE-SPECIFIC PUBLICATIONS. THESE PUBLICATIONS HAVE BEEN DESIGNED TO WORK TOGETHER IN THE DAY-TO-DAY PRACTICE OF LAW AS AN INTEGRATED SYSTEM IN WHAT IS CALLED THE "TOTAL CLIENT-SERVICE LIBRARY® (TCSL®). EACH LCP PUBLICATION IS COMPLETE WITHIN ITSELF AS TO SUBJECT COVERAGE. YET ALL HAVE COMMON FEATURES AND EXTENSIVE CROSS-REFERENCING TO PROVIDE LINKAGE FOR HIGHLY EFFICIENT LEGAL RESEARCH INTO VIRTUALLY ANY MATTER AN ATTORNEY MIGHT BE CALLED UPON TO HANDLE.

INFORMATION IN ALL PUBLICATIONS IS CAREFULLY AND CONSTANTLY MONITORED TO KEEP PACE WITH AND REFLECT EVENTS IN THE LAW AND IN SOCIETY. UPDATING AND SUPPLEMENTAL INFORMATION IS TIMELY AND PROVIDED CONVENIENTLY.

FOR FURTHER REFERENCE, SEE:

AMERICAN JURISPRUDENCE 2D: AN ENCYCLOPEDIC TEXT COVERAGE OF THE COMPLETE BODY OF STATE AND FEDERAL LAW.

AM JUR LEGAL FORMS 2D: A COMPILATION OF BUSINESS AND LEGAL FORMS DEALING WITH A VARIETY OF SUBJECT MATTERS.

AM JUR PLEADING AND PRACTICE FORMS, REV: MODEL PRACTICE FORMS FOR EVERY STAGE OF A LEGAL PROCEEDING.

AM JUR PROOF OF FACTS: A SERIES OF ARTICLES THAT GUIDE THE READER IN DETERMINING WHICH FACTS ARE ESSENTIAL TO A CASE AND HOW TO PROVE THEM.

AM JUR TRIALS: A SERIES OF ARTICLES DISCUSSING EVERY ASPECT OF PARTICULAR SETTLEMENTS AND TRIALS WRITTEN BY 180 CONSULTING SPECIALISTS.

UNITED STATES CODE SERVICE: A COMPLETE AND AUTHORITATIVE ANNOTATED FEDERAL CODE THAT FOLLOWS THE EXACT LANGUAGE OF THE STATUTES AT LARGE AND DIRECTS YOU TO THE COURT AND AGENCY DECISIONS CONSTRUING EACH PROVISION.

ALR AND ALR FEDERAL: SERIES OF ANNOTATIONS PROVIDING IN-DEPTH ANALYSES OF ALL THE CASE LAW ON PARTICULAR LEGAL ISSUES.

U.S. SUPREME COURT REPORTS, L ED 2D: EVERY REPORTED U.S. SUPREME COURT DECISION PLUS IN-DEPTH DISCUSSIONS OF LEADING ISSUES.

FEDERAL PROCEDURE, L ED: A COMPREHENSIVE, A-Z TREATISE ON FEDERAL PROCEDURE—CIVIL, CRIMINAL, AND ADMINISTRATIVE.

FEDERAL PROCEDURAL FORMS, L ED: STEP-BY-STEP GUIDANCE FOR DRAFTING FORMS FOR FEDERAL COURT OR FEDERAL AGENCY PROCEEDINGS.

FEDERAL RULES SERVICE, 2D AND 3D: REPORTS DECISIONS FROM ALL LEVELS OF THE FEDERAL SYSTEM INTERPRETING THE FEDERAL RULES OF CIVIL PROCEDURE AND THE FEDERAL RULES OF APPELLATE PROCEDURE.

FEDERAL RULES DIGEST, 3D: ORGANIZES HEADNOTES FOR THE DECISIONS REPORTED IN FEDERAL RULES SERVICE ACCORDING TO THE NUMBERING SYSTEMS OF THE FEDERAL RULES OF CIVIL PROCEDURE AND THE FEDERAL RULES OF APPELLATE PROCEDURE.

FEDERAL RULES OF EVIDENCE SERVICE: REPORTS DECISIONS FROM ALL LEVELS OF THE FEDERAL SYSTEM INTERPRETING THE FEDERAL RULES OF EVIDENCE.

FEDERAL RULES OF EVIDENCE NEWS

FEDERAL PROCEDURE RULES SERVICE

FEDERAL TRIAL HANDBOOK, 2D

FORM DRAFTING CHECKLISTS: AM JUR PRACTICE GUIDE

GOVERNMENT CONTRACTS: PROCEDURES AND FORMS

HOW TO GO DIRECTLY INTO YOUR OWN COMPUTERIZED SOLO PRACTICE WITHOUT MISSING A MEAL (OR A BYTE)

JONES ON EVIDENCE, CIVIL AND CRIMINAL, 7TH

LITIGATION CHECKLISTS: AM JUR PRACTICE GUIDE

MEDICAL LIBRARY, LAWYERS EDITION

MEDICAL MALPRACTICE—ALR CASES AND ANNOTATIONS

MODERN APPELLATE PRACTICE: FEDERAL AND STATE CIVIL APPEALS

MODERN CONSTITUTIONAL LAW

NEGOTIATION AND SETTLEMENT

PATTERN DEPOSITION CHECKLISTS, 2D

QUALITY OF LIFE DAMAGES: CRITICAL ISSUES AND PROOFS

SHEPARD'S CITATIONS FOR ALR

SUCCESSFUL TECHNIQUES FOR CIVIL TRIALS, 2D

STORIES ET CETERA—A COUNTRY LAWYER LOOKS AT LIFE AND THE LAW

SUMMARY OF AMERICAN LAW

THE TRIAL LAWYER'S BOOK: PREPARING AND WINNING CASES

TRIAL PRACTICE CHECKLISTS

2000 CLASSIC LEGAL QUOTATIONS

WILLISTON ON CONTRACTS, 3D AND 4TH

FEDERAL RULES OF EVIDENCE DIGEST: ORGANIZES HEADNOTES FOR THE DECISIONS REPORTED IN FEDERAL RULES OF EVIDENCE SERVICE ACCORDING TO THE NUMBERING SYSTEM OF THE FEDERAL RULES OF EVIDENCE.

ADMINISTRATIVE LAW: PRACTICE AND PROCEDURE

AGE DISCRIMINATION: CRITICAL ISSUES AND PROOFS

ALR CRITICAL ISSUES: DRUNK DRIVING PROSECUTIONS

ALR CRITICAL ISSUES: FREEDOM OF INFORMATION ACTS

ALR CRITICAL ISSUES: TRADEMARKS

ALR CRITICAL ISSUES: WRONGFUL DEATH

AMERICANS WITH DISABILITIES: PRACTICE AND COMPLIANCE MANUAL

ATTORNEYS' FEES

BALLENTINE'S LAW DICTIONARY

CONSTITUTIONAL LAW DESKBOOK

CONSUMER AND BORROWER PROTECTION: AM JUR PRACTICE GUIDE

CONSUMER CREDIT: ALR ANNOTATIONS

DAMAGES: ALR ANNOTATIONS

EMPLOYEE DISMISSAL: CRITICAL ISSUES AND PROOFS

ENVIRONMENTAL LAW: ALR ANNOTATIONS

EXPERT WITNESS CHECKLISTS

EXPERT WITNESSES IN CIVIL TRIALS

FORFEITURES: ALR ANNOTATIONS

FEDERAL LOCAL COURT RULES

FEDERAL LOCAL COURT FORMS

FEDERAL CRIMINAL LAW AND PROCEDURE: ALR ANNOTATIONS

FEDERAL EVIDENCE

FEDERAL LITIGATION DESK SET: FORMS AND ANALYSIS

PREFACE

Readers who take the time for this preface will gain a useful appreciation of the logic and utility of the text and immediately know better how best to utilize it for maximum benefit. Many readers will not read a preface, though it is the author's opportunity to emphasize important features of the book and explain the purpose of material that might otherwise appear enigmatic.

Scope

Law office accounting is a complex and demanding area. Neither general accounting knowledge nor clerical law office experience alone will permit a new staff member to enter a law firm and work effectively with the accounting system from the first day. This book is designed to provide the specialized knowledge all law firm personnel must have to use accounting information in their daily work.

Not every reader will get the same type of benefits from this book, nor will all educators see the same values. For most formal learning situations, there is more than enough material to justify a rigorous thirty-hour credit course and lab time. With careful planning a well-prepared class can cover the core material in eighteen hours. Regardless of the formal time assigned to study and discussion, the major benefits of this book may accrue to readers after they complete the course. The level of a particular staff member's responsibilities and interests in accounting functions usually varies, with substantial expertise required in one area, but only basic knowledge in another. Most readers will find far more here than they need immediately, but will be able to expand their knowledge as required.

With this combination textbook, desk book, reference, and "helpful hints" guide in hand, anyone who works in a law office will find a choice of approaches to various subjects, from simple explanation of a process within the law office, to several examples of how that process is different in other firms, to some commonly encountered problems and possible solutions, to ways to prevent such problems.

There is no substitute for solid technical skills in any job, but to really excel in law office accounting workers need to integrate every technical step with the purpose behind it. This integration is impossible without an appreciation for the support aspect of accounting. Certain behavior-related illustrations might seem at first glance to be unsuitable for an "accounting book," but experienced managers know the difference a positive attitude makes not only in the office environment but also in objectively measurable performance. Attitude is important enough to merit attention in even the most minimal coverage of this material.

Language

Those who like certainty may object to the frequent use of generalizations and qualifiers, but words like many, most, usually, sometimes, and often all have real meaning in English and are not simply ways for an author to hedge. Qualifiers indicate to the reader that matters are not always thus, but no one should be surprised if such is encountered in real life. The nature of some of the material is that it reflects certain rules and standards that are not optional, and readers must be able to distinguish these from things that often are, but do not necessarily have to be, so.

Many terms used in general conversation have specific meanings in the context of accounting and/or the law office. Clear and authoritative communication in law offices depends in part on the mastery of these terms. When a particular term is first introduced as a key term, it is defined at the bottom of the page. The term may have been used before in an example, but it is defined where it is first used as essential to the discussion. The Glossary provides the same definition. Terms that correspond to *Ballentine's Legal Dictionary and Thesaurus* (Delmar/LCP, 1995) are indicated by a dagger (†).

Features

Examples in the main text are used to clarify points that may be difficult to understand without reference to a realistic situation. They are not necessarily the most commonly encountered situations nor even typical ones. They were chosen because they are straightforward and have few confusing incidental factors.

Figure illustrations were designed with the same criteria in mind. The fictitious law firm of Carpenter & Cook, Attorneys at Law, is used to provide consistency in figures that illustrate progressive steps in an accounting function. This firm is introduced in the memorandum preceding the text and is also used in some exercises.

Some readers may question the concentration on manual systems, believing that they are no longer used (they are), or at least will not be around much longer. Understanding manual systems is important because in a formal learning setting, they must be mastered before investigating any automated system. While there may be great variety in law office accounting software packages, they all basically emulate manual systems, and understanding different software packages is easier if each is compared to the manual system, *instead of to another software package.*

Practical applications enhance the reader's ability to apply material learned to realistic situations. They are not entirely fictitious. Clients, colleagues, and class participants contributed many of the central ideas behind them. Although there is no single right answer for any question, and some answers are better than others, the most important function of the questions is to promote an appreciation of the range of options available to solve real problems in the workplace. The practical applications do not relate to the firm of Carpenter & Cook, as they depict situations in firms of different sizes and compositions.

Cases are real, although necessarily summarized to reflect the accounting-related professional issues addressed by lawyer-litigants and the courts. In almost all examples, the issues surrounding disciplinary action go beyond mere accounting, but in each case accounting concerns contributed significantly to the material facts and/or judgment. The added emphasis in boldfaced type refers to the most important point in the case from the perspective of the related discussion, not the most important judicial points. Cases are reasonably current, but they have not been investigated as to their present status or jurisdictional authority and should not be given any weight in making real life decisions. Unlike cases in substantive law texts, almost all cases in this book deal with lawyers' disciplinary issues, so the names and jurisdictions have been omitted as not being sufficiently important to be in the main text. The Table of Cases gives the citation and name for anyone who wishes to further investigate a case.

Comprehensive exercises at the end of each chapter will be helpful to all readers, not just those who have been assigned them for grading purposes. Exercises that include designing checklists can be used not only by students as a thorough review of the chapter but also by anyone in a law office who wants clarification about who does what and how and why in the accounting department.

The ABA Model Rules of Professional Conduct illustrate the basic legislation and regulations found in most states. The reader should investigate state legislation and related enactments when faced with actual problems or questions.

Included software allows interested readers to explore a limited-use copy of a real product available on the market.

The instructor's guide contains curriculum samples, lesson plans, discussion overhead masters, suggested responses to questions, discussion topics for cases, and a test bank.

ACKNOWLEDGMENTS

I thank my family and friends who consistently supported me in the incredibly involved process of taking the idea for this book and doing what I had to do to produce the finished product. In particular, I thank my brother Roy Langston for his editorial guidance and encouragement, my Seattle ally Douglas Gold CPA, Brenda Hersh CMA, and Phillip Sherring.

I also thank the following reviewers, whose comments were invaluable:

Jean Morton
College of Legal Arts
Portland, OR

Cheryl Kirschner
Bentley College
Newton, MA

Arnold Cirtin
Ball State University
Muncie, IN

Anthony Piazza
Dyke College
Cleveland, OH

Marcia Chaifetz
Bryant and Stratton Business Institute
Albany, NY

Diane Koble
Fresno City College
Fresno, CA

Susan Demers
St. Petersburg Jr. College
Clearwater, FL

TABLE OF CASES

Welcome to the Firm of Carpenter & Cook

Carpenter & Cook

MEMORANDUM

TO: Robin Butler
FROM: Marty Fisher, Administrator
DATE: January 4, 1999
RE: Employment

I am very pleased to welcome you to the firm of Carpenter & Cook. As you know, I will be leaving in a few weeks for a year of traveling. To support your orientation phase, I have prepared some basic background of the firm and its personnel, as well as an outline of your duties.

C&C, as we call ourselves, is a general practice formed last September 1 by a merger of the practices of Pat Carpenter, the senior and managing partner, and Sandy Cook. Terry Baker is the only employee-associate; Lee Mason is a semi-retired independent lawyer who is of counsel to the firm. Everyone in the firm is on a first-name basis, and we pride ourselves in our reputation for being professional and cordial with everyone in the community.

Paralegal Kim Gardener and senior secretary Dale Miller work most closely with Pat and Terry (Pat's "team"). Senior secretary Chris Weaver and junior secretary and receptionist Leslie Steward work most closely with Sandy and Lee (Sandy's "team").

You will be assuming my combined role of paralegal (with Sandy's team), legal administrator, and accountant. The paralegal work will consume about half of your time.

Pat is familiar with much of the administration, and Sandy's team will help with the paralegal work, so you will have lots of support in those areas. I am most anxious to spend time with you on the accounting side of things, as you will be much on your own in that area. Also, we did not have time when the firm was first formed to acquire and establish a proper computerized accounting system; that will be your job, I believe. We did at least set up a coding system that should be compatible with most software, so people are getting used to that way of doing things.

Staff meetings are held during business hours as topics arise, but not usually less frequently than twice per month. On the second Friday of each month, we have an in-house gathering from 4:00 p.m. on. This is purely social and is optional, but we encourage everyone to attend if possible.

I am acquainted with your accounting training program and know that you are well-prepared for this position. However, every law firm has its own special way of doing things, and I invite you to ask any questions you need to ask. Everyone in the office realizes that there is no such thing as a silly question. Serious problems can occur when questions are not asked. If you have any concerns about information you receive, or you do not receive adequate answers when you ask, be sure to take it up with me or one of the partners.

We all look forward to seeing you Monday morning.

Regards

||||

CHAPTER 1

ACCOUNTING FUNDAMENTALS

In business organizations like law firms, accounting is one of the most important support functions. It not only tells managers where the organization has been, but also can help predict where it is going and where it should go. The sole purpose of accounting is to provide information, and the sole purpose of information is to help people make decisions. Sometimes a law firm's accounting information is used by people outside the firm, and the decision is whether or not the firm meets the strict standards of professional responsibility lawyers must observe.

Case 1–1   Found: Lawyer's conduct included: entering into business agreement with client, **failing to maintain contemporaneous books and records sufficient to demonstrate compliance with disciplinary rules, false certification to court that such records are maintained,** and commingling of funds.

Ordered: Public reprimand and probation for three years.

Many beginning students of accounting are surprised to find that accounting is a dynamic process, far removed from the stereotype of a tedious and costly inconvenience that requires adherence to arbitrary rules and that simply records historical data and contributes little to "real" business. This awareness is essential, because the true value of accounting is lost unless its potential benefits are recognized and maximized by people who prepare accounting information and by people who use it to make decisions.

Until recently, only accounting specialists within law offices recorded lawyers' time, produced bills, processed client payments, and provided records of trust transactions. Technological advancements and changing staff configurations in law firms now encourage a movement away from centralized accounting departments to more distributed duties, and these new responsibilities mean that nonaccounting personnel need to understand basic accounting. Everyone in the firm who is responsible for any part of the accounting function or who needs to use accounting information, in other words, everyone in the firm, will benefit from exposure not only to simple bookkeeping procedures, but also to accounting theory, objectives, and some guiding principles accountants use when preparing information.

Elements of Accounting Information

There are many steps in the accounting process. Accountants spend years studying how these steps can be used to produce two main types of information from raw data:

- **Financial information** is the basis for preparing financial statements, tax returns, and reports to governments, banks, and others who have a legitimate interest in the finances of the firm. **Financial statements** are standardized presentations of the activity and position of the firm. The **balance sheet** shows the firm's financial *position* at a given point in time, usually the end of a month or year. The **income statement** summarizes the firm's income-earning *activity* (financial performance) during a given period.

- **Management information** provides supplementary schedules and reports for making the decisions that affect the direction and future of the firm: how it will be managed, changes that are needed, and even staff remuneration and advancement. Management information is used primarily inside the firm, although some reports are submitted to banks to support credit arrangements.

Most financial data can be verified outside the firm through financial (monetary) transactions or is subject to rules and conventions that reduce the possibility of misinterpretation. It is mostly historical, reflecting events that have already happened (a client paid a bill) or that people have agreed will happen (a client has been sent a bill and is expected to pay it).

Most management data is also historical, although not necessarily based on monetary transactions. The finer level of detail and flexibility in presenting the resulting information allows managers to determine trends and identify problems earlier than they could using financial information alone. Much of the data used for compiling management information is generated internally, however, and cannot be verified by external references, so accuracy in recording and processing this type of data is essential.

TERMS

financial information Data related to the economic monetary events in an organization accumulated and classified to support decisions.

financial statement A financial report in accepted form; balance sheet, income statement, statement of retained earnings, cash statement.

balance sheet A classified list of assets, liabilities, and equity showing the financial situation of an organization at a specified point in time.

income statement A classified list of revenues, direct costs against revenues, operating expenses, and gains and losses showing the financial activity during a specified period.

management information Data related to all economic events in an organization accumulated and classified to support decisions.

The Accounting Entity

Business accounting assumes that a particular set of transactions constitutes the activities of a specific **economic entity**, which also usually has a separate legal identity. For accounting purposes, law firms are one of the following:

- a **personal service corporation** (one or more lawyer-shareholders),
- a **proprietorship** (one lawyer-owner), or
- a **partnership** (several lawyer-owners).

Accounting *could* be performed for three different components in each law firm:

1. *The professional practice,* which is responsible for all client-related transactions. Accounting functions are time and disbursement recording, client billings and accounts receivable, and trust accounting.

2. *The administrative operation,* which manages the business organization side of the practice such as employee and supplier relations, business investments, acquisition of operating assets, and office maintenance. Accounting functions relate mostly to managing overhead expenses. Sometimes a separate management company supervises all of these responsibilities for a fee charged to the professional practice.

3. *The equity,* which may be held by individual lawyers or law corporations, among whom income is allocated at least annually for tax purposes. True equity holders are persons (natural or corporate) that are entitled to make decisions (vote) regarding the management of the practice. In law firms, the *owners* are generally lawyers, although some jurisdictions allow a limited type of nonvoting "ownership" by other individuals. Accounting functions relate to capital requirements and transactions and to income measurement and division.

In traditional law practices, these three accounting components are combined into *the firm,* but changes in both tax and legal professions

---
TERMS
---

economic entity   A separately identifiable unit of material activity and substance.

personal service corporation   An incorporated limited-liability business organization whose purpose is to increase the wealth of its shareholders through the provision of professional services to the public.

proprietorship   An unincorporated unlimited-liability business organization whose purpose is to increase the wealth of a sole professional practitioner-owner through the provision of professional services to the public.

partnership   An unincorporated unlimited-liability business organization whose purpose is to increase the wealth of two or more professional practitioner-owners through the provision of professional services to the public.

legislation encourage many firms to legally separate these entities. This book deals mostly with accounting for the professional practice, although effects on other parts of the firm are addressed as necessary.

The entity concept has special meaning in law firms. Because of the high degree of confidence that clients place in lawyers, lawyers often have access to the client's property, the handling of which is discussed in depth in Chapter 7. The lawyer's duty to the **client** and others requires that the records and substance of the property entrusted to the lawyer *be at all times* kept separate from the firm's property. Failure to do so is referred to as **commingling**, the simple fact and detection of which can lead to disciplinary action. If commingling results in a loss to a client, a professional **malpractice** suit also can result.

Case 1–2

Found: Lawyer made false statements and failed to reveal information to the state bar; **failed to place funds of a client in a bank account; commingled funds; failed to maintain complete records of the handling, maintenance, and disposition of a client's funds;** failed to deliver the funds to the client promptly when requested; and converted funds of client.

Ordered: Suspension for one year.

Balance Sheet Elements

The balance sheet is a categorized division of the **accounting equation**, which is:

$$\text{Assets} - \text{liabilities} = \text{equity}$$
$$\text{or}$$
$$\text{Assets} = \text{liabilities} + \text{equity}$$

Many accountants prefer the first equation, because it reflects the inherent *residual* nature of equity.

Formerly, balance sheets were presented with the assets on the left and liabilities and equity on the right. Now most balance sheets display comparative information from prior years, which would be crowded in

---

TERMS

client A consumer of legal services provided by a law firm, whether or not compensated.

commingling† The act of an agent, broker, attorney, or trustee in mingling his own property with that of his client, customer, or beneficiary.

malpractice† The failure of a professional person to act with reasonable care; misconduct by a professional person in the course of engaging in his profession.

accounting equation Assets – liabilities = equity.

the traditional form, so the parts follow in sequence, as illustrated in Figure 1–1. The **balance sheet equation** is:

$$\text{Assets} = \text{liabilities} + \text{equity}$$

Assets are tangible and intangible resources owned by the firm or under its control, such as:

- petty cash,

- money in bank accounts,

- **bills** rendered to clients but not yet paid (accounts receivable),

- unbilled legal services,

- unbilled **disbursements** (advanced on behalf of clients),

- office furniture and equipment, and

- goodwill and deferred charges (seldom of concern to law office staff).

The first five are commonly encountered by both accounting and nonaccounting staff in law firms. Unbilled services (time) and disbursements are referred to as **WIP (*work-in-process*)**.

In order to qualify as assets, resources must provide probable future economic benefit. An irreparably broken piece of equipment is not an asset except to the extent of its scrap value. A bill to a client is not an asset unless payment can reasonably be expected.

Liabilities are amounts owed to other parties including:

- suppliers,

- lending institutions,

- taxation authorities, and

- employees.

Liabilities are legal obligations to pay specified amounts, although some kinds of liabilities are traditionally recorded as estimates.

TERMS
---

balance sheet equation   Assets = liabilities + equity.

asset   Tangible property and intangible rights to resources under the control of an entity, which arise from the economic activity of the entity and provide ultimate future benefits to owners.

bill   A statement submitted to a client or other party detailing the obligation to the firm for services rendered and/or costs incurred in a legal representation.

disbursement   Payment for an item or service by the firm on behalf of the client.

work-in-process (WIP)   Legal services already rendered, and disbursements already incurred by the firm, but not yet billed to the client.

liabilities   Obligations to pay a specific amount to a person or entity.

FIGURE 1–1

Balance Sheet:
Accrual Method

Carpenter & Cook

BALANCE SHEET
December 31, 1998

Current Assets		
Petty Cash	$ 100	
General Bank Account	9,746	
Accounts Receivable	35,836	
Unbilled Disbursements	7,793	
Prepaid Expenses	7,260	
		$60,735
Fixed Assets		
Furniture	7,500	
Computers	20,100	
		27,600
Total Assets		$88,335
Liabilities		
Computer Loan	10,000	
Payroll Taxes Payable	5,261	
Sales Tax Payable	1,917	
Accounts Payable	6,715	
		23,893
Equity		
Contributions		
- P Carpenter	36,500	
Less: Drawings	12,000	
		24,500
Contributions		
- S Cook	29,000	
Less: Drawings	12,000	
		17,000
Current Period Income		
(Unallocated)		22,942
Total Liabilities		
and Equity		$88,335

This is a copy of the draft balance sheet that the partners wanted me to prepare on a modified accrual basis. M.

Equity is the amount that the owners invest in a business entity or the right to the *residual value* of the business. If all of the assets were sold and all of the liabilities satisfied, the remainder would be available to the owner. Sources of equity in proprietorships and partnerships include:

- initial or periodic cash contributions from owners;

- owners' contributions of personal assets (property), such as furniture and books;

- owners' share of allocated earnings that have not been paid to the owner; and

- unallocated (current period) income.

In corporations, an amount, sometimes nominal, is specified as **capital stock.** It must remain in the corporation as long as the shareholder has an ownership interest. Income that has been subject to income tax but is not yet designated to be paid out as dividends is **retained earnings.** Dividends that have been declared but not paid are liabilities of the firm to the shareholders. Personal service corporations like law corporations pay the bulk of their income out to lawyer-shareholders as employment income because of strong tax disincentives to pay dividends or keep retained earnings within the firm.

Income Statement Elements

The **income statement equation** is:

$$\text{Revenue} - \text{expenses} = \text{income}$$

Theoretically, the income statement, formerly called the profit and loss statement, need not exist because all of the activity summarized in it is really a constituent of the period's earnings as accumulated in the equity portion of the balance sheet. Since revenues are increases in assets and expenses are depletions of assets, all revenue and expenses could simply be recorded in one place. This method would not be useful for most organizations, however, because it provides little information about the firm's operations. Figure 1–2 illustrates an income statement.

TERMS

equity   The remaining value of an entity's assets after all obligations are met; net worth.

capital stock   An amount of equity an owner is required to maintain in a corporation to secure a specific portion of ownership.

retained earnings   The balance of income earned in all previous accounting periods that has not been distributed to owners as dividends.

income statement equation   Revenue – expenses = income.

FIGURE 1–2

Income
Statement:
Accrual Method

Carpenter & Cook

INCOME STATEMENT
Four months to December 31, 1998

Revenue		
Fees Billed	$125,416	
Disbursement Recovery	11,219	
Other Revenue	912	
		$137,547
Direct Costs		
Associates' Salaries	21,400	
Associated Counsel Fees	15,455	
		36,855
Expenses		
Staff Salaries	45,867	
Rent	6,800	
Equipment Rental	4,738	
Telephone	3,794	
Stationery and Supplies	1,524	
General Office Expense	2,385	
Library and Subscriptions	2,702	
Professional Dues and Memberships	4,504	
Promotion	3,850	
Accounting	520	
Bank Service Charges	90	
Interest Charges	278	
Bad Debts	698	
		77,750
Net Income		$22,942

This is the draft income statement that corresponds to the accrual balance sheet. M.

Nonaccountants tend to use the terms *revenue, income, profit, earnings,* and even *gains* interchangeably. This may be acceptable in general conversation, but accountants attach strict definitions to these terms:

- **Revenues** are increases in the assets of a firm resulting from its normal operation (providing legal services) and certain other sources such as interest on its investments.

--------------------------------------- TERMS ---------------------------------------

revenue   Increases in the assets of a business resulting from its normal operation and certain other sources.

- **Income** generally means net income of the firm or the excess of total revenues over total expenses. It also refers to an individual's remuneration from business or employment.

- **Profit** may mean net income of the firm, but it is more often used to describe the excess of regular business revenues over their *related* costs. A law firm that realizes a large gain on the sale of its office building but loses money on providing legal services is not "profitable," even if the year's net income is positive, because a law firm's business is not property speculation.

- **Earnings** may also mean net income but more often refer to individual partners' shares of the firm's net income.

- **Gains** usually refer to value received in excess of the recorded ("book") value on the disposition of assets, such as the sale of a photocopier for more than its net (depreciated) value on the balance sheet. Gains are unrelated to the main activity of the firm, that is, providing legal services, and are nonrecurring and unanticipated.

Expenses are decreases in assets incurred in supporting normal business activity. They are distinct from **losses**, which arise from nonrecurring and unanticipated decreases in assets. **Net loss** is the equivalent of negative net income.

Accounting Conventions

For accounting information to be valuable, it must be compiled and communicated within a framework that is both consistent and easily understood. If business organizations did not have a uniform structure

---

TERMS

income   The excess of total revenues over total expenses.

profit   The excess of regular business revenues over their related costs.

earnings   An individual owner's share of net income.

gains   Nonrecurring and unanticipated value received in excess of the recorded value on the disposition of assets; increases in resources unrelated to the main activity of the firm.

expenses   Decreases in assets incurred in supporting or incidental to normal business activity.

loss   Nonrecurring and unanticipated decrease in assets.

net loss   Equivalent to negative net income.

for understanding accounting, information within and between organizations would not be comparable or useful.

Even nonaccounting personnel should be aware that there are a number of guidelines for deciding how to compile and present accounting information. They exist for very good reasons and in general are followed by law firms.

Principles and Concepts

Accounting principles provide guidance in recording transactions and making adjustments. Once data is received, procedures and controls help to ensure that it is recorded promptly, correctly, and completely. There are also *concepts* and *assumptions* that help people make decisions when questions arise about how to record or report accounting information.

The **going-concern concept** assumes that the entity being accounted for has an indefinite life; that is, it is not being sold, and the owners anticipate that it will continue into the foreseeable future.

Except under unusual circumstances, law firms follow the **stable-dollar assumption** that a dollar today is worth the same as a dollar yesterday. There are no accounting adjustments for the effects of inflation or for changing relative values of items.

Periodicity is a convention that divides accounting information into periods so it can be collected and summarized regularly. Law firms generally summarize and "close" some records (books) on a monthly basis, and other records, such as those relating to income tax, on an annual basis. Quarterly summary periods are required by some taxation authorities. Separation of economic activity into these periods is quite arbitrary and can cause confusion if supplementary information about prior time periods, and educated projections about future ones, are not included where necessary.

——————————————————— TERMS ———————————————————

accounting principle   Rules and guidelines that promote accuracy and consistency of financial information.

going-concern concept   The assumption that an entity will continue in its current enterprise into the indefinite future.

stable-dollar assumption   The assumption that the value of a dollar is constant over time.

periodicity   The somewhat arbitrary division of accounting information into periods.

**Practical
Application
1–1**

Mr. Finch: I don't think the accounting really reflects how much money we're making. It seems that if we get a big settlement in one month, or have to pay a big invoice, our numbers are way out of whack. I can't see why we don't take all of the year-to-date figures and divide them by the number of months since the beginning of the year to get our average monthly figures. That's really more important than what happens to occur in a given month.

Why does Mr. Finch think the "numbers are way out of whack"? What accounting principles are being applied? What other information would help Mr. Finch better understand his accounting reports?

Although all accounting principles are important, the most significant in day-to-day law office accounting are:

- **Matching.** Recorded expenses should relate to the revenues they help produce. For example, rent paid in advance for a subsequent month should not be recorded as an expense in the current month. Also, recorded revenues should relate to the expenses used to produce them.

- **Materiality.** Taking the trouble to ensure that each and every small amount is recorded precisely may cost more than the added worth of absolutely perfect information. Data is often received after information is needed to make a decision and outdated perfect information may be valueless. Timely information of reasonable accuracy is often of great value.

- **Consistency.** Recording methods must be consistent from one period to the next if comparative information is used to make a decision. For example, if WIP time is recorded in the general ledger in one month and not the next, the two months cannot be compared to make a decision, such as financing requirements, based on revenue or asset growth.

Any reports sent to external parties such as lenders usually must conform to additional principles including, but not limited to:

TERMS

matching principle   The recording of corresponding revenues and expenses in the same accounting period.

materiality principle   Disregarding negligible differences and transactions as being not worth recording.

consistency principle   Congruity of accounting applications between accounting periods.

- **Cost.** Transactions are recorded at the value of money exchanged or, if there is no exchange of money, at the best possible estimate of the market value. From the time they are recorded, the value does not change. Some assets may be worth more in the hands of the firm than they cost, but they are nonetheless recorded at the price the firm paid for them.

- **Objectivity.** Consistent with the cost and stable-dollar principles is objectivity. Using the dollar as a unit of measure removes the requirement for accounting staff to judge the actual "value" of a transaction.

- **Conservatism.** Where matters of judgment arise, the guiding principle is that net income and asset values should be shown at the most conservative (lowest) value.

- **Revenue recognition.** The stage in the accounting process at which *revenue* is *recognized* (recorded as being earned in the accounting sense) is the point when *all* of the following have occurred:

  - The value (price) of the revenue is determinable.

  - The transaction is essentially complete.

  - The costs related to the revenue are known or can be reasonably estimated.

If a principle has been accepted by professional accounting bodies, broadly within industry or business sectors, and/or in authoritative accounting literature, it is referred to as a "generally accepted accounting principle," collectively referred to by accountants as **GAAP (*g*enerally *a*ccepted *a*ccounting *p*rinciples).**

The application of any accounting principle or concept will necessarily be imperfect because there will always be a compromise between competing advantages. For example, the strictest application of the objectivity principle may be compromised by the strictest application of

--- TERMS ---

cost principle   The true value of financial transactions is reflected by the actual number of dollars exchanged in the transaction.

objectivity principle   Dollars exchanged in a financial transaction is the best measurement of the value of the transaction.

conservatism principle   Where there is a question of the true value, the value reflecting the lowest reasonable value for assets and income.

revenue recognition principle   Revenue is recorded in the financial data when the transaction is complete, the value is determinable, and the related costs can be matched.

generally accepted accounting principles (GAAP)   The set of principles adopted by professional accounting bodies, industry, government, and educators providing guidelines for the preparation of financial information.

the materiality or conservatism principles. Sometimes the most important determining factors are timeliness and simplicity, and the choice of primary principles depends on the particular use of information.

Opal: Sometimes the partners disagree about who gets how much equity. It doesn't matter because the firm will just go on and on, and they will never have to worry about how much they would get if the firm discontinued business. I thought the going-concern concept meant that you don't worry about closing down. The partners should be more concerned with profits than with equity.

How are profits and equity related? Why would equity be important to partners?

One of the aspects of accounting systems that governs which principles are primary and which are secondary is the accounting method. There are really only two theoretically consistent methods: the accrual method and the cash method. A number of hybrid methods are used in practice, especially when a method must be adapted to conform to income tax or other regulations.

The Accrual Method

The **accrual method** is a "complete" accounting method in that it takes into consideration all of the identifiable money-related transactions of the firm, whether or not any money has yet changed hands. It provides financial and management information consistent with each other. The balance sheet illustrated in Figure 1–1 is prepared using the accrual method.

Basically, accrual accounting recognizes revenue when it is *earned,* and expenses when they are *incurred,* and the balance sheet displays a full range of assets and liabilities. The concepts and principles that are maximized by accrual methods are the going-concern concept, the matching principle, and the consistency principle.

There are limited instances in which the accrual method is not *permitted* as a tax reporting method for law firms under federal or state legislation. This method is rarely used unless required because it results in earlier payment of taxes in profitable and growing businesses.

TERMS

accrual method   A system of preparing financial information that reflects all identifiable economic transactions as they occur.

The Cash Method

As can be inferred from the name, the **cash method** relies upon the cash (or bank) account as the primary source of accounting data. Although generally inferior to the accrual method in the value of information that it can provide, cash method accounting supplemented by schedules and reports can provide most required information.

Because it uses only cash, this method recognizes revenue when it is *received* and expenses when they are *paid,* and so requires fewer balance sheet accounts. Accounts receivable and many other assets are not recorded until they are converted to cash. Accounts payable, sales taxes payable, salaries payable, and bank loans are not recorded until the liability is satisfied from the bank account. The cash method maximizes the stable-dollar assumption and the materiality, cost, and objectivity principles. Figure 1–3 illustrates the balance sheet and income statement in Figures 1–1 and 1–2 as they would appear using the cash method.

The major weakness of the cash method is that it does not conform to the entity concept, except in cash-based businesses. In law firms, "revenue" figures reflect the ability or inclination of clients to pay, not the firm's performance. Similarly, "expense" figures represent management decisions about whom to pay and for what and when, not the firm's true cost of doing business.

Despite its deficiencies as an information tool, the cash method is very popular because it confers the advantages of some tax deferrals. State and federal legislation may restrict the application of the cash method for certain types of organizations, but most law firms can and do use the cash method.

Practical Application 1–3	Marcel: I think the cash method is better than the accrual method. Let's face it—you're not paid until you're paid. The ultimate test of success is the bank balance, not some "estimate" of what you think you will eventually be paid who knows when. Look at the bank balance. That's all the "management information" any law firm needs.

Discuss the pros and cons of Marcel's opinion.

TERMS

cash method   A system of preparing financial information that reflects economic transactions only when there is an exchange of money.

FIGURE 1–3
Balance Sheet and
Income Statement:
Cash Method

Carpenter & Cook

BALANCE SHEET
December 31, 1998

Assets
Petty Cash   100
Firm Operating Account   9,746
Computers   10,100
    Total Assets   19,946

Equity
Contributions - P Carpenter   29,000
  Less: Drawings   12,000
                                         17,000

Contributions - S Cook   29,000
  Less: Drawings   12,000
                                         17,000

Current Period Income (Loss)   (14,054)

    Total Liabilities and Equity   19,946

INCOME STATEMENT
Four Months to December 31, 1998

Revenue
Fees Collected   98,176
Disbursements Collected   15,432
Sales Tax Collected   2,645
Other Revenue   912
                                        117,165
Direct Costs
Associate Salary   20,000
Associated Counsel Fees   12,200
Client Disbursements   18,760
Sales Tax Paid   1,525
                                         52,485
Expenses
Staff Salaries   42,006
Rent   9,560
Equipment Rental   4,738
Telephone   3,794
Stationery and Supplies   1,524
General Office Expense   2,385
Library and Subscriptions   1,863
Professional Dues and Memberships 9,004
Promotion   2,972
Accounting   520
Bank Service Charges   90
Interest Charges   278
    Total Operating Expenses   78,734

    Net Income (Loss)   (14,054)

*We normally do our financial accounting on a cash basis for tax purposes. As
you can see, the results are quite different from the accrual basis. M.*

Transaction Data

The first phase of accounting is **bookkeeping**, the process of recording raw data into the firm's "books" (set of accounts) and summarizing the effects of transactions to produce information. Although there is no absolute boundary dividing bookkeeping from the rest of accounting, bookkeeping generally refers to the process of establishing and maintaining records, and accounting refers to interpreting and communicating the resulting information.

An essential aspect of bookkeeping is the assumption that all **accounting transactions** (economic events) affect **accounts** (economically significant components of the firm's operations). **Double-entry bookkeeping** requires that all transactions affect at least two accounts, one as a **debit** and one as a **credit**, and that the total of all debits equals the total of all credits. For example, payment of a client bill results in a reduction of what can be expected to be collected from clients in the future (a credit to accounts receivable) and an increase in the amount of money the firm has in the bank (a debit to the bank account).

To those who are not familiar with bookkeeping, credits are often thought of as being "good" and debits are considered "bad," perhaps because of the way banks present account statements. Credits are deposits, representing the accumulation of wealth, whereas debits are checks (money paid out). It seems better to have more credits. Bank statements, however, are presented from the bank's viewpoint of debits and credits. The account holder's position is the exact opposite.

Debits and credits are simply conventions adopted in bookkeeping for recording the changes in the status of the firm's accounts. Debits increase (and credits decrease) assets and expenses. Credits increase (and debits decrease) liabilities, equity, and revenue.

TERMS

---

bookkeeping The accounting function concerned with establishing and maintaining economic records.

accounting transaction An economic event affecting the entity.

account An economically significant component of the entity's operation.

double-entry bookkeeping A system of recording financial transactions in which each transaction has an equal and opposite effect in two or more accounts.

debit An entry in double-entry bookkeeping that increases assets and/or expenses, and/or decreases liabilities, equity, and/or revenue.

credit An entry in double-entry bookkeeping that decreases assets and/or expenses, and/or increases liabilities, equity, and/or revenue.

Debits are often abbreviated as "Dr," although there is obviously no "r" in "debit," and credits as "Cr." Other common conventions used to differentiate the two are:

Debits	**Credits**
left side of journals and ledgers	right side of journals and ledgers
no "+" or "−" sign	"−" sign
no "( )"	"( )"

Handling Checks

Checks are very important documents in almost all businesses. They provide a secure and timely way to transfer funds from one entity to another, but they are only as good as their form. Checks are one example of form superseding substance in accounting, and everyone in the firm should be familiar with the elements of a check, illustrated in Figure 1–4.

FIGURE 1–4

Elements of a Check

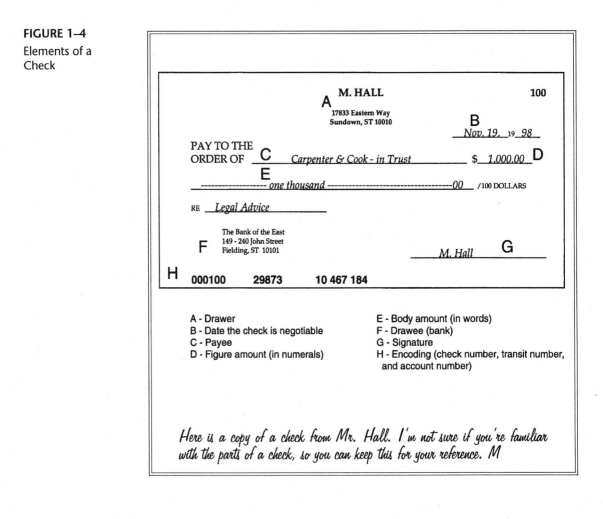

A - Drawer
B - Date the check is negotiable
C - Payee
D - Figure amount (in numerals)

E - Body amount (in words)
F - Drawee (bank)
G - Signature
H - Encoding (check number, transit number, and account number)

Here is a copy of a check from Mr. Hall. I'm not sure if you're familiar with the parts of a check, so you can keep this for your reference. M

Checks coming into the office need to be **proofed** (scrutinized) to ensure that the check will be accepted by both the firm's bank and the drawee. Areas to examine are:

- *The date,* which must be current, not older than six months (**stale-dated**) and not in the future (**postdated**). During January many people inadvertently use the previous year, which renders a check stale-dated. It may be possible to negotiate stale-dated money orders and certified checks, but the drawee should be consulted first.

- *The payee* must be the firm, a lawyer in the firm, or a payee who has endorsed the check to the firm.

- *The drawee bank.* If it is a foreign bank, the currency might not be United States dollars.

- *Body and figure must match.* This is rarely a problem when a check-writer is used, but errors can occur.

- *Signatures* must be present and complete.

- *Changes* that are not initialed could cause a check to be returned.

The back of the check is reserved for the **endorsement**, a signature or other mark that tells the drawee bank that the payee has received value for the check. If the check is made payable to the firm or a lawyer in the firm, the person preparing the check for deposit endorses the back with the firm's name and bank account number or uses a special endorsement stamp. If the payee on the face of the check is not the firm and there is a previous endorsement on the back of the check, the firm should ensure that the endorsement conforms to state check-clearing rules. Multiple successive endorsements may create problems when the check is presented to the drawee bank. Under no circumstance should the firm negotiate a check if it knows a prior endorsement is forged.

Case 1–3

Found: Lawyer misappropriated client funds leading to conviction for grand theft, **negotiated client's draft with knowledge that endorsements were forged,** represented conflicting interests, abandoned numerous clients, and wrote checks with insufficient funds.

Ordered: Disbarment.

──────────────────────────────── **TERMS** ────────────────────────────────

proofing Scrutinizing a check to ensure that all necessary elements are present and correct.

stale-dated A date on an uncertified check that is older than six months.

postdated A date on a check that is some time in the future.

endorsement A mark on the back of a check that signifies that the maker of the mark has received value for the check.

When a check is issued by the firm, the person preparing the check must make sure that it is properly prepared:

- *The check date* is usually the date the check is prepared. Month numbers should not be used. Instead, a policy of consistently spelling months in full, or using *standard and unique* letter abbreviations, reduces the possibility that a stale-dated check will be accepted by the bank.

- *The payee* must be printed carefully. If the check is for an advance payment on an item and is sent back to the firm to be reissued with the correct payee, needed goods and services could be delayed substantially.

- *The amount* must be clear, with no changes. If the amount is written incorrectly, the check is voided and reissued, especially if it has already been recorded.

- *The reference line* assists the payee in identifying the payment. Including a supplier's reference or file number helps ensure that the payment is not misdirected.

Sometimes a check must be voided because it has been completed incorrectly or in error. Voiding checks is usually handled only by accounting staff who:

- *Remove* the signature area and destroy it.

- *Print* "VOID" in bold letters across the face of the check.

- *Retain the remainder* of the check. If there are check stubs, the void check is stapled to the stub. Otherwise, it is filed in a "Void Check" file or kept with the bank statement *for the month in which it was voided.*

- *Reverse the check,* if it has been entered.

- *Retain all documents* pertaining to the reason for voiding the check.

If the check is no longer in the hands of the firm and is stale-dated, it is not negotiable unless it has been certified, but some firms also stop payment on stale-dated checks. If the check is lost, stolen, or mislaid before it is negotiated, payment should be stopped only on written request from a lawyer, and the **stop payment** approved by a bank signatory (preferably a partner). Stop payment requests, however, may not be legally binding upon the bank. If the check is subsequently negotiated, the firm may be responsible for honoring it.

───────────────────────── TERMS ─────────────────────────

stop payment   An order by a drawer to the drawee bank to refuse payment of a check when presented.

Steven: Norm made a mistake preparing a check, and instead of making the change and asking me to initial the change, he reissued the check. I realize everyone is human and makes mistakes, but his procedures were a waste of time. He not only has to void the old check, reverse it, and everything else, but he also has to get duplicate documentation for the new one. I don't want to make a mountain of a molehill, but this time-wasting must add up over a month or year.

Victoria: The procedures can be frustrating, but let me tell you what happened at my last firm. We issued a trust check, then realized the date was wrong. The trust clerk changed it, and I initialed the change. The client kept the check for over a year. It was for quite a bit of money, so I called the client. She said she'd lost the check, so we reissued it. But the client misunderstood, hunted around for the check, found it, and changed the old check date and cashed it. The bank accepted it because the change was initialed. Then the client cashed the new check we'd sent as well, which made our trust account short by over five hundred dollars. In fact, the account was more or less dormant, held only small old trust balances, and actually became overdrawn. If our bank personnel hadn't been on their toes, other trust checks would have been returned NSF! The time it took to document and correct the whole thing was incredible, not to mention that I had to contact the client, who refused to pay the money back. I wish we'd had Norm in charge there, I can tell you.

Write a brief memo to a partner like Steven, explaining the importance of handling checks properly.

While all elements are important in the efficient issue and negotiation of checks, those that are particularly critical in specific transactions are reviewed in appropriate subsequent sections.

Source Documents

The recording of most day-to-day transactions is initiated by a **source document**, which is usually a piece of paper, but may be an electronic record produced by a computerized data-capture system. Source documents provide the *data* (facts, measurements, and evidence) necessary to record transactions. This seems unquestionable, but people often attempt to use insufficient data to record transactions. For example, an invoice from a supplier for a specific item is usually an acceptable source document, but a promotional brochure offering the same item for sale usually is not. A bank statement is not usually an acceptable source document for recording checks or deposits, but usually is for recording bank service charges and interest.

TERMS

source document   The first complete record of a transaction.

Most source documents that originate outside law firms are supplier invoices, bank memoranda, and remittance notices from clients. Internally generated source documents include timekeeping data, disbursement logs (such as the transmit/receive lists printed by fax machines), bills to clients, and records of payments to suppliers.

Accounting Journals

Transactions are first recorded in the accounting system in journals (books of original entry). Technically, a **journal** is any record of a complete transaction between two or more accounts. More commonly, the term is applied to a set of related **journal entries,** each of which is complete in itself, with the total value of the debits *always* equal to the total value of the credits. Law firms use **special journals** to simplify recording similar transactions, such as cash receipts and client billings. A general journal is used to record transactions that cannot or should not be recorded in a special journal.

The minimum data required to create a journal entry is:

- *Effective date of the transaction,* which may be different from the date the entry is recorded.

- *Identification of the account(s) to be debited*, account title and/or account number, and the *amount of each debit entry*. By convention, debit entries are listed before credit entries.

- *Identification of the account(s) to be credited* and the *amount of each credit entry.*

A brief description of the purpose or detail of the entry is also included, unless the reason for the entry is completely obvious. Another common notation is a unique *reference* (label) for the entry (some combination of letters, numbers, and other characters) to simplify identification of the entry if questions arise. Account numbers, *in addition* to titles, are often used to identify accounts, especially in automated systems that do not recognize account titles. Figure 1–5 illustrates a standard form of general journal entry.

TERMS

journal   A complete record of a financial transaction; a collection of related journal entries.

journal entry   A complete record of a financial transaction.

special journals   A collection of related journal entries used to simplify recording transactions in ledgers.

FIGURE 1–5
General Journal
Entry: Bank
Service Charges

G12-6
December 15, 1998

Dr. Bank Service Charges	6520	23.75	
Cr. General Bank Account	1100		23.75

To record general bank debit memo re: exchange on Canadian check on November 17, 1998.

This is a short form of general journal entry that I use—in this case, to record a bank debit memo that was not explained until the middle of December. It was a charge for a Canadian check that was taken as U.S. funds, and this is the exchange difference. I just charged it to bank service charges. M.

Special journals do not follow this form, because their formats are designed specifically to reduce the labor and error incidence inherent in recording general journal entries. In automated systems, each special journal is a separate menu item, and groups of entries are arranged in *batches* or edit lists.

Practical Application 1–5

Penny: I'm not sure why the debits always have to equal the credits. If you have more revenue, the credits have to increase. You don't want more debits because that's an increase in expenses. Why not just add up all the credits and subtract all the debits to get net income?

What is Penny confused about? Explain to her the function of the accounts. Draw a simple illustration if that helps. Design a diagram that will help her remember which are debits and which are credits.

The Cash Synoptic

In small firms employing the cash method, a cash **synoptic**, illustrated in Figure 1–6, is often used to record transactions through the operating bank account. Synoptics are large columnar sheets where transaction amounts are entered in separate columns for each type of revenue or expense. At the end of the month, the columns are totaled

---
TERMS

synoptic   A combination journal and ledger, usually for a bank or petty cash account.

Carpenter & Cook

GENERAL BANK SYNOPTIC

Month November 1998   Page 2 of 2

Date	Description	File #	Ck #	Client Pay.	Client Disbs.	General Office	Staff Salaries	Promo-tion	Draw	Other GL A/C	Amount	P	Balance
11/08	Brought Fwd from p. 1												20,631.70
11/10	Pd.: Century Textiles	1844.0		840.34								P	21,472.04
11/10	Sundown Search & Serv.	1673.3	1412		25.00							P	21,447.04
11/12	Pd.: Northwest	1073.6		5,422.59								P	26,869.63
11/12	Trust Transfer			1,922.77								P	28,792.40
11/15	Transfer to Payroll A/C		1413				5,980.00			5100	2,500.00		20,312.40
11/20	Lee Mason		1414							5200	1,250.00		19,062.40
11/25	Fielding Office Supplies		1415			288.63							18,773.77
11/28	Pd: Sundown Market	1673.3		1,000.00								P	19,773.77
11/28	Dean Business Cons.	2409.1	1416		678.00							P	19,095.77
11/30	Transfer to Payroll A/C		1417				5,980.00			5100	2,500.00		10,615.77
11/30	Gotcha Video Service	2302.8	1418		256.00			320.00				P	10,039.77
11/30	P. Carpenter - Draw		1419						3,000.00				7,039.77
11/30	S. Cook - Draw		1420						3,000.00				4,039.77
11/30	Bank Charges									6520	12.00		4,027.77

This is November's general (operating) bank account synoptic. This type of synoptic is the bank journal and bank ledger combined. M.

FIGURE 1–6   Cash Synoptic: General Bank Account

and balanced (footed), and the totals are entered into the account ledgers. Synoptics are bulky, time-consuming to add, and subject to addition and allocation errors. They are common only in firms where there are few bank transactions.

Accrual Journals

In firms using the accrual method, special journals expedite recording noncash transactions efficiently. Like synoptics, manual special journals use columns to group and balance transactions and to minimize allocation errors.

A common special journal is the accounts payable journal, as illustrated in Figure 1–7. All credits are posted to the accounts payable liability, and the corresponding expenses are posted to the expense ledgers.

Account Ledgers

Account ledgers contain all the information entered in the journals that relate to a particular account, with a running balance that is updated after each transaction (entry). Ideally, journals are **posted** to (recorded in) the ledgers in chronological order, but this is not always possible. Figure 1–8 illustrates the ledger effects of the journal entry in Figure 1–5.

Some ledgers are not related to transactions that are included in the firm's financial accounts. These are referred to as **memorandum (memo) ledgers** (or accounts) and are common in firms using the cash method. A memo account serves the same purpose as a financial account in summarizing transactions related to a particular activity, such as billing.

TERMS

account ledgers   A chronological listing of all transactions affecting an account; ledger.

posting   Recording a line from a journal in a ledger.

memorandum ledger   A ledger that is not part of regular financial transactions, but provides information for anticipated or nonfinancial transactions; a list or schedule.

Accounts Payable Journal

Month of ___December 1998___   Journal # ___AP/1298___

Date	Supplier	File #	P	Client	Amount	Debit G/L A/C	Total Bill	A/P Total
Dec 5	Northern Legal Reports	1673.3		Sundown Market	460.00	1250	460.00	460.00
Dec 16	Archer Professional Magazines				566.00	6210	566.00	1,026.00
Dec 16	Gotcha Video Service Inc.	2186.5		Fielding Sports	730.00	1250		
					878.00	6350	1,608.00	2,634.00
Dec 23	Lawyers' Legal Library Ltd.				273.00	6210	273.00	2,907.00
Dec 31	Sundown Search & Service	2409.1		United Inv. Corp	119.00			
		1673.3		Sundown Market	212.00			
		2186.5		Fielding Sports	157.00			
		"		"	65.00	1250	553.00	3,460.00
Dec 31	Lee Mason - December collections				3,255.00	6050	3,255.00	6,715.00

I listed these accounts payable at the end of December to prepare the accrual method statements. M.

FIGURE 1–7   Special Journal: Accounts Payable

FIGURE 1–8

Account Ledger:
Bank Service
Charges

Bank Service Charges				G/L # 6520
Date	**Reference**	**Debit**	**Credit**	**Balance**
09/30/98	BS/09	10.00		10.00
10/31/98	BS/10	28.25		38.25
11/30/98	BS/11	12.00		50.25
12/15/98	G12-6	23.75		74.00

This is the bank service charges account ledger, showing the general journal entry for the exchange charges on December 15. M.

The General Ledger

The complete set of ledgers comprising all the firm's financial accounts is referred to as the **general ledger (G/L)**, the comprehensive list of which is called the **chart of accounts**. Figure 1–9 illustrates a chart of accounts for the general ledger used to create the financial statements in Figures 1–1 and 1–2. Balance sheet accounts appear before the income statement accounts, and the accounts are usually numbered because of potential confusion between some assets and expenses.

There are four levels of detail in recording transactions to the general ledger, depending on the type of account:

- **Control accounts** are always balance sheet accounts. The totals of special journals (such as accounts payable and billing journals) are posted to the general ledger, with an *equal and concurrent (not opposite)* entry made to subsidiary ledgers, so that the control account balance always equals the total of all subsidiary ledgers.

- **Accumulation accounts** may be balance sheet or income statement accounts. As with control accounts, the entries arise mostly from a

─────────── TERMS ───────────

general ledger (G/L)   The complete set of ledgers for financial accounts.

chart of accounts   The complete listing of general ledger accounts and their corresponding numbers or abbreviations, if any.

control account   A general ledger or memorandum account that controls transactions through its related subsidiary ledgers.

accumulation account   An account reflecting only the totals of special journals, instead of each transaction.

FIGURE 1–9

Chart of Accounts

Carpenter & Cook

Chart of Accounts
(Accrual Method)

Assets
- 1000   Petty Cash
- 1100   General Bank Account
- 1200   Accounts Receivable
- 1250   Unbilled Disbursements
- 1300   Prepaid Expenses
- 1600   Furniture
- 1700   Computers

Liabilities
- 2500   Computer Loan
- 2600   Payroll Taxes Payable
- 2700   Sales Tax Payable
- 2800   Accounts Payable

Equity
- 3100   Contributions - P Carpenter
- 3150   Drawings - P Carpenter
- 3200   Contributions - S Cook
- 3250   Drawings - S Cook

Revenue
- 4000   Fee Revenue (Billed)
- 4200   Disbursement Revenue (Recovery Billed)
- 4500   Other Revenue

Direct Costs
- 5100   Associates' Salaries
- 5200   Associated Counsel Fees
- 5300   Client Disbursements

Expenses
- 6000   Staff Salaries
- 6100   Rent
- 6120   Equipment Rental
- 6140   Telephone
- 6160   Stationery and Supplies
- 6180   General Office Expense
- 6210   Library and Subscriptions
- 6230   Professional Dues and Memberships
- 6350   Promotion
- 6410   Accounting
- 6520   Bank Service Charges
- 6540   Interest Charges
- 6600   Bad Debts

This is the chart of accounts that I made for the general ledger (accrual method). M.

special journal, only there is no equal corresponding entry to a subsidiary ledger. General bank account and fee revenue are typical accumulation accounts.

■ **Clearing accounts** are special balance sheet accounts used to control several types of transactions related to the same function, such as tax remittances and payroll. Within a short period of time, usually a month, all of the reconciling (outstanding) entries at the end of the month are expected to clear (by a corresponding and opposite entry being recorded). Because clearing account transactions often arise from general journals, the description of each transaction is usually recorded in the account ledger. Special clearing accounts called suspense accounts may be set up to post journals where one side must be posted immediately but the appropriate ledger for the other side is not known. For example, if a general check must be posted to keep the general bank balance current in the records, but the debit is identified only as "library," which may be either an expense or an asset, the debit is posted to the suspense account, then transferred to the correct account when it is identified.

■ **Detail accounts** show the full particulars of every entry posted to the account. Most detail accounts appear in the debit side of the trial balance, such as expenses, fixed asset acquisitions, and draw accounts. Except for other revenue and bank loans, credit detail accounts are usually used only at year-end to record accumulated depreciation, allowances for doubtful accounts, and capital transactions. *All* accounts that affect equity should be detail accounts.

Periodically, especially at the end of each month and year when financial reports are prepared, the balance of each account is listed in a **trial balance** (listing of all general ledger account balances at a certain date). The total of all debit balances is compared to the total of all credit balances to ensure that they are equal. If they are not equal, the general ledger is out of balance and the error(s) must be found and corrected before proceeding with the following period. However, the fact that the general ledger is in balance does not necessarily mean that every entry and balance is correct.

――――――――――――――――――――― TERMS ―――――――――――――――――――――

clearing account   A balance sheet account containing related transactions that regularly clear through another account.

detail account   An account that always contains a record of each separate transaction affecting the account.

trial balance   A periodic list of the balances of all of the general ledger accounts, where the total of all debit balances is compared to the total of all credit balances; a list used in preparing financial statements.

Terry: Why don't we just record the source document data right into the account ledger and not bother with the journals? Journals waste a lot of time and paper and really don't tell you anything that you can't find in the ledger eventually.

Why are journals used? How do they make bookkeeping easier?

The other main purpose of the trial balance is preparation of the financial statements. Most banks that extend credit to law firms request informal monthly financial statements, which are usually simply formatted trial balances produced from an automated system. Figure 1–10 illustrates the trial balance used to create the informal financial statements illustrated in Figure 1–3.

Proper formal financial statements for distribution outside the firm should *not* be prepared by anyone who is not familiar with the accepted standards for financial statement preparation.

Subsidiary Ledgers

Subsidiary ledgers (or subledgers) support general ledger control accounts by classifying transactions in a meaningful way. For example, separate accounts payable subledgers list all transactions for each individual supplier, with the sum of the subledger balances equaling the accounts payable control account balance in the general ledger.

Each transaction in a subledger is also recorded in the account ledger, but often in less detail, or as part of a summary total from a special journal. In law firms, the most important subledgers relate to client file activity and are called client ledgers.

Transactions relating to each client must be kept separate so that the firm can readily access information when making decisions regarding individual clients. For example, each client's billing and payment history must be kept in a separate place, with the entries and balances related only to that client. If a separate ledger were not maintained, it would be difficult for the client's lawyer to determine whether the client had been billed for services and had paid for them. Figure 1–11 illustrates a comprehensive client ledger.

TERMS

subsidiary ledger   One ledger in a set of related ledgers, which in aggregate correspond to a control account; subledger.

FIGURE 1–10
Trial Balance

Carpenter & Cook

Trial Balance
December 31, 1998

G/L #	Account Name	Debits	Credits
1000	Petty Cash	100	
1100	General Operating Account	9,746	
1700	Computers	10,100	
3100	Contributions - P. Carpenter		29,000
3150	Drawings - P. Carpenter	12,000	
3200	Contributions - S. Cook		29,000
3250	Drawings - S. Cook	12,000	
4000	Fee Revenue (Collected)		98,176
4200	Disbursement Revenue (Collected)		15,432
4300	Sales Tax Collected		2,645
4500	Other Revenue		912
5100	Associates' Salaries	20,000	
5200	Associated Counsel Fees	12,200	
5300	Client Disbursements	18,760	
5400	Sales Tax Paid	1,525	
6000	Staff Salaries	42,006	
6100	Rent	9,560	
6120	Equipment Rental	4,738	
6140	Telephone	3,794	
6160	Stationery and Supplies	1,524	
6180	General Office Expense	2,385	
6210	Library and Subscriptions	1,863	
6230	Professional Dues and Memberships	9,004	
6350	Promotion	2,972	
6410	Accounting	520	
6520	Bank Service Charges	90	
6540	Interest Charges	278	
	Totals	175,165	175,165

I used this trial balance to draft the cash-basis financial statements. M.

Carpenter & Squire

CLIENT FILE LEDGER CARD

Page: 1

File Opened: July 1, 1998

Name: Isosceles Investments, Inc.

File Number: 4011-1

Lawyer: P. Carpenter

Re: Tax Matters

						BALANCES FORWARD		

Date mm/dd/yy	Description	Memo	Trust Funds		Disbursements		Accounts Receivable			Current Balances		
			Received	Disbursed	Billed	Incurred	Payment	Fees	Tax	A/R	Trust	Disb.
07/02/98	Courier	18765				5.00						5.00
07/05/98	Courier	18792				10.00						15.00
07/08/98	Copies	PC-3/8				3.30						18.30
07/22/98	Courthouse PC	GD-3/22				8.10						26.40
07/22/98	Fax	FX-3/22				23.00						49.40
07/24/98	Courier	1884 1				36.00						85.40
07/25/98	L.D. Calls	LD-3				184.12						269.52
07/29/98	Tax Refund	TR-7	65,000.00								65,000.00	
07/29/98	State Authority	GC-281				500.00						769.52
07/30/98	Courier	1926				32.00						801.52
07/30/98	C & S Bill	319			801.52			15,000.00	450.00	16,251.52		0.00
07/30/98	Trust Transfer	TC-484		16,251.52			16,251.42			0.00	48,748.48	
07/30/98	Isosceles Inv Inc	TC-485		48,748.48						0.00	0.00	0.00

We used to have these ledger cards at the old firm of Carpenter & Squire. Some of the clients' files came with us to the new firm, so you may still see a few of these around. M.

FIGURE 1–11 Full Client Ledger

Internal Controls

Internal controls are the methods, procedures, forms, and approval requirements incorporated into the firm's accounting structure to:

- *Safeguard assets.* Liquid assets such as cash, or easily exploited ones such as metered postage, are not the only assets that require protection. Firms must control their general resources, such as office supplies, copying facilities, refreshments, and idle equipment. Any threat to economic benefit, intentional or not, represents a possible loss to the firm.

- *Prevent and detect errors.* Mistakes are not only time-consuming to correct, but they also lead to misinformation and poor decisions if not detected at all. Especially strong controls are needed where errors involve professional liability or misconduct issues.

- *Ensure policies are followed.* For many policies, adherence cannot be verified by passive observation, and special controls are needed. With some planning and consideration for their purposes, they can be designed to create minimal extra work or to serve more than one control purpose.

- *Ensure the accuracy and reliability of accounting data.* One of the most important overall controls is prompt data input, which supports error detection through regular reporting and checking. The longer an incorrect entry remains undetected, the less likely it will ever be detected.

A well-designed control is an integral part of the overall system, not a clumsy appendage. In many cases, the mere visibility of controls encourages diligence and integrity, and although most controls are recognizable as such, those intended to detect staff misappropriations may be designed to be inconspicuous. Other controls in specific accounting areas are addressed in subsequent chapters, as are the effects of a lack of them.

Case 1–4	Found:	(in part) Although lawyer cannot be held responsible for every detail of office procedure, **he must accept responsibility to supervise the work of his staff.**
	Ordered:	(for this, commingling, and other issues, notwithstanding absence of misappropriation) Public reproof.

--- TERMS ---

internal controls A comprehensive set of methods, procedures, forms, and approval requirements incorporated into the accounting system to safeguard assets, prevent and detect errors, ensure policies are followed, and ensure the accuracy and reliability of accounting data.

Levels of Controls

There are three basic levels of controls in accounting procedures:

- *Primary controls* ensure that what is supposed to happen actually happens. These include appropriate approval processes, proper communication of instructions, and adequate access to essential resources. Practically everyone in the firm contributes to these in some fashion by providing clear instructions for performing transactions and by following instructions correctly and completely. Failure of primary controls results in **substantive errors**, or "things that actually go wrong" and must be rectified through some action.

- *Secondary controls* ensure that what happened is properly recorded and otherwise communicated. Practically everyone in the firm contributes to these as well by providing accurate and complete records of transactions that have already occurred and by processing and providing accurate information. Errors in recording transactions (**recording errors**) frequently cause substantive errors because they depict something that did not actually happen, and other transactions are executed on the assumption that the records are correct.

- *Tertiary controls* support primary and secondary controls. They are mostly reviews, reports, and double-checks that identify both substantive and recording errors, rather than prevent them. Preparing a trial balance is, in part, a tertiary control to help locate omissions and addition errors. Again, almost everyone in the firm contributes to ensuring these controls are in place and operating effectively, even by simply distributing reports promptly to the appropriate people.

Because controls are designed to minimize errors at the earliest point, primary controls usually (and appropriately) receive the greatest attention. However, undervaluing the importance of secondary controls (for example, by allocating inadequate human and computer resources to accounting functions) can undermine the effectiveness of primary controls. The greatest obstacle in properly applying tertiary controls is the temptation to use them to fix blame, rather than to control the incidence and practical effects of errors.

TERMS

substantive errors   Incorrect or untimely accounting events.

recording errors   Errors in the recording of an otherwise correct and timely event.

Bonny: Some of these new procedures look like they're intended to make me look bad! I get a whole bunch of data to enter, but some of it is wrong. I can't tell it's wrong, because I don't know what the right figures are. Then when it's time to put it all together, my supervisor brings all sorts of corrections to me to enter into the system. I know she knows they're not all my fault, but she's under so much pressure that she's mad about the mistakes, no matter who made them. The corrections take a long time to fix and my other work gets behind. I haven't been here very long and I want to make a good impression, since Joan is leaving soon and I would like to get promoted to her job. If I seem like I can't keep up, or if I complain, I won't have much of a chance for a promotion. I end up working through my lunch break, on my own time, so that I won't look lazy or incompetent.

What should Bonny do?

Bookkeeping Errors

There are several types of errors in accounting, but this book deals in depth with only two, recording errors, which occur mostly in the bookkeeping function, and substantive errors. Recording errors require only the amendment of how an event was recorded. Most law firms amend records by following such typical conventions as:

- Correcting through the original journal (or input program) whenever possible.

- Reversing the *entire* original entry, noting the reversal in the description section, then posting the transaction *correctly,* noting the correction in the description section.

- Using the original posting reference number (journal reference number or check number), unless it was incorrect.

- *Never* simply netting the adjustment of incorrect amounts.

- Using the original date (the actual date of the transaction) if the monthly records have not been closed. If the month is closed, both the reversal and correction usually must be posted as at the date the correction was made.

- In a pegboard system (discussed in Chapter 2), using parentheses "( )", not a "–" sign, to note a reversal in the *original* column (reverse checks in the check column and reverse deposits in the deposit column).

- In an automated system, using the reversing sign shown in the software manual (usually a "–" sign preceding the amount).

Substantive errors require action, not just a change in the records, to correct their effects. These errors are dealt with in subsequent relevant chapters. Figure 1–12 illustrates a reversed and corrected entry in both journal and ledger.

Practical
Application
1–8

Violet: I don't know how to figure out what happened with these entries. There were some wrong entries. They weren't Bonny's fault; she fixed them, but only sort of. Either she or I missed a few correcting entries, but because most of the corrections are for the same amount, and she just entered the difference instead of reversing the original and reentering the data, I can't figure out which entries still need to be corrected. I know she's had a lot of work with the change in procedures. Maybe because it's quicker to make one entry than two, she opted for the quickest way. I guess I need to sit down and talk to her, but I'm so busy. I don't want to seem like I'm blaming her for the original mistakes, but incorrect corrections are mistakes, too!

What should Violet do?

FIGURE 1–12
Journal Entry
Correction: Journal
and Ledger

G12-9
December 19, 1998

Dr. General Bank Account	1100	23.75	
Cr. Bank Service Charges	6520		23.75

To reverse journal entry # G12-6 general bank debit memo re: exchange on Canadian check on November 17, 1998.

Bank Service Charges				G/L # 6520
Date	**Reference**	**Debit**	**Credit**	**Balance**
09/30/98	BS/09	10.00		10.00
10/31/98	BS/10	28.25		38.25
11/30/98	BS/11	12.00		50.25
12/15/98	G12-6	23.75		74.00
12/19/98	G12-9		23.75	50.25

G12-10
December 19, 1998

Dr. Accounts Receivable	1200	23.75	
Cr. General Bank Account	1100		23.75

To record general bank debit memo re: exchange on Canadian check on November 17, 1998.

When I explained to Pat and Sandy about the exchange charge, they wanted it billed back to the client's accounts receivable, so I reversed it out of the bank service charges ledger. M.

Comprehensive Exercises

A. Using the cash method trial balance in Figure 1–10 (used to create the financial statements in Figure 1–3), the accounts payable journal in Figure 1–7, the client ledger in Figure 1–11, and the following information, create journal entries and post them to the general ledger accounts illustrated in Figure 1–9, which will then agree with the financial statements in Figures 1–1 and 1–2.

1. When the firm signed the lease for office space, a deposit of $2,760 was required as a security and key deposit and to secure the signing incentive of the first two months' rent being free. The whole amount will be refunded providing that at the end of the lease, there is no damage to the premises and all of the keys and electronic access cards are returned.

2. Pat Carpenter supplied $7,500 worth of personal furniture that is now used in the reception area and coffee room and is integral to the practice (i.e., if it were not already supplied, it would have to be bought in any event).

3. There is a $10,000 loan for computer equipment, on which interest must be paid every month, with optional payments at any time in $1,000 increments, providing that the loan is paid in full by October 31, 1999.

4. The accounts receivable at the end of December totaled $36,579—$27,240 is fees, $8,521 is disbursements, and $818 is state tax.

5. There is one bad debt to be recorded as illustrated in Figure 6–10. State tax liability is reversed for recorded bad debts, and the disbursement is charged to the disbursement recovery account.

6. At the end of December, payroll taxes withheld for Terry Baker were $1,400, and for the other staff $3,861.

7. The unbilled disbursements amount at the end of December, and after all of the above transactions are recorded, is $7,793.

B. Jay: There are definitely advantages to the accrual method, but all in all, cash is better. It's more objective. A dollar is always a dollar. It takes less time, and everyone can understand it.

Mike: Sometimes other things are important. How can you plan if you don't know how much your clients owe you or how much you owe your suppliers? You can get a drastically wrong impression if you only look at the bank balance. The only decision the cash basis helps you make is how much tax to pay.

Jay and Mike both have points. What aspects of law firm management are most affected by the differences between the two methods? On what accounting principle are the two methods least alike? How does the cash method not reflect the entity concept? To illustrate your opinions, use the information in question A.

‖‖

CHAPTER 2

ACCOUNTING WITHIN
THE LAW OFFICE

Businesses require many systems to ensure that they operate efficiently. Law firms have special needs for sound infrastructure because of the rules that govern the legal profession and the serious professional conduct and liability issues lawyers face if their practices are not organized properly.

Case 2–1

Found: Lawyer failed repeatedly to perform services for clients. **Neither busy practice nor secretarial problems mitigate misconduct.**

Ordered: 180-day suspension, and proof of passing professional responsibility examination within one year.

Lawyers are personally responsible for the adequacy of the firm's accounting and are naturally concerned that all systems function smoothly and produce all necessary records. The purpose of this chapter is not to demonstrate how to establish a suitable system; rather, it describes typical systems to illustrate the ways system components interact to promote efficiency.

In medium-sized and large firms, the *accounting department* is usually:

- staffed by specialist accounting personnel,

- located in a separate area or areas of the office, and

- required to report directly to the partners and/or management committee, even though the staff provide support to everyone in the firm.

Accounting functions within firms are increasingly being distributed to staff members whose primary job is not accounting. In this book, these staff members are nonetheless referred to as "accounting staff" if they perform the accounting function under discussion. The term "accounting system" refers to the people, procedures, communication, paper, and machines that work collectively to accomplish accounting tasks within the firm.

The primary information functions of accounting staff are:

- *Recording source data.* Accounting staff do not usually *generate* source data, except when their duties overlap with other legal support functions or when they are asked to keep records of how their own time is spent.

- *Converting data into information.*

- *Acting upon informed decisions of others through adequate instructions.*

- *Processing information into reports.*

Although they seem routine, nonaccounting staff are often unaware of how these steps contribute to the major decisions that guide the management of the firm.

George: Sometimes I think the people in accounting are working in a different firm than I am. I give them straightforward instructions and basic data and ask them to do something simple. From there who knows what happens? I get back either more or less than I want, and I can't begin to figure out what is extra or missing. Scot wanted to "have a chat" about what the accounting staff does with the things I send them, but who has time? I'm a busy attorney! He starts talking on and on about sticking to accounting principles and working with the system. I want answers, not an accounting course.

Assuming he knows about George's frustrations, what should Scot do?

Office Structure

To some degree, all law offices conform to a certain structure, partly because they are required to under state professional conduct rules, but mostly because the accepted structure is sound and practical. **ABA Model Rule** 5.4 illustrates how a lawyer's independence of professional judgment and actions must be supported by the way in which management and financial decisions are controlled within the practice.

RULE 5.4
Professional Independence of a Lawyer.

(a) A lawyer or law firm shall not share legal fees with a non-lawyer, except that:

(1) an agreement by a lawyer with the lawyer's firm, partner, or associate may provide for the payment of money, over a reasonable period of time after the lawyer's death, to the lawyer's estate or to one or more specified persons;

(2) a lawyer who purchases the practice of a deceased, disabled or disappeared lawyer may, pursuant to the provisions of Rule 1.17, pay to the estate or other representative of that lawyer the agreed-upon purchase price; and

(3) a lawyer or law firm may include nonlawyer employees in a compensation or retirement plan, even though the plan is based in whole or in part on a profit-sharing arrangement.

(b) A lawyer shall not form a partnership with a nonlawyer if any of the activities of the partnership consist of the practice of law.

(c) A lawyer shall not permit a person who recommends, employs, or pays the lawyer to render legal services for another to direct or regulate the lawyer's professional judgment in rendering such legal services.

──────────────── TERMS ────────────────

ABA Model Rules Rules governing professional conduct promulgated by the American Bar Association and adopted to some degree in most states.

(d) A lawyer shall not practice with or in the form of a professional corporation or association authorized to practice law for a profit, if:

(1) a nonlawyer owns any interest therein, except that a fiduciary representative of the estate of a lawyer may hold the stock or interest of the lawyer for a reasonable time during administration;

(2) a nonlawyer is a corporate director or officer thereof; or

(3) a nonlawyer has the right to direct or control the professional judgment of a lawyer.

Case 2–2 Found: **Lawyer practiced law in form of a professional association where nonlawyers were corporate officers and directors,** failed to notify or provide quarterly reports to state Bar concerning employment of disbarred lawyer performing accounting and legal-related services, and permitted disbarred lawyer to be a signatory on and to disburse funds from the trust account.

Ordered: Disbarment.

Partners (or other lawyer-owners) are responsible for the operation of the professional practice. In large firms with many partners, business decisions are delegated to a management committee consisting of partners who vote on decisions, and senior staff who serve in an advisory capacity. Nonpartner lawyers (associates) are supervised directly or indirectly by the partners. These lawyers have no management decision-making authority, although their opinions are sometimes sought on management issues. Both state rules and common law decisions regarding the responsibilities of partners and supervisory lawyers are reflected in ABA Model Rule 5.1.

RULE 5.1
Responsibilities of a Partner or Supervisory Lawyer

(a) A partner in a law firm shall make reasonable efforts to ensure that the firm has in effect measures giving reasonable assurance that all lawyers in the firm conform to the Rules of Professional Conduct.

(b) A lawyer having direct supervisory authority over another lawyer shall make reasonable efforts to ensure that the other lawyer conforms to the Rules of Professional Conduct.

(c) A lawyer shall be responsible for another lawyer's violation of the Rules of Professional Conduct if:

(1) the lawyer orders or, with knowledge of the specific conduct, ratifies the conduct involved; or

(2) the lawyer is a partner in the law firm in which the other lawyer practices, or has direct supervisory authority over the other lawyer, and knows of the conduct at a time when its consequences can be avoided or mitigated but fails to take reasonable remedial action.

Paralegals and legal assistants often perform functions similar to those of junior associates, except they are not permitted to perform certain legal services for clients and must be diligently supervised directly by a lawyer.

Case 2–3

Found: **Lawyer failed to adequately supervise lay personnel,** resulting in neglect of client matter, and must stand responsible for the quality of the
work done by them.

Ordered: Public censure.

Legal support staff are nonlawyer administrative, legal secretarial,
and clerical employees who are supervised at some level by a **legal administrator** (or law office manager). Support staff roles in law firm management are restricted by professional conduct rules.

Legal administrators are necessarily very discerning when hiring and
training employees. References are thoroughly checked and office behavior and job performance are monitored for the first few months of
employment. Hiring people with the wrong background and/or skills
can have disastrous consequences.

Case 2–4

Found: Lawyer failed to exercise minimal care over client trust accounts; **failed to
check history of employee or to dismiss her after finding that she
had embezzled funds, whereupon embezzlement continued, constituting gross negligence;** and violated disciplinary rules governing client trust accounts.

Ordered: 90-day suspension.

Management's relations with employees should be well-defined in
writing, and all new employees should be informed about:

- How policy and procedure directives are communicated, who has input into formulating them, and who is expected to follow them and
to what degree.

- Who can legitimately demand information from whom, what type of
information, when and how often, and in what depth.

- Who is expected to cover whose duties during both planned and un-
planned absences.

People understand the general need for supervision and accountability, but may not realize that tasks are organized in a certain way to
promote efficiency, provide control, or conform to specific information
standards. Except in unusual circumstances, such as dealing with highly
sensitive information or investigating impropriety, people who know
why they are asked to provide material to others in the firm are much
more cooperative and thorough.

--- **TERMS** ---

legal administrator   The senior staff member in a law firm who oversees
organizational, personnel, accounting, and support matters; law office administrator.

Practical
Application
2–2

Bud: Heather wants us to get the client bills done before the end of the month so that they go in this month's figures. I can't see why it matters if it's the end of this month or the beginning of next month. It won't make any difference to how quickly we're paid, really. She says she needs "figures for management." What does she mean by that?

Answer Bud's question.

Administrative Supervision

Busy law firms cannot afford to have their partners and senior lawyers engaged full time in the administration of the practice and are obliged to delegate some administrative duties to senior nonlawyer administrators. Delegation of duties, however, is not delegation of responsibility, as illustrated in ABA Model Rule 5.3.

RULE 5.3
Responsibilities Regarding Nonlawyer Assistants

With respect to a nonlawyer employed or retained by or associated with a lawyer:
  (a) a partner in a law firm shall make reasonable efforts to ensure that the firm has in effect measures giving reasonable assurance that the person's conduct is compatible with the professional obligations of the lawyer;
  (b) a lawyer having direct supervisory authority over the nonlawyer shall make reasonable efforts to ensure that the person's conduct is compatible with the professional obligations of the lawyer; and
  (c) a lawyer shall be responsible for conduct of such a person that would be a violation of the Rules of Professional Conduct if engaged in by a lawyer if:
    (1) the lawyer orders or, with the knowledge of the specific conduct, ratifies the conduct involved; or
    (2) the lawyer is a partner in the law firm in which the person is employed, or has direct supervisory authority over the person, and knows of the conduct at a time when its consequences can be avoided or mitigated but fails to take reasonable remedial action.

In medium-sized and large firms, the administrator/office manager is responsible for such nonlegal tasks as:

- staff meetings and policy adherence;

- day-to-day personnel issues, benefits, and payroll;

- vacation scheduling and replacement staff;

- choice of suppliers and supplier relations;

- physical plant and equipment maintenance;

- records management;

- internal celebrations and receptions; and

- advertising and promotional activities.

In small firms, the managing or senior partner typically shares these responsibilities with the bookkeeper and a senior secretary or paralegal.

Where the administrator is also the accounting supervisor, there are special control concerns because both positions confer considerable access to assets and information. When the bulk of senior administrative tasks are performed by one busy person, there is a natural tendency toward expediency rather than thoroughness. The temptation to bypass procedures can be curbed through additional reporting practices, including:

- A structured routine for reporting to the administrative partner.

- A designated partner who approves payment of overhead expenses.

- Use of an external payroll service, with the records reviewed by a designated partner.

- Periodic review of accounting procedures and task structure by the external accountant.

- Approval of suppliers by a designated partner.

- Annual inventory of physical assets.

- Budget guidelines for operating costs.

- Cross-training all administrative and senior accounting functions with at least one other person who has access to the records for that function.

- Periodic review of the general ledger detail by the accounting firm.

The best universal control over any administrative position is a set of policies that is clearly communicated to everyone in the office and, most importantly, has the visible support of the partners and management committee.

Case 2–5   Found: **Lawyer failed to adequately supervise employee.** Lower court found:

> [U]pon the recommendation of one of his clients, [lawyer] hired [employee] . . . as a secretary. Subsequent to her hiring, [employee] was given increasing responsibilities, resulting in her position in the nature of an office manager. She had the responsibility to see that the pleadings were prepared from [lawyer's] dictation, the cases properly filed, dates properly calendared, the keeping of the financial books and records, and authority to sign checks from the office account and clients' trust account.
>
> There came a time while in the employment of [lawyer] that [employee] failed to prepare the necessary pleadings, documents or papers required to be done. As she got increasingly behind, she would remove the files and not

calendar them, preventing the lack of progress on those files from coming to the attention of [lawyer]. In order to cover her inactivity on these files, [employee] then started going through all of the office mail, removing any letters that had reference to the work that had not been done. She also removed any phone messages and intercepted calls to [lawyer]. She made excuses or misrepresentations as to why the work had not been done in some instances and falsely represented that the work had been done in others. Checks received from clients were not deposited in the appropriate account, and from the exhibits it would appear that un-authorized checks were drawn by [employee] for improper purposes. She further intercepted letters from the Attorney Grievance Commission.

From the testimony presented, there is no evidence that Respondent, [lawyer], was aware of any of the activities of [employee] until the time of her termination. . . ."

Ordered: 30-day suspension.

Records Administration

The records of a law firm include:

- Client folders and other collections of records pertaining to the legal aspects of the firm's representation. Separate folders may contain correspondence, pleadings, case law, and client bills and trust statements.

- Firm accounting records containing both client accounting information and the firm's general operating financial and management information.

- Personnel records for each partner and employee including basic personal information, dates of salary and performance reviews, salary increases, and behavior and attitude evaluations.

- Administrative files relating to partnership agreements, office leases and janitorial contracts, equipment leases or purchases and service contracts, firm-owned vehicles, and other assets and contracts.

- Central calendar and/or **bring-forward** records that are used to ensure that important client-related dates are not forgotten. Individual client **limitation dates**, use of the firm's meeting rooms, staff vacation schedules, and firm-sponsored receptions and community activities are registered either in a central calendar at the main reception desk or in an automated calendaring system.

TERMS

bring-forward   Record a future date for attention to a specific matter, usually a client-related matter; diarize.

limitation date   A date that limits or restricts when an action can be taken—for example, the date by which a lawsuit must be initiated.

Along with the central calendar, each secretary and lawyer also keep calendars and/or appointment books as detailed reminders of more routine appointments and deadlines.

Case 2–6

Found: Lawyer grossly negligent in permitting circumstances to exist by which employee not authorized to practice could sign lawyer's name to legal documents and **grossly negligent in failing to establish any internal calendaring system to record deadlines with regard to limitations and in failing to reveal to client that statute of limitations had run on claim.**

Ordered: Three-month suspension.

The firm's archives provide a secure place to store information that is no longer required in the main filing area but must be kept for some time pursuant to regulation, professional accountability requirements, or firm policy. Properly maintained archives store information so that it can be easily *retrieved*. Unfortunately, archiving procedures can become biased strongly toward ease of getting rid of papers rather than of finding them again if and when necessary.

Most accounting records are stored by fiscal year after the financial statements have been prepared. Access to accounting material and other sensitive firm records such as personnel files and partners' banking records should be restricted to partners and one senior staff member. With automated systems, the accounting information is backed up and permanently stored on electronic media on a separate schedule from the firm's other data.

When storing client file material, firms use a cross-index system so that misfiled information is easier to find. A simple cataloging system is a pair of index cards prepared for each closed file. One set of cards is arranged alphabetically by client name and the other numerically by file number. If the number is recorded inaccurately, the file can be located through the alphabetical set.

Proper archiving registers save time when files are scheduled to be destroyed. If an external records management company is used, it is easier and less costly to request that files be destroyed if they are all in one area or box. Larger firms that decide their volume of material cannot be stored cost-effectively for very long microfilm the material and destroy all the paper after a shorter retention period.

Increasingly, firms consider adherence to environmental policies a priority and insist that all waste paper be sorted and collected by a recycling company. If the paper contains confidential client and/or firm information, as most paper in a law office does, it is shredded before leaving the office.

Practical Application 2–3

Wade: I must say, law firms generate a lot of paper. When I was with an engineering firm, we had twice the staff and a quarter of the paper. And it's hard to find these files I'm supposed to retrieve. They were filed alphabetically in each month the firm closed files. The receptionist was supposed to keep track of where they were, but she was European and not used to putting the month number before the day number, so she got it mixed up sometimes. Here I was wondering why she thought there were 15 months in a year! There is no cross-index, and sometimes the plaintiff's name is used for a file when we were actually representing the insurance company. Working with engineers is much easier.

What are some of the faults of the archiving system? What should be changed?

Client-Lawyer Relations and the Firm

The relationship between client and lawyer is a **fiduciary relationship**, meaning that the client places a high degree of confidence and trust in the lawyer's abilities and ethics. Lawyers in turn are required to be loyal and honest with clients, place their clients' interests above their own, and be diligent in their clients' interests, as stated in ABA Model Rule 1.3.

RULE 1.3
Diligence

A lawyer shall act with reasonable diligence and promptness in representing a client.

Conflicts of Interest

Before accepting a file, the firm must be certain that the client's work will not present a **conflict of interest**, that is, that it will not conflict with the interests of the firm or its other clients. **Conflict search** systems are used in firms that may handle either side in a particular field of practice to ensure that a new client matter does not conflict with an existing file or a lawyer's personal business, as illustrated in ABA Model Rule 1.7.

———————————————————— TERMS ————————————————————

fiduciary relationship† A relationship between two persons in which one is obligated to act with the utmost good faith, honesty, and loyalty on behalf of the other.

conflict of interest† The existence of a variance between the interests of the parties in a **fiduciary relationship**.

conflict search The investigation in a law firm's records to ensure that the interests of a client will not present a conflict of interest for the firm.

RULE 1.7
Conflict of Interest: General Rule

(a) A lawyer shall not represent a client if the representation of that client will be directly adverse to another client, unless:

(1) the lawyer reasonably believes the representation will not adversely affect the relationship with the other client; and

(2) each client consents after consultation.

(b) A lawyer shall not represent a client if the representation of that client may be materially limited by the lawyer's responsibilities to another client or to a third person, or by the lawyer's own interests, unless:

(1) the lawyer reasonably believes the representation will not be adversely affected; and

(2) the client consents after consultation. When representation of multiple clients in a single matter is undertaken, the consultation shall include explanation of the implications of the common representation and the advantages and risks involved.

Often the system is a card index with a card for *each client* and a card for *each opposing party,* along with the file references. Large multifield firms have a special need for this procedure because they handle so many files, but it is often incorporated into an automated system. A potential conflict that is often overlooked in corporate litigation is the possibility of conflicting interests between clients and the firm's suppliers, bankers, and other business connections. Any staff member who identifies a conflict should report it immediately to a lawyer or supervisor.

Case 2–7   Found: **Lawyer repeatedly violated responsibilities to clients by placing personal interests first,** improperly keeping records, improperly using trust account, and commingling trust and business expenses.

Ordered: One-year suspension.

Ensuring a lack of conflict of interest is not the same as supporting a client to an unreasonable degree. In fact, there are restrictions on the types of assistance that lawyers may provide to clients, as discussed in Chapter 4. Just as a lawyer may not place unreasonable terms in a fee agreement (discussed in Chapter 5), a client may not make extreme demands on the resources of the lawyer.

Case 2–8   Found: **Lawyer who properly refused to lend money to client, whereupon client discharged lawyer, was unjustly discharged and not in breach of employment contract.**

Ordered: Fees to discharged lawyer on quantum meruit basis.

Practical Application 2–4	Dawn:	Ms. Pepper is a nice client, but I don't know if I should do what she's asking. Her doctor bills are adding up and she won't get her malpractice settlement for some time yet. She says her doctor doesn't mind waiting for a while, as long as we guarantee that he will get paid from the settlement. She wants me, as Ms. Lane's secretary, to tell the doctor we can do that. But Ms. Lane says she isn't sure there will be much money left after our bill is paid. Ms. Pepper says that lawyers should be more generous and agree to be paid last, instead of first like it says in the fee agreement. Ms. Pepper is telling me that Ms. Lane isn't very professional or kind, but I'm sure this isn't true.

How reasonable is Ms. Pepper's request? How reasonable is Ms. Lane's proposal? Write a brief summary of the related rules in your state. Research the terms *barratry* and *champerty* and discuss how each is related to this example. Would it make a difference if Ms. Lane was convinced that the settlement amount would be more than enough to cover both the firm's bill and Ms. Pepper's doctor's bills?

Confidentiality

The principle of *confidentiality* of client information explained in ABA Rule 1.6 also extends to nonlawyer staff. No law office personnel should discuss a client's affairs outside the firm, even after the client's file has been concluded. Confidentiality also applies to situations in which a lawyer provides only a free initial consultation, after which the client decides not to continue with the matter.

RULE 1.6
Confidentiality of Information

a) A lawyer shall not reveal information relating to representation of a client unless the client consents after consultation, except for disclosures that are impliedly authorized in order to carry out the representation, and except as stated in paragraph (b).

(b) A lawyer may reveal such information to the extent the lawyer reasonably believes necessary:

(1) to prevent the client from committing a criminal act that the lawyer believes is likely to result in imminent death or substantial bodily harm; or

(2) to establish a claim or defense on behalf of the lawyer in a controversy between the lawyer and the client, to establish a defense to a criminal charge or civil claim against the lawyer based upon conduct in which the client was involved, or to respond to allegations in any proceeding concerning the lawyer's representation of the client.

Practical Application 2–5

Chester: I'm dying to know what will happen on the Bridges divorce case. Mr. Bridges was my high school basketball coach, and I still remember the Monday he came in with a black eye. He said it was from some game, but the rumor was his wife gave it to him. Maybe I'll stay late and peek in his wife's file. I won't tell anyone, of course. It's just to satisfy my own curiosity.

Discuss Chester's plan. Does it make a difference if Chester is a lawyer? Paralegal? Clerical staff? Legal administrator?

Advertising and Promotion

While both lawyers and nonlawyers must be extremely careful regarding statements made outside the office about confidential client information (including making a response to someone else's statements), they must also be cautious in making statements about the firm. Representations concerning the quality of the firm's services and expected outcomes are limited by state regulations corresponding to ABA Model Rule 7.1.

RULE 7.1
Communications Concerning a Lawyer's Services

A lawyer shall not make a false or misleading communication about the lawyer or the lawyer's services. A communication is false or misleading if it:

(a) contains a material misrepresentation of fact or law, or omits a fact necessary to make the statement considered as a whole not materially misleading;

(b) is likely to create an unjustified expectation about results the lawyer can achieve, or states or implies that the lawyer can achieve results by means that violate the Rules of Professional Conduct or other law; or

(c) compares the lawyer's services with other lawyers' services, unless the comparison can be factually substantiated.

Media advertising is also a sensitive issue in some situations and is limited by the provisions of ABA Model Rule 7.2.

RULE 7.2
Advertising

(a) Subject to the requirements of Rules 7.1 and 7.3, a lawyer may advertise services through public media, such as a telephone directory, legal directory, newspaper or other periodical, outdoor advertising, radio or television, or through written or recorded communication.

(b) A copy or recording of an advertisement or written communication shall be kept for two years after its last dissemination along with a record of when and where it was used.

(c) A lawyer shall not give anything of value to a person for recommending the lawyer's services, except that a lawyer may

(1) pay the reasonable costs of advertising or written communication permitted by this Rule;

(2) pay the usual charges of a not-for-profit lawyer referral service or legal service organization; and

(3) pay for a law practice in accordance with Rule 1.17.

(d) Any communication made pursuant to this rule shall include the name of at least one lawyer responsible for its content.

Firms are usually wise not to quote fees or other information that might become obsolete during the time period the advertising material is expected to be applicable.

Case 2–9   Found: Lawyer employed nonlawyer as president of legal clinic and **published false and misleading advertisements,** indicating that a change of name would be perfected for a fee of $75 plus costs, and in fact charging client $100 in fees and $44 in costs; lawyer advertised that clinic would provide free initial consultation and charged client $35 for a five-minute consultation.

Ordered: Public reprimand; lawyer to make restitution and pass ethics portion of state Bar Examination within one year.

Even direct contact with prospective clients is restricted in many jurisdictions through regulation similar to ABA Model Rule 7.3.

RULE 7.3
Direct Contact with Prospective Clients

(a) A lawyer shall not by in-person or live telephone contact solicit professional employment from a prospective client with whom the lawyer has no family or prior professional relationship when a significant motive for the lawyer's doing so is the lawyer's pecuniary gain.

(b) A lawyer shall not solicit professional employment from a prospective client by written or recorded communication or by in-person or telephone contact even when not otherwise prohibited by paragraph (a), if:

(1) the prospective client has made known to the lawyer a desire not to be solicited by the lawyer; or

(2) the solicitation involves coercion, duress or harassment.

(c) Every written or recorded communication from a lawyer soliciting professional employment from a prospective client known to be in need of legal services in a particular matter, and with whom the lawyer has no family or prior professional relationship, shall include the words "Advertising Material" on the outside envelope and at the beginning and ending of any recorded communication.

(d) Notwithstanding the prohibitions in paragraph (a), a lawyer may participate with a prepaid or group legal service plan operated by an organization not owned or directed by the lawyer which uses in-person or telephone contact to solicit memberships or subscriptions for the plan from persons who are not known to need legal services in a particular matter covered by the plan.

Large urban firms and small suburban firms usually engage in *general practice,* meaning that they handle many types of client matters. Small urban firms tend to have practices restricted to a few related fields, such as personal injury or family law. Figure 2–1 illustrates a number of related fields of practice.

A firm's latitude in communicating its major or preferred **field of practice** (type of legal work) is limited by state regulations similar to ABA Model Rule 7.4.

RULE 7.4
Communication of Fields of Practice

A lawyer may communicate the fact that the lawyer does or does not practice in particular fields of law. A lawyer shall not state or imply that the lawyer is a specialist except as follows:

(a) a lawyer admitted to engage in patent practice before the United States Patent and Trademark Office may use the designation "Patent Attorney" or a substantially similar designation;

(b) a lawyer engaged in Admiralty practice may use the designation "Admiralty," "Proctor in Admiralty" or a substantially similar designation; and

(c) [for jurisdictions where there is a regulatory authority granting certification or approving organizations that grant certification] a lawyer may communicate the fact that the lawyer has been certified as a specialist in a field of law by a named organization or authority but only if:

(1) such certification is granted by the appropriate regulatory authority or by an organization which has been approved by the appropriate regulatory authority to grant such certification; or

(2) such certification is granted by an organization that has not yet been approved by, or has been denied the approval available from, the appropriate regulatory authority, and the absence or denial of approval is clearly stated in the communicaiton, and in any advertising subject to Rule 7.2, such statement appears in the same sentence that communicates the certification.

(c) [for jurisdictions where there is no procedure either for certification of specialties or for approval of organizations granting certification] a lawyer may communicate the fact that the lawyer has been certified as a specialist in a field of law by a named organization, provided that the communication clearly states that there is no procedure in this jurisdiction for approving certifying organizations.

The structure and identity of the firm must be clear to the general public. Firms may not use a name or other label that misrepresents or misleads the public, as confirmed in ABA Model Rule 7.5.

RULE 7.5
Firm Names and Letterheads

(a) A lawyer shall not use a firm name, letterhead or other professional designation that violates Rule 7.1 A trade name may be used by a lawyer in private practice if it does not imply a connection with a government agency or with a public or charitable legal services organization and is not otherwise in violation of Rule 7.1.

――――――――――――――― TERMS ―――――――――――――――

field of practice   A classification of an area of legal service.

Fields of Practice

CONTRACT
- 10 Personal Contract—General
- 11 Personal Contract—Plaintiff
- 12 Personal Contract—Defense
- 14 Commercial Contract—General
- 15 Commercial Contract—Plaintiff
- 16 Commercial Contract—Defense
- 18 Builders' Lien
- 19 Collection

TORT
- 20 General Tort—Claims
- 21 Personal Injury—Claims
- 22 Professional Malpractice—Claims
- 23 Product Liability—Claims
- 25 General Tort—Defense
- 26 Personal Injury—Defense
- 27 Professional Malpractice—Defense
- 28 Product Liability—Defense

INSOLVENCY
- 31 Bankruptcy
- 32 Receivership
- 33 Creditors Claims

ADMINISTRATIVE
- 35 General Administrative
- 36 Professional Bodies
- 37 Workers' Compensation
- 38 Employment Standards

FAMILY
- 40 General Family
- 41 Divorce
- 42 Division of Assets
- 43 Custody
- 44 Maintenance
- 49 Family—Appointed

LABOR
- 50 General Labor
- 51 Grievance
- 52 Negotiation
- 53 Arbitration
- 54 Mediation

IMMIGRATION
- 56 General Immigration
- 57 Refugee
- 59 Immigration—Appointed

CRIMINAL
- 60 General Criminal
- 61 Impaired
- 62 Motor Vehicle Offenses
- 63 Summary Conviction
- 64 Indictable
- 69 Criminal—Appointed

CORPORATE
- 70 General Corporate
- 71 Incorporation
- 72 Corporate Records
- 73 Securities
- 74 Merger/Acquisition

REAL PROPERTY
- 76 Transfer—Residential
- 77 Transfer—Commercial
- 78 Mortgage
- 79 Development

TAXATION
- 80 General Taxation
- 81 Income
- 82 Excise
- 83 Sales and Use

WILLS AND ESTATES
- 85 Wills
- 86 Trusts
- 87 Estate Administration

We handle cases for these fields of practice. The codes are for easy reference for the nonlegal staff. M.

FIGURE 2–1   Fields of Practice

(b) A law firm with offices in more than one jurisdiction may use the same name in each jurisdiction, but identification of the lawyers in an office of the firm shall indicate the jurisdictional limitations on those not licensed to practice in the jurisdiction where the office is located.

(c) The name of a lawyer holding a public office shall not be used in the name of a law firm, or in communications on its behalf, during any substantial period in which the lawyer is not actively and regularly practicing with the firm.

(d) Lawyers may state or imply that they practice in a partnership or other organization only when that is the fact.

Case 2–10

Found: **Lawyer practiced under name of partnership after former partner relinquished ownership interest** and arranged for third party to provide loans to client.

Ordered: Public remand.

Practical Application 2–6

Clint: Why should it matter to a potential client whether our firm is a partnership or a sole practitioner with several lawyers as employees? And why would they care whether the firm is a corporation or not? As long as the work is done competently and diligently, who could complain?

Answer Clint's questions.

Client File Systems

Accounting systems serve a central function in many parts of client file control, even though the people responsible for the systems may never look at a client folder. Lists of open and closed files, compiled using various criteria, are often generated directly from the accounting system.

A **client file** is an abstraction, a convenient way to divide a complex set of information into manageable components. Some firms open (establish) files for every small component of a client's matter, and others only open one file for each client regardless of how many legal matters (issues) the firm handles for that client.

--------------------------------- TERMS ---------------------------------

client file   A specific matter undertaken by a lawyer on behalf of a client (not a file folder).

Ivy: Rose gave me a file opening form for her new motor vehicle personal injury client. For the conflict search, she has put down the name of the other driver's insurance company because she's not sure what the other driver's name is or who actually owns the car. I guess I'll need to check the conflicts again when she gets those names.

What should Rose and Ivy find out as soon as possible? Who should be responsible for this? What are the possible problems?

Opening Client Files

When a client secures the firm's services, a client file is opened and a **responsible lawyer,** who has primary conduct of the file and approves all large transactions, is assigned to it. The responsible lawyer also negotiates the fee agreement with the client and determines whether the client must provide a fee advance to be held in trust by the firm as security against future bills. In some firms, only partners are permitted to have primary conduct of a file, or if an associate has conduct, a partner must approve the firm's commitment to the file.

Sometimes no formal file is opened, even though the lawyer performs a service for the client, such as notarizing a document or providing a brief opinion. Many firms record the accounting transactions for these matters under a "miscellaneous" file. This is a weak system because there is usually no conflict-checking ability.

Several files may be opened for one client if a number of separate matters are handled by the firm. These are given identifying tags, such as a unique file number, a file extension, or a short matter description. In firms that do not have file numbering systems, the files are referred to by name, and by matter if the client has more than one file. File numbers are assigned consecutively or by using a more complicated character string including letters, periods, and dashes, as illustrated in Figure 2–2.

Those who design file numbering systems may be tempted to introduce too much significance into a rather short character string, which causes numerous problems:

- If some of the characters are not on the calculator pad of enhanced keyboards, data entry usually takes longer.

- Nonconsecutive numbers give no information as to the relative age of the file and do not help in identifying missing file numbers.

TERMS

responsible lawyer The lawyer in a law firm who has primary contact with the client and primary responsibility for the conduct of a client's matter.

FIGURE 2–2
Client File
Numbering Systems

EXAMPLES OF CLIENT FILE NUMBERING SYSTEMS

123   simple numeric sequence, each file number is unique

123.1   first file for this client, all clients have unique numbers and the file extension is simply the nth file in the firm for each client

123.01   "01" is the area of practice, all file numbers are unique

D123   initial of client's last name, or the business name begins with "D"; number may or may not be unique

97-123   123rd client file in 1997 for the firm, or the number may be unique, and the "97" is simply for reference

6-123   123rd client for lawyer number 6, or the file number may be unique, and "6" is simply for reference

1234.4   first four digits are unique for each file, and the extension is the check digit.

When we started up the firm, these file numbering systems were suggested. We use the last system. M.

- Putting too much meaning into the numbering system complicates reassigning a different number to the file if the original one was inappropriate.

- Consecutive numbers are unique (names and other complicated combinations may not be) and remain constant, even if other client or lawyer information changes.

- Incorporating alphabetic characters encourages reliance upon changeable or ambiguous information. If there are several clients on a file, which name is listed first is often an arbitrary decision, and locating the file number is more difficult.

- Modern accounting software usually provides more appropriate fields for data—such as responsible lawyer, field of practice, "alpha-sort" order, and date opened—that enhance reporting capabilities.

Although consecutive numbers may be the easiest characters to use as references in automated word processing and accounting systems, care should be used when setting up the system. For example, the character string denoting the client file should never parallel any other character string used to denote such accounting information as general ledger account numbers, check numbers, or journal numbers.

Check digits are used where possible to ensure that each client file number is at least two digits different from any other number. Some automated systems limit the character type or field size, so this is not always possible. Check digits are calculated as follows:

Start from right.
Double first and every other digit.
Keep other numbers the same.
Add new digits, keeping double digits as $1 + n$.
Subtract from next highest ten.
        E.g.:   1   6   6   5   7
                    2 + 6 + 1+2 + 5 + 1+4 = 21
Subtract from 30 = 9

Use of a standard file opening form, such as the one illustrated in Figure 2–3, ensures that all pertinent information needed for internal administration of the file is supplied as soon as possible. The minimum information required is:

- file number, where file numbers are used;

- client's name, address, telephone number (including work number if necessary), fax number, and contact name;

- subject matter (often called the "re: line") and opposing party name;

- lawyer responsible for the file and any lawyers who have secondary responsibilities;

- date the file was opened (when work on it began);

- notation of any special tax treatment;

- billing limits specified in a fee agreement; and

- person who performed the conflict check and other duties, such as typing client index cards and adding the file to supplementary lists.

Other common entries in automated systems include:

- notation of a limitation date (used with an integrated diary system),

- estimated fee value of the file (for the firm's budgeting process),

- name of any referring lawyer (one who brought the client to the firm but is not handling the case),

- field of practice (for statistics and marketing programs), and

- special billing information such as frequency or whether the client should be charged interest on overdue bills.

――――――――――――――――――――― TERMS ―――――――――――――――――――――

check digit   A single digit added at the end of a numeric sequence to ensure that all numeric sequences are at least two digits different.

FIGURE 2–3

Client File Opening
Form

Carpenter & Cook

CLIENT FILE OPENING FORM

prepared by: __C W__ on: _Oct. 9, 1998_

FILE NUMBER: _2409.1_	CLIENT NAME: _United Investment Corp._
DATE OPENED: _Oct. 10, 1998_	RE: _Acquisition: Cross Town Towing_
DAYTIME PHONE: _486-1204_	CLIENT ADDRESS:
FAX: _488-7917_	Street: _1798 14th Ave._
OTHER NUMBER: _page 691-1700 #429_	City: _Seaside_
CONTACT: _Ms. Ivy Cantor_	State: _ST_ Zip Code: _10002_
RESPONSIBLE LAWYER: _S.C._	FIELD OF PRACTICE: _74_
SPECIAL BILLING INFORMATION: _Use premium rate for L M and S C, standard for all other; paralegal time not billable, but TASK should be recorded._	LIMITATION DATE: _N/A_ FIRST B/F: _Jan. 12, 1999_ CALENDARED: _L S_ CONFLICT CHECKED BY: _C W_
ESTIMATED FEES: _$15,000_	BILLING LIMITS: _L.M. limit is $5,000_
SPECIAL INSTRUCTIONS:	REFERRING LAWYER: _L.M._

This is the file opening form for one of Sandy's more recent clients. M.

The original of the form is kept in the main folder of the file, with copies kept in the accounting department's binders and in a master binder in the reception or central filing area. In automated systems, a printout verifying the accuracy of the input is produced and attached to the opening form. This is especially important if the accounting records are used for conflict searches because misspellings and nonstandard abbreviations may compromise the accuracy of the check.

In firms that handle a large variety of files involving companies and individuals, a file opening list naming all involved parties should be circulated at least weekly so that lawyers and staff can identify potential conflicts.

When a lawyer leaves a firm, the files that will remain with the firm must be reassigned to ensure that there is always a lawyer who is responsible to the client.

Mike:	I think we need to have a client file numbering system that reflects the field of practice for each file. Probably the first two digits should be the field of practice, the next four indicate the client, the seventh and eighth should be the responsible lawyer's initials, and the last should be a check digit.
Penny:	How will the ledger cards be filed then? It's best to put the lawyer's initials first so that each lawyer or secretary will only have to look through the ledger cards for their own files to find the one they want.
Frank:	Everyone knows their clients best by their names. The best and simplest system is to file ledger cards by the client surname or by the corporate name.
Mike:	But what if there is more than one client on a file? They may have different surnames.
Penny:	We could just always put the name of the oldest client first.
Frank:	Are *you* going to ask a couple which one of them is oldest?

Client file systems have advantages and disadvantages. What are some pros and cons of the above suggestions?

Maintaining Client File Information

Most secretaries maintain the client folders themselves and arrange active file folders near their work areas using some system other than numeric, such as alphabetically by client name, grouped by field of practice, or ordered by bring-forward date. The accounting staff rarely need to refer to these folders, but when they do, the secretary is asked to produce a specific document or piece of information. Not only is it usually considered discourteous for accounting staff to simply remove or rearrange active file folders, but information is likely to be refiled improperly or lost.

Basic client information that accounting staff need includes changes in telephone numbers and addresses and the court registry (docket) number once an action has been filed. All changes are documented, dated, and filed in logical sequence once the changes have been recorded where needed. A special change-of-information form, or simply a file opening form marked "change," specifies the file identity and *only* the information to be changed.

People find making small changes to client information tedious even though they recognize the value of current information. One way to encourage people to report changes is to provide special colored forms, the presence of which reminds people that corrections are important. Verbal instructions to change client information are less desirable because they are difficult to verify, trace, and distribute to all necessary staff, whereas forms are easy to photocopy and file in the permanent places needed. Firms that wish to minimize paper usage design a form to be passed along to all necessary staff (such as those responsible for index card files and other supplementary lists) in sequence, with a space for the initials of each person who has dealt with the change. As with all tasks that require controls to work properly, responsibilities within the office should be clear and, where necessary, subject to the responsible lawyer's approval.

Closing Client Files

The file closing process is one of the most important administrative systems in law offices. Adequate file closing procedures help firms:

- avoid misplaced information,

- reduce storage expense, and

- identify documents and material that should be returned to the client at the conclusion of a matter.

Secretaries like to close files because it clears their work areas and reduces the number of files that must be reviewed regularly (such as at billing time). The process, however, tends to be more haphazard than file opening or maintenance, because while active files are considered "assets," closed files are just "liabilities." There is little incentive to organize them because the time it takes does not represent a future benefit to the secretary or lawyer. Their jobs are not made easier by organizing closed file folders. For this reason, file closing methods must be very clear and closely managed.

Guidelines for culling files of unnecessary and redundant materials require special attention because the firm may need certain information to substantiate its activities long after the file is closed. However, excess paper creates other problems. Old paper just gets older and more costly to store and soon no one remembers why it was kept. Culling is usually best done by the lawyer and secretary together, as it is difficult to delegate to someone not familiar with the file.

The closing procedure is initiated by the responsible lawyer when the client work is concluded and the file records are no longer needed. With an appropriate system, the accounting department may monitor file balances for small amounts that should be deleted or produce a "last active date" list and bring to the lawyer's attention any files that look like they should be closed.

Issuing a closed file number at the beginning of the closing procedure helps to identify missing file closure forms or those that have not been attended to. If the locator code is not sequential, the closed file number should be. This makes storage more efficient because no spaces need be left, as would be the case if the files were stored alphabetically or by open file number.

A file closure form specifying the procedures to be followed and the areas to be checked, such as the example in Figure 2–4, ensures that the folders and records are not moved from the office to storage prematurely. The form includes spaces for:

- file identification (name, number, and matter description);
- approval from the responsible lawyer to begin the closing process;
- the accounting department verification that there are no balances in any part of the client ledger;
- verification by the secretary that all original material to be returned to the client, case law to be filed in the library, and redundant documents have been culled from the file;
- verification by the secretary that the word processing system has been cleared of the client's documents and precedents have been kept if needed;
- indication of client information to be kept permanently in the office (such as the client's last known address and telephone number in case they must be contacted later or for greeting card and announcement lists);
- verification of entry into the firm's permanent conflict reference file;
- closed file number;
- the date the file was removed from the office;
- the location of any remaining folders (perhaps with new counsel); and
- recommended destruction date.

Before a file is closed accounting staff determine whether there are outstanding accounts receivable or WIP time or disbursements to be dealt with. A client file must never be closed if there are funds held in trust or if there is an uncleared trust check against the file. Firms whose specialty is conveyancing find this policy difficult to follow. A simple policy of holding files for one month before transferring them to permanent off-site storage is usually an acceptable compromise.

FIGURE 2–4
Client File Closing
Form

	FILE CLOSING REQUEST	

A

Open File Number: _1058.7_

File Name: _Moss, Peter_

Re: _Dean, Jack: Copyright Infringement_

_____

C

Closed File Number: _C98-406_

Date File Closed: _Dec. 12, 1998_

Date Material Removed: _Jan. 19, 1999_

Locator Code: _B - 704 - 906 - 1_

Destruction Date: _Jan. 2009_

B Verified Function	Initial	Date
Approval to Close (Lawyer)	P.C.	11/17/98
Accounting Balances Nil	M.F.	11/20/98
All Dossiers Culled	K.G.	11/28/98
Word Processing Documents Deleted/Archived	D.M.	11/28/98
Client Information to Announcement List	L.S.	11/28/98
Permanent Conflict List	M.F.	12/2/98

We use this form so that we don't forget anything when we're closing files. M.

Practical Application 2–9

Opal: Baron's old partner, Dell, always said that there is no such thing as a closed file. You may need to contact the client later about something so you need to know what happened on the file. Even if the last time anyone looked at the file was twelve years ago, we always had to keep them in the back room.

What are the pros and cons of Dell's ideas?

Accounting Systems

Accounting systems are more than recording methods and equipment. They are complex combinations of interdependent components like people, paper, controls, forms, and methods that work together to accomplish accounting-related tasks.

Because all systems are unique, every firm benefits from having a comprehensive accounting procedures manual. New and temporary staff are accustomed to different systems and may omit important steps or perform them in an inappropriate sequence. This can create control problems, confusion, and conflicts with others in the firm.

Practical Application 2–10	Herb: In our office, the accounting system is very well designed and so straightforward that we don't need an office accounting manual. Anyone who's new to the firm can tell by commonsense what to do. Even if they make mistakes, that's how people learn—by making mistakes.

Comment on Herb's views.

Documenting procedures also helps save the external accountant's costly time, as the accountant must understand the procedures to review the documents properly.

Basic Books and Documents

To comply with state regulations governing professional conduct with respect to record-keeping and to conform to minimum standards of documentation required for tax and other purposes, the firm must keep a basic set of books and documents. In well-designed systems, these records are already part of the established bookkeeping routines and controls and are not onerous to produce and retain. For example, most firms carefully monitor the issue and flow of accounting documents by using numbered receipts, checks, and bills as a tertiary control. These procedures verify conformity to proper record-keeping by providing evidence of the *uniqueness* of each transaction and the *completeness* of each collection of records.

Journals are kept for:

- general (operating) bank accounts, often separated into check and receipt journals;

- trust bank accounts, often separated into check and receipt journals; and

- client billings.

Depending on the form of the general ledger, firms may also have journals for clients' unbilled time and disbursements, a general journal for adjustments, and an accounts payable journal. All journals bear some unique reference number and provide a space to indicate that the entry has been posted to the applicable ledgers.

All of the general ledger accounts must have ledgers. Firms must also keep the following client ledgers:

- client trust transactions, and

- client accounts receivable.

Other common client ledgers include client unbilled time and unbilled disbursements. If clients are billed for disbursements, records of the charges must also be kept for each client, though not necessarily in a formal client ledger.

Client trust and accounts receivable ledgers must be kept but may be combined on the same card in manual systems. Firms that keep unbilled time and disbursement ledgers often combine trust, accounts receivable, and unbilled disbursements on the same card. Usually time is kept as a separate card or set of records. In automated systems, the *totals* of each client ledger may be displayed together in an inquiry, but all *details* are in separate client ledgers.

Additional documents that must be kept are:

- all bank statements with canceled checks,

- validated copies of all bank deposit slips,

- passbooks for nonstatement trust bank accounts, and

- accounting copies of client bills.

Memoranda authorizing accounting transactions are filed in a logical and easily retrievable fashion. All verbal instructions should be verified by memo to ensure they are clear, and initialed or signed by the lawyer responsible for the file.

Figure 2–5 illustrates the flow of information between the accounting records, and the impact on the general ledger.

Manual Accounting Systems

Many small law offices use a completely manual system where entries are made in special journals, posted as they occur to the client ledgers, and summarized monthly and posted to the general ledger. In very small practices, each entry in a journal is posted separately to both the general ledger and client ledger, although this is rare. Firms that use completely manual systems tend to be small or not very active.

The general and trust bank account journals are often kept in large columnar books, and the general ledger in a binder so pages can be added as necessary. Trust and accounts receivable ledgers are kept on sheets in binders, on cards in trays, or in some other fashion that allows ledger pages or cards to be added, removed, and interfiled. The ledger page or card number should be noted at the top even on the first page. Subsequent pages should be stapled or otherwise attached to the *front* of the previous page so that the most current balances are readily available. Client ledgers are kept in numerical order in firms with file numbering systems. The only other system in common use is alphabetic.

FIGURE 2–5
Impacts of Firm
Accounting
Records on the
General Ledger

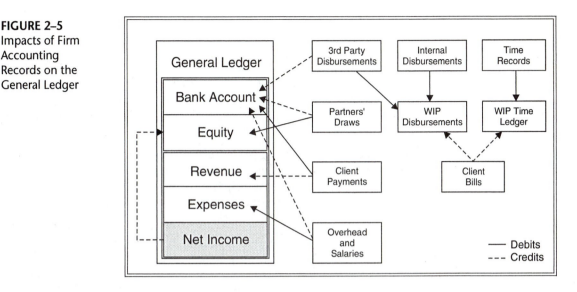

A more common and efficient form of manual system is a **pegboard system** using carbon and/or noncarbon reproduction (NCR) to post to client ledgers as the journal is created. Checks are usually provided with a carbon strip to record the details in the synoptic journal, as NCR coatings are difficult to endorse in ink. The removable journal pages are summarized monthly and posted to the general ledger. Pegboard systems provide some improvement on traditional manual systems because both sides in a transaction are entered at the same time, which helps to reduce posting errors and omissions. Advanced controls are difficult to build into a manual system without generating considerable extra paper, such as long supplementary lists and proof of extensive cross-checks. Manual systems that support more than one lawyer and are accessed by more than one support staff member usually require more thorough control mechanisms because:

- Producing exact copies of ledgers or client file summaries for others in the office is so time-consuming, awkward, and expensive that file information tends not to be reviewed often enough.

- Reports are easy to generate only after the monthly accounting period has been closed. Trust and billing errors not found during the month they occurred are troublesome to correct.

- Access to the ledger card information is necessarily limited. In certain fields of practice such as conveyancing where the trust and billing

—————————————————— **TERMS** ——————————————————

pegboard system   A manual accounting system using pressure-sensitive reproduction methods to record journals, ledgers, and subledgers concurrently.

cycles are very short, this inaccessibility leads to missed disbursements and trust errors.

- The journals and ledgers themselves are so large and bulky that accounting staff find it easier to wait for enough similar transactions (for example, trust receipts or disbursements) to justify batch work in a special journal. Often, this means that posting is delayed and/or items are missed.

- Differences in handwriting styles and neatness, the possibility of skipping important details (which would cause a transaction to be rejected in an automated system), and delays in subtotaling columns to ensure that the whole journal balances contribute to many errors.

Manual systems raise difficult security issues. The current set of records is usually quite heavy, bulky, and difficult to store in a locked cabinet or vault. Journal pages and ledger cards are easily mislaid and difficult to reconstruct if not located. Fire, flood, large-scale vandalism, and malicious pilfering are genuine threats to the accessibility of records, and often mean permanent loss.

Automated Accounting Systems

There is little question in the minds of most law office managers, both lawyers and administrative staff, that using an automated accounting system is cost-effective in all but the smallest of firms. Advantages include:

- The ledgers are automatically updated as the journals are entered, which avoids time-consuming adding and balancing of figures.

- Performance reports are more complete and can often be customized for the firm's needs.

- Reports are more timely and on-line inquiries can be made.

- Audit trails are more complete.

Firms often partially automate the accounting function or have more than one automated system:

- Time and disbursement details are kept in a separate program (either word processing or database) that is used to generate client bills. The WIP details are never entered into the main accounting system, but the bill totals are posted to the client ledger.

- Only the general ledger is automated. All client ledgers are kept manually and verified monthly to each general ledger control account.

- The general ledger is kept on a separate system from a complete set of client ledgers. The totals of the client ledgers are easily generated and compared to the general ledger control total.

Ideally, in-house forms are designed to conform to system menus and input formats. It is much faster for an experienced data entry operator to take the necessary information directly from the next space on a form than to have to search for it. Data entry systems should include double-checks to ensure that the information is entered properly. For example, many systems display the client name immediately after the file identification is entered. On the form, the name should be in the space following the client number so the operator remembers to check it.

Automated systems often improve internal controls by allowing faster information access, conflict checks, and other analyses that are time-consuming in manual systems. Information quality, however, is dependent on the operators' data entry skill and precision and on the caliber of input controls. Some systems allow obviously incorrect dates to be entered even though they print "date-sensitive" reports. This can cause client ledger totals to be out of balance with the control account at the effective date.

Shared information configurations are becoming more popular, with the accounting information on the hard disk (or network server) accessible to both accounting and nonaccounting staff. Firms require a special sign-on password to enter the accounting program or assign special passwords within the program to restrict access to sensitive information.

All systems allow some sort of screen inquiry in addition to printed reports. With increasing consideration for environmental concerns, many firms encourage screen inquiries instead of printouts. Large multiuser systems allow secretaries and lawyers to monitor accounting information on their clients' files as needed. There are usually several levels of inquiry, such as:

- balances at a certain date,

- activity between specific dates,

- all details, and

- details exceeding a certain dollar or hour value.

An important security measure is to ensure that the system is backed up regularly and that a backup disk set or tape is kept off-site in case of fire or other physical damage. The frequency of backups depends on the volume of information entered, but even small firms back up their accounting data files at least weekly.

Certain routines, such as purging billed client WIP details, are done as necessary, either to clear space on the hard drive or to improve processing speed. File closures may also be done on demand, but only with proper caution. Many systems purge *all* the client information, and reports printed at month-end for clients with activity during the month of closure may be out of balance (if the transaction is dropped in the summarizing process) or missing the file name. Most firms close a file and purge the information only after the last month containing a transaction on the file has been closed.

In automated systems, entries made into journals are affected by a certain type of data record (using a program subroutine) that forces a particular calculation or replacement or allows a default entry if no other is made. Called **master profiles** (or templates, or simply masters or profiles), these records are designed to control and simplify the arrangement of data within the system and to increase processing speed. Master profiles that support specific accounting functions are addressed in subsequent sections, but it is important to understand that they control many bookkeeping operations.

Almost all master profiles affect journal entries in some way, even if only to replace a simple input code (such as a two-digit alpha sequence) with a full word or phrase that will display in full whenever an inquiry regarding the entry is made. Other master profiles affect several types of journals. The one most often encountered is the client master profile, which can control:

- the rate at which lawyers' fees are recorded in the time journal,

- the unit price for photocopies in the disbursement journal, and

- the tax rates applicable to each client in the billing journal.

When they are designed and used properly, master profiles are a valuable foundation for accuracy and efficiency in all areas of bookkeeping. When they are poorly designed or not used properly, they cause errors, dropped entries, and corrupted electronic files. Whenever they are part of a system, data entry operators should be knowledgeable about their structure and application.

Practical Application 2–11

Brad: Our firm doesn't use computers to do accounting. It's too easy to make a mistake and you have to reverse it on a computerized system. With a manual system, you just erase it or use white-out. A manual system is much neater, especially if you just do the bookkeeping once a month. Computers are too expensive for any benefits they might provide.

Chip: You have to use a computer to keep everything up-to-date. Computerized systems also make sure that everything is entered properly. And you can't back up a manual system. Our backup disks are all in the supply cabinet, right next to the magnetic paper-clip holders.

Brad and Chip both have inaccurate ideas about their own and other systems. How would you explain the benefits and disadvantages of both manual and computerized accounting systems?

---------------------------------- TERMS ----------------------------------

master profile   A standardized arrangement of conventions that regulate the recording of data.

System Controls

Nonaccounting support staff, especially those new to the law office environment, may fear that the presence of system controls indicates that they are not trusted by management. While understandable, this fear is groundless. Controls are simply part of good procedure, and awareness of common types of controls and their purposes should reassure staff that the firm is simply well run, not suspicious. Examples of common system controls are:

- *Task separation.* If several individuals are responsible for various sequential operations, they will be more likely to discover each other's errors and imprudence. For example, the receptionist opens the mail and lists the client payments received or makes a receipt, and the list is then compared to the bank deposits prepared by a cash receipts clerk. At the same time, employment criteria, especially impeccable references and bondability, are often different for accounting staff than for other support staff, and the level of exposure to cash assets must be carefully considered.

- *Numbering and counting.* Check and bill numbers are used to alert staff to missing items. Physical counts of small, valuable items should be made frequently and irregularly. To discourage excessive staff usage of noncash resources, firms use photocopy tracking devices and other systems to determine levels of staff usage. The firm may not actually charge the staff member, but it is quite common to do so, especially for actual outlays such as long-distance calls.

- *Reconciling.* Petty cash and the bank accounts are reconciled at least monthly. Supplier statements are checked carefully and the *originals* of supporting documents (packing slips and individual invoices) attached. Most checks that are outstanding on the bank reconciliation for more than two months are investigated to protect the relationship with the payee, in case the check went missing.

- *External checks.* Sending account statements to clients encourages them to contact the firm if they have paid a bill but the payment has not been recorded. An important external check is the ongoing involvement of the external accounting firm.

- *Shifting people regularly.* Although staff stability is desirable for the most part, staff changes often bring attention to inefficiencies and problems not addressed by the previous worker. Firms may be wary of a payroll clerk who does not appear to be ambitious to move ahead or a trust clerk who refuses to schedule a vacation for longer than one week.

- *Recording the same information in more than one way.* Standard accounting documents are supplemented by in-house or customized forms, usually to facilitate requests made by others to the accounting staff. The forms have a space for the client name as well as the file number to verify that the number was recorded and read properly.

- *Plausibility checks.* Often comparisons to the previous accounting period or a simple review of the general ledger detail will pinpoint errors and system weaknesses. A substantial and unsupported change in disbursement recovery rates, overhead expenses, or payroll expenses should prompt an investigation.

- *Observing behavior.* Unfortunately, many people experience stresses in their personal and career lives that cause them to use poor judgment or commit indiscretions at work. Sudden changes in behavior and increased absenteeism may be the first signs that an employee should be directed to seek professional help.

Accurate recording of data alone does not ensure quality information, and staff should understand that the GIGO (garbage in, garbage out) principle applies to all systems, not just computerized ones. The accounting department may be able to catch many data errors (such as incorrect file numbers on a time sheet) incidentally, but the people responsible for providing the data must understand that the value of information depends upon their efforts.

Practical Application 2–12	Simon: I don't think Ms. Wells trusts me very much. Mr. Cairns used to let me just handle things on my own. Here, you've got to do some things twice, and you don't get the full job to do—just parts of it. I know it's a much bigger firm—that Mr. Cairns was just practicing on his own—but I miss my boss realizing I know what I'm doing. Maybe I should go into restaurant management or something.

What might be some reasons for Simon's concern? If you were the administrator and Simon voiced his concerns, what would you say to him?

Case 2–11 (continuation of 2–5)	Found: The court found: [T]here were instances in which deeds were not recorded and pleadings were not timely filed; **that disbursement was not properly made on sums collected for the account of clients, . . . that [lawyer]'s escrow account showed negative balances from time to time; that [lawyer] never examined monthly bank statements; that at the time [employee] came to work for [lawyer] she was on probation in [jurisdiction] as a result of embezzling funds from a title company there; that in an earlier incident she had misappropriated funds from yet another title company, which did not bring criminal charges because of its desire to avoid publicity;** that when [lawyer] ultimately terminated the services of [employee] as a result of his investigation

following a fellow employee's complaints to him, undeposited checks totalling more than $11,000 were located; and that among items found in that investigation were unopened communications from the Attorney Grievance Commission of [jurisdiction].

. . . An attorney may not escape responsibility to his clients by blithely saying that any shortcomings are solely the fault of his employees. He has a duty to supervise the conduct of his office. **A very telling aspect here is that although at one time the escrow account showed an overdraft of nearly $40,000 (possibly brought about by [employee]'s apparent tardiness in depositing a check), [lawyer] was unaware of this because he never at any time took the simple precaution of running his eye over bank statements at the end of the month.**

. . . We understand the difficulties of a busy sole practitioner, which is what [lawyer] was during most of this time. We also understand that one cannot watch every single thing which takes place in his office. It would appear here, however, that [lawyer] just did not adequately supervise his employee. He is fortunate, under the circumstances, that there appears to have been no actual loss to his clients by virtue of the negative balances in his escrow account.

Nonetheless, the public must be protected. Lawyers must be impressed with the fact that at all times they have a responsibility to their clients. This responsibility necessarily includes adequate supervision of their employees. . . .

Reporting

Complex accounting information is most effectively communicated in writing. Reports, interpretive memoranda, schedules, and narrative descriptions are used to summarize and clarify the many transactions that comprise the firm's economic activities.

Comprehensive information related to the overall performance and financial status of the firm is restricted to relatively few people, normally partners and the senior accounting staff. Authorized access to financial information should be clearly articulated in firm policy, as balancing the need for control over sensitive material and free access to other information can become a source of conflict between accounting and nonaccounting staff. If there is any question about the legitimacy of a request, the partners or management committee should be consulted to obtain their written approval to release the material.

Proper reporting methods and topics ensure that those who receive a report understand:

- The sources of the data and the recording and processing methods used.

- The reason they are getting the report (that is, the decision they are expected to make).

- How and to whom questions about the report should be directed.

- What types of supplementary and supporting information are available.

- The recommended retention period and location for the report.

Batches of reports that are routinely distributed after the monthly accounting records have been closed are accompanied by an explanatory memo detailing highlights of the period, any deficiencies in the data that may cause interpretation problems or, at a minimum, an invitation to ask questions about the reports. Some reports, such as client file lists, are produced and distributed regularly to everyone in the office and the old reports are destroyed.

<table>
<tr>
<td>

Practical Application 2–13

</td>
<td>

Grace: We get all of these reports every month, but I honestly don't know what I'm supposed to do with them. There are so many numbers that I can't tell good news from bad news. Anyway, all of the events have already happened and I can't change anything. I'd feel silly asking about this; partners are supposed to know these things.

What is not happening that needs to happen? How would you help make it happen? How valuable is the "information" in the reports?

</td>
</tr>
</table>

Cash Management

Cash management is a joint effort in law firms, although many people are unaware of how they can contribute to or hamper it. Senior administrators and managing partners usually deal with the bank-related financing activities, but everyone in the firm helps by:

- preparing regular and timely client bills,

- contributing to quick bill collection by answering client inquiries promptly,

- ensuring that fee advances are transferred as soon as possible,

- preparing interim disbursement bills,

- advising the accounting department of any unusually large client disbursements that will be incurred, and

- keeping client information current so that bills and collection letters will be sent to the right address and contact person.

The accounting staff improve cash management by circulating aged accounts receivable reports, providing sample collection letters approved by the partners, and promptly supplying additional information as requested.

Temporary cash shortages might be handled by the use of supplier credit, but if used too often and/or for too long, this compromises valuable relationships with suppliers.

General Bank Accounts

Partners frequently ask accounting staff to report general (operating) bank balances daily or weekly and assist with cash management, so that the firm can use revolving loans or lines of credit to manage cash flow fluctuations effectively.

Access to the firm's **general bank account** must be monitored as in any business. While others not directly involved with accounting might prepare checks, the accounting supervisor must ensure that withdrawals are appropriate and approved. The usual safeguard is that a partner of the firm must sign each general check, although other staff may be authorized as secondary signatories. In large firms, it is common to require two signatures on all general checks. Supplies of checks should be kept in a safe place, preferably under lock and key, with access limited to the senior member of the accounting department and one or two partners.

Bank accounts are reconciled at least monthly. Figure 2–6 illustrates the steps in bank reconciliation. The completed reconciliation is illustrated in Figure 2–7.

Accounting staff sometimes perform banking and bookkeeping services for partners. However, any funds that come into the firm's hands should be deposited to the firm's bank accounts, and not taken by partners as an offset to other funds due to them.

Petty Cash

Office **petty cash** is used for buying small items such as:

- housekeeping supplies,

- birthday cards and other celebration supplies,

- postage for special items that must be taken to the post office, and

- photocopies from a courthouse or university library.

-- TERMS --

general bank account   The firm's operating bank account.

petty cash   A small amount of currency and coin kept in the office to pay for items that can only reasonably be paid in cash.

FIGURE 2–6

Bank
Reconciliation
Steps

Bank Reconciliation Steps

1. Determine the adjusted bank balance. Reviewing the statement will identify almost all items that will require listing and/or posting adjustments.

    a) Verify that the bank statement dates match the ledger dates. Multipage bank statements require special attention.

    b) Verify the cleared (canceled) checks to the statement, watching for clearing errors (where the check amount does not match the amount charged to the account), which are quite common.

    c) Sort the cleared checks into numerical order.

    d) Obtain a numerical list of checks outstanding from the previous month and checks issued in the current month.

    e) Verify the cleared checks to the list, again looking for clearing errors. List and total the outstanding checks.

    f) Compare the statement deposit total to those recorded in the current month and outstanding from the previous month. Note any differences and list adjustments required, which may include dishonored deposited checks.

    g) List and total any outstanding deposits, investigating any older than three banking days.

    h) Identify any bank statement items that are not verified. These are usually bank service charges or unrecorded items. Make any necessary adjustments in the ledgers.

    i) List reconciling items and adjust the bank statement balance accordingly to obtain the adjusted bank balance.

2. Compare the *adjusted* totals (bank records and account ledger). If these figures do not reconcile, investigate the following common problems:

    a) Verify the bank statement opening balance to the previous month's closing balance.

    b) Add the previous month's outstanding checks to the current month's checks and subtract the bank statement "total debits" (less any bank errors or returned receipts). These should total the outstanding checks.

    c) Discrepancies divisible by nine often indicate that there is a figure transposition error. Divide the discrepancy by nine to determine the difference in the two transposed figures.

Here is a list of steps I use in reconciling bank accounts. M.

FIGURE 2–7
Bank
Reconciliation:
Illustrated

**General Bank Account Reconciliation
at November 30, 1998**

State Eastern Account #18872-2

Balance per Bank		$8,970.42

Outstanding Checks

1388	179.66		
1409	219.11		
1412	25.00		
1415	288.63		
1416	678.00		
1418	576.00		
1419	3,000.00		
		(4,966.40)	

Adjusted Bank Balance		$4,004.02
Balance per Bank Synoptic	4,027.77	
Debit Memo Not Posted	(23.75)	
(adjusted Dec. 15, 1998)		
Adjusted Ledger Balance		$4,004.02

Approved: ___*Pat Carpenter*___   Date: ___*Dec. 19, 1998*___

This is November's general bank account reconciliation. M.

The use of petty cash as a lending institution should be discouraged. However, as it is often partners or senior lawyers who request petty cash "loans," most accounting staff find it difficult to enforce this policy.

Sometimes petty cash must be advanced to make a purchase, with any change returned to the petty cash. Petty cash voucher forms (as illustrated in Figure 2–8) supply the following information:

- Date petty cash was taken.

- Signature or initial of the person taking it (not the person it is for).

- Client file identification, if for a disbursement, with an area indicating whether the entry has been posted to the client WIP disbursements ledger.

- Nature of the expenditure.

- Amount removed (adjusted later if change is brought back).

FIGURE 2–8
Petty Cash Voucher

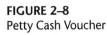

Date: *Dec 10, 1998*	Amount $ 13.38	Taken By: __*L.S.*__
For: *Postage - Special Delivery*		

Client Disbursements	**Office Expenses**	**Draw**
File Number: __*2409.1*__ Disb. Code : __*16*__	Charge to: _____	Partner: _____
File Name : __*United Inv*__	Approved: __*L.M.*__	Posted: __*M.F. 12/18/98*__

Here is a sample of our petty cash vouchers. Lee and Terry are allowed to approve disbursements up to $100. M.

Supporting documents such as cash register receipts are attached to all voucher forms. Sometimes staff will reimburse the firm for such items as photocopies and postage. These are noted as credits on the voucher.

The amount held in petty cash depends on the size of the firm, expected frequency of usage, and types of usage. Firms limit the petty cash "float" to $100 to $200, and if needs are expected to be high, the petty cash is replenished more frequently, as opposed to having a higher float. Supplying proper denominations ensures that clients who pay in cash and need change can be reimbursed promptly from petty cash.

Petty cash reconciliations result in either a check written for the amount depleted or a journal entry, depending on how checks to replenish petty cash are written. If they are written when petty cash is needed but not coinciding with the reconciliation, a journal entry is used to adjust the petty cash to the actual amount on hand. If a check is written only when the petty cash is reconciled, then the debit will be to the various expenditure accounts and the petty cash general ledger account is not affected. A standard reconciliation form may be used, as illustrated in Figure 2–9.

Firms expect to absorb small discrepancies between cash on hand plus total vouchers and the theoretical balance. There should be some policy, however, as to the limits. Regular, large, or suspicious outages should be reported to the partners. Often, stronger controls will reduce or eliminate these outages.

Carpenter & Cook

PETTY CASH RECONCILIATION

Float	100.00
To: _Dec. 20, 1998_ Cash on Hand	12.96
Journal #: _PC/1298_ Check Amount	87.04

Client Disbursements						
Date	File #	File Name	Description	Code	Amount	
Dec. 4	1073.6	Northwest	Postage	16	7.50	
Dec. 9	1350.8	Standard	Taxi	53	20.00	
Dec. 10	2409.1	United Inv.	Postage	16	13.38	
			Total	1250		40.88

Firm Expenses	G/L Account		
Stationery and Supplies	6140	23.93	
Miscellaneous Office Expense	6170	11.21	
Promotion	6350	17.61	
Other Staff Postage	6180	(9.66)	
	Total		43.09
Outage Under/(Over)	6180	3.97	

Check #: G 4319   Date: Dec. 21, 1998   Paid to: L. Steward

Denominations Required	
Bills _____ x $20 = _____	Coin __32__ x .25 = __6.00__
__4__ x $10 = __40.00__	__5__ x .10 = __.50__
__6__ x $5 = __30.00__	__10__ x .05 = __.50__
__10__ x $1 = __10.00__	__4__ x .01 = __.04__
Received by: __M. Fisher__ on __Dec. 21, 1998__	

I try to reconcile the petty cash when it gets below $20. Leslie cashes the check and gets the denominations I specify. M.

FIGURE 2–9   Petty Cash Reconciliation

Practical
Application
2–14

Glen: Heather seems upset that petty cash is out by five dollars and I don't understand it. There is actually five dollars more than there is supposed to be. Even
if it were short five dollars, it doesn't seem like a big deal. Last month it was
short by three dollars and she spent about half an hour trying to track it
down. Dot offered to just give her the three dollars, and Heather got quite ir-
ritated. What's the big deal? It probably all works out over time.

Explain to Glen why Heather is concerned about the outages. Is Heather over- react-
ing? Why or why not? If you were Heather, what would you do to help minimize
outages in the future?

Expense Accounts and Firm Credit Cards

In many fields of practice, it is almost impossible for lawyers to work
without incurring the kind of expenditures that cannot practicably be
paid by firm check and are too large or frequent to reimburse from petty
cash. These are usually:

- taxi, ferry, and bus fares;

- meals (both subsistence and entertainment); and

- unanticipated or emergency client disbursements.

Expense account forms like the one illustrated in Figure 2–10 are
used to reimburse staff for amounts paid in cash or on a personal credit
card and for mileage. As with any expenditure, the appropriate approvals must be obtained before reimbursement.

Firms often issue credit cards to partners, and sometimes to senior
lawyers and staff. Considerable confidence is implicit in issuing these
cards, as the charges made on them are not subject to the same advance
scrutiny as other expenditures. However, partners are aware that when
they approve issuing these cards, the holder possesses the equivalent of
a presigned firm check.

Credit card statements are reviewed carefully and approved before
being paid, with special attention given to due dates. Late payments can
affect the firm's credit rating with its bank, as the cards are usually issued through the same institution. Recently, firms have been obliged to
adopt policies regarding the "extras," such as frequent-flier points that
credit card companies offer as a reward for using the card. The ownership of these privileges is determined in advance by firm policy and
communicated clearly to all cardholders.

TERMS

expense account   An approved reimbursement to personnel who purchase items
and services on behalf of the firm from their own funds.

FIGURE 2–10
Staff Expense
Report

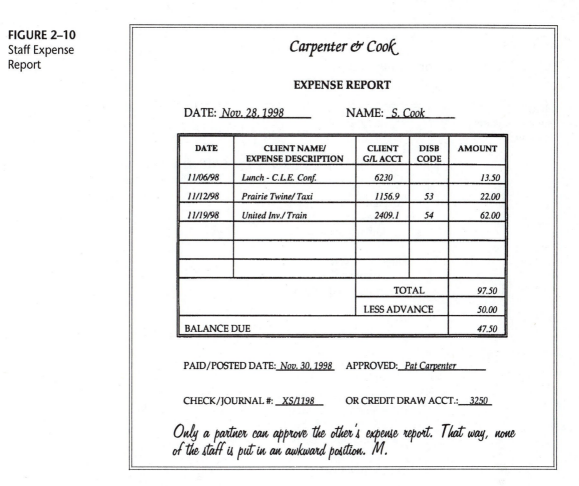

Carpenter & Cook

EXPENSE REPORT

DATE: _Nov. 28, 1998_   NAME: _S. Cook_

DATE	CLIENT NAME/ EXPENSE DESCRIPTION	CLIENT G/L ACCT	DISB CODE	AMOUNT
11/06/98	Lunch - C.L.E. Conf.	6230		13.50
11/12/98	Prairie Twine/ Taxi	1156.9	53	22.00
11/19/98	United Inv./ Train	2409.1	54	62.00
			TOTAL	97.50
			LESS ADVANCE	50.00
BALANCE DUE				47.50

PAID/POSTED DATE: _Nov. 30, 1998_   APPROVED: _Pat Carpenter_

CHECK/JOURNAL #: _XS/1198_   OR CREDIT DRAW ACCT.: _3250_

Only a partner can approve the other's expense report. That way, none of the staff is put in an awkward position. M.

Budgets

Many medium-sized and large firms use budgets to provide guidance to staff and information to management, most commonly in the form of comparisons to budget and to the previous year to date or previous year's month. Budgets are usually incorporated into an automated system, as they are time-consuming to maintain and report on in manual systems.

Many firms like to work with budgets to provide both incentives and feedback. Budgets are usually prepared and maintained for:

- lawyers' logged and billed time and billing variances,

- collected and written-off fees, and

- firm overhead expenses.

Advanced budgets also include expected levels of WIP and accounts receivable carried by the firm at any time. Figure 2–11 illustrates a firm's operating budget.

FIGURE 2–11
Budget: Income
Statement

Carpenter & Cook

BUDGET INCOME STATEMENT
Four Months to December 31, 1998

Revenue		
Fees	120,000	
Other Revenue	1,000	
		121,000
Direct Costs		
Associate Salary	20,000	
Associated Counsel Fees	15,000	
		35,000
Expenses		
Staff Salaries	40,000	
Rent	7,000	
Equipment Rental	3,500	
Telephone	3,500	
Stationery and Supplies	1,500	
General Office Expense	2,500	
Library and Subscriptions	2,500	
Professional Dues and Memberships	4,000	
Promotion	2,500	
Accounting	500	
		67,500
Net Income		18,500

This is the budget that the partners made for September to December 1998. M.

Compensation

All law firm personnel are concerned with how and when they will be compensated, not only in base salary, but in benefits, perquisites (privileges), and bonuses. Federal and state income tax reporting laws, partnership and employment agreements, professional regulations, and employment laws restrict various types of compensation for certain individuals.

Almost all employees are subject to **source deductions** (amounts remitted by the employer to government taxation branches on behalf of employees) from their paychecks. The employer is also obliged to contribute to social security and compensation plans. Types and amounts of deductions vary somewhat by state.

Some types of benefits and perquisites are taxable in the recipient's hands and others are not. The composition and timing of many law firm compensation plans are increasingly driven by income and other tax rules. For example, depending on marital, parental, and investment situation, it may be in an employee's best interest to have a personal retirement plan instead of participating in the firm's retirement plan.

In reality, compensation is a very complex issue in law firms and this section is intended simply to introduce a number of basic concepts and common situations, not advocate one legitimate system over another. The practice of fee-splitting is addressed in Chapter 5.

Partners and Shareholders

Only lawyers may participate as partners or voting shareholders (in a law corporation). Aside from bonus or profit-sharing plans, partners and shareholders participate in the equity of the firm, which is the theoretical value that is remaining after liabilities are paid and assets are liquidated. Because of the going-concern concept, this amount is necessarily an estimate to a certain extent but is used as a basis for assigning compensation between owners.

Partners receive **draws** (or drawings) on a regular basis (usually monthly or semi-monthly) as an advance against the portion of the net income that they will be assigned at the end of the **fiscal year**, which is almost always December 31. They may or may not receive the full amount in cash throughout the year, but they must nonetheless pay tax on it. The distribution of net income among partners is subject to the partnership agreement and may be a set percentage or a complicated formula reflecting the partners' billing and collection amounts, new files brought to the firm, and compensation to administrative partners for nonbillable time they are obliged to spend in managing the firm.

Although all partnerships are limited to a specific set of partners and the admission or withdrawal of a partner technically creates a new

---

TERMS

source deductions   Amounts withheld from an employee's pay for remittance by the firm to a government agency.

draw   A sum of money advanced to a proprietor or partner in anticipation of distribution of related net income.

fiscal year   The period for which net income is distributed and taxed.

partnership, many large partnerships admit and remove partners with little visible affect on the practice. Small firms tend to be completely dissolved and the partners enter or form other partnerships. Termination of an active partnership does not, however, extinguish the liabilities of the partners with respect to the obligations of the partnership. Written partnership agreements are essential in determining the rights and obligations of partners upon dissolution.

Case 2–12	Found:	**Absent a provision in the partnership agreement, aggregate of fees collected would be allocated according to percentages specified in the agreement for the distribution of profits and losses, rather than on the basis of time spent on individual cases after dissolution;** services rendered by one partner in winding up affairs of partnership are not recoverable as arm's-length services from the four remaining partners.
	Ordered:	Collected fees awarded in proportion as business partners, not as professionals rendering service to clients.

Shareholders in a law corporation are compensated with a salary and/or dividends. Tax laws generally favor the former for a full-time shareholder. Salaries are based on the capacity of a shareholder to increase the net income of the firm through expertise, working long hours, and/or by bringing new business to the firm. Dividends are paid on the basis of shares of ownership. Shareholders who own more capital stock of the firm will be paid more dividends. Unlike partnerships, the legal existence of a corporation is not dependent on a particular group of owners. When a shareholder leaves an incorporated law practice, that portion of the ownership is either repurchased by the other partners (who then have a larger percentage of the ownership) or is bought by another lawyer joining the firm.

Practical Application 2–15	John:	I want to join a another law firm, but it's a partnership and I'm concerned that they aren't a law corporation. Partnerships seem to be a lot more hassle and it's easier to get into financial trouble. I don't want to be responsible if another partner makes a mistake on a file or if an employee files a harassment suit against another partner. How much difference does a corporation really make?

Research state, federal, and case law and answer John's question.

Associate Lawyers

Associates usually receive salaries, which may be supplemented by bonuses based on the net income of the firm or the individual lawyer's performance (billing and collecting fees) but are at least based on some minimum expected level of performance.

Practical Application 2–16

Donna: I think this new bonus program will be very good for us junior associates. It means we can earn more if we work harder and do a really good job. The base salary is lower than most other firms offer, but you can get stuck in a rut and be undermotivated if you aren't challenged enough. It's not that tough to work another three or four hours each day, is it?

What could be some short-term problems arising from the perception Donna has of the bonus program? What about long-term problems? What is the effect of the bonus program if there is a fixed bonus pool where one lawyer's extra bonus is another's lost bonus?

In firms with a high ratio of associates to partners, competition is often keen among associates to be offered partnership (to "make partner") by the existing partners. A major consideration in making partner is bringing a substantial amount of money into the firm. Partners are aware that very successful associates expect to be offered partnership or they will leave to join another firm as a partner.

Compensation may also include receiving a percentage of fees billed by the lawyer or by the whole firm. All compensation agreements with associates should be in writing and should stipulate the disposition of their files and payment for outstanding bonuses if the associate leaves the firm.

Case 2–13

Found: Associate had agreement with firm to receive 50% of fees for files she brought to the firm and subsequently brought in a significant negligence contingency case. Associate resigned from firm, taking client's contingency matter with her to new firm. Old firm sued for 50% of total fees after matter settled. Associate performed half of all work done on the file at old firm and half at new firm. *No provision was made in the employment contract for associate leaving before file settled:*

> Both parties testified at the evidentiary hearing, however, that because of the euphoric atmosphere that usually prevails when parties conclude a new deal [employment of associate], neither gave any thought to what would happen if [associate] left the firm. This case may demonstrate more than anything that we lawyers, also need lawyers.

Ordered: Old firm received 25% (50% of 50%) of fees, balance to associate.

──────── **TERMS** ────────

associate (lawyer)   Lawyers who are employees of the firm and hold no equity.

Lawyers of Counsel

Lawyers who are neither partners, shareholders, nor associates of the firm but who are associated with the firm for limited purposes in a special field of expertise are called **lawyers of counsel.** These lawyers (**associated counsel**) are traditionally semi-retired lawyers and law professors associated with only one firm. As with any compensation agreement, firms should ensure that the terms are clear and provide for termination of the agreement other than through full performance.

Case 2–14

Found: Attorney of record associated with a two-member law firm on a contingency case with the understanding that for 50% of the fees recovered, *senior member of the firm would perform essentially all services under the agreement. Senior member was appointed to bench before agreement was completed.* When agreement does not specify compensation for partial performance, fee is prorated for percentage of the services rendered.

Ordered: Two-member firm awarded fee on a prorated basis.

Some restrictions on a firm's options in associating lawyers of counsel are discussed in Chapter 5.

Nonlawyer Employees

Nonlawyer employees include:

- Paralegals, legal assistants, and law students, whose work is related to client files.

- Legal secretaries and clerical staff, who work partly on client matters and partly on firm-related tasks and general lawyer support .

- Administrative and accounting staff, who may assist in client-related tasks, but only as they relate to the firm.

Most of these employees are paid salaries or wages, although some firms also pay bonuses based on *overall firm profitability.* In most jurisdictions, it is not permissible to pay bonuses to nonlawyers on the basis of the profitability of an individual client file.

--------------------------- TERMS ---------------------------

lawyer of counsel   A lawyer who contracts services to a firm.

associated counsel   Lawyer of counsel.

Case 2–15

Found: Lawyer communicated settlement offer directly to adverse party knowing that party was represented, placed trust funds belonging to clients in general account, engaged in law practice under trade name, **paid salary to employee contingent upon legal clinic fee receipts, and elected nonlawyer as secretary of legal clinic.**

Ordered: Suspension for three months and one day, and thereafter pending passage of ethics portion of state Bar Examination.

Practical Application 2–17

Guy: It really isn't fair about these bonuses lawyers will be getting if they bring in more money. We paralegals don't get to participate in the program, at least to the same extent. We get the same types of bonuses the rest of the nonlawyer staff get, but we actually bill our time, which they don't do. It's not clear to me why the "rules" are that we can't get a portion of our billings. It wouldn't have to be a big percentage—it's mostly symbolic, I guess—more pay for harder work.

Write a brief explanation to Guy explaining why paralegals are not permitted to participate in bonus systems that directly reward on the basis of billings or collections.

Comprehensive Exercises

1. Create a checklist of points that should be addressed by a new staff member joining a law firm. Cover each of the major points of this chapter and others come to mind (such as hours of operation and evening telephone service coverage). The checklist should have at least 50 points such as fields of practice and reporting structure. Any reasonable form is acceptable. List basic information about the firm and responsibilities for procedures.

2. Draw an organization chart for a firm in which you have worked. If possible, ask a co-worker to review it. Are your impressions consistent? If not, why not? If you have never worked in a law firm, design an "ideal" organization for a mid-sized firm.

3. Draft a procedures manual for Carpenter & Cook for opening, maintaining, and closing files that is consistent with their current procedures. What changes would you recommend? Describe the current and recommended procedures in terms of controls.

IIII
CHAPTER 3

TIME RECORDS

The entire revenue cycle of law firms starts with legal staff spending time on client work. In years past, when the profession was generally less competitive and clients more affluent and less knowledgeable about the legal profession, many lawyers were not especially concerned about recording time spent on a file. Today, however, lawyers' services regularly come under review by clients, courts, and other lawyers.

Case 3–1

Found: **Lawyers charged fees of $9,000 for services that were worth only $1,500, and in support of which no records were kept.**

Ordered: Lawyers sanctioned.

Most time recording systems used in law firms are automated to some extent because manual systems are so clumsy and expensive to maintain that they are worse than having no system at all. Poorly designed systems with inadequate controls can cause lost revenue, inaccurate performance measurement, misunderstandings with clients, and embarrassing allegations of professional misconduct.

Time recording systems vary greatly in complexity and usefulness. The simplest systems produce only bill preparation documents, and the most elaborate have many components and procedures that are used to produce complex reports. While not included in all systems, the following components are common and may appear in various combinations:

- Original **time data** (time data source documents) written or otherwise recorded by the lawyer or secretary.

- *Time journals* that organize the hour and dollar values by lawyer and file.

- Client **WIP time ledgers** that chronicle the hours spent for each lawyer on the file and may include service details.

- *Supplementary reports* that support client-related decisions as well as management decisions.

- *Entries to the general ledger* if the general ledger is affected before billing or payment.

Time records are treated very differently by different firms. Some firms track only *billable* time that is expected to be recovered from clients. Others track all time, including time spent on professional and client development and on administrative tasks. In practice, recording, posting, and summarizing methods are combined in many variations.

————————————————————————— TERMS —————————————————————————

time data   Original records of time spent by lawyer and other timekeepers.

WIP time ledgers   Subsidiary ledger for unbilled (WIP) time on a client file.

Objectives of Time Recording

Maintaining a time recording system properly involves integrating the firm's information objectives, personnel structure, and support resources. It is not enough to simply complete time data source documents properly. They must be recorded into the system in a way that serves the information needs of the firm. Generally, law firms keep records of lawyers' time logged (worked) for such purposes as:

- *Creating a diary of services to a client.* This benefits the firm by providing detailed evidence of the services provided by individual lawyers, which are often not performed in the presence of the client.

- *Providing clients with itemized bills for services rendered.* In many fields of practice, the client bill contains a very detailed description of all services the firm has provided.

- *Enhancing profitability.* Unrecorded time is unlikely to be remembered, and thus unlikely to be billed.

- *Improving cash flow.* Time records may be used to generate reports identifying files that should be billed promptly and/or files where fee advances are available to be transferred from a trust account.

- *Promoting efficiency.* Time reports help identify client files that should be billed or closed.

- *Measuring productivity.* Individual lawyers' logged hours are compared to billed hours to measure performance. Performance measures are often used to determine remuneration for associate lawyers or income shares for partners. Firms may establish target budgets for recording time and evaluate performance on that basis.

- *Determining realization rates* or the effectiveness of time spent on fixed-fee and contingency files or in specific fields of practice. Firms need to know whether further investment in research capability and specialized staff in a particular field is worthwhile.

- *Providing other information,* such as a record of an individual lawyer's work experience (in more advanced systems), or tracking nonbillable time, such as client development and time off. Advanced systems provide a "work-in-hand" estimate for budget planning by subtracting billed and unbilled fees from the estimated total fee on each file.

Some firms do not keep the type of time records discussed here, especially where:

- Few files are billed on a fee-for-service basis and an itemized bill or service diary can be created from a simple review of the file documents.

- The practice does not generally bill on an hourly basis (for example, criminal defense, conveyancing, personal injury).

- There are few lawyers, and performance measurement is not an issue.

It is advisable to keep time records in some form, as records of services performed for a client may be required if the client disputes a bill or alleges professional negligence.

Practical Application 3–1	Randy: In my firm, we do mostly personal injury contingency work, and we sometimes do real property transfers and wills for established clients. We don't record time because there is no need. The contingency fee is based on the amount recovered, and the conveyances and wills are all fixed-fee quotes. The only hourly rate work we do is estates and the file is always handy, so we keep track of time spent on a piece of paper in the front of the file. I have no partners and only four associates and two paralegals, so I never have to justify my actions or time. Recording every six minutes of a workday is a waste of time and makes the legal staff feel like I don't trust them. I know if my staff aren't pulling their weight.

Discuss the pros and cons or Randy's viewpoint. Would you feel differently about the current system if you were one of his associates? One of the paralegals?

Time Data Source Documents

Data documentation methods include:

- *Timesheets* that are completed by the lawyer or secretary each day or at other fixed intervals. Timesheets provide an entry control total that can be used in both manual and automated systems and is effective for tracking lawyer time. However, timesheets can make preparation of an itemized bill awkward in manual systems unless the description of services is kept in a separate word-processing billing document. Figure 3–1 illustrates a completed daily timesheet.

- *Time slips,* which are similar to timesheets except that a separate slip is completed for each block of time spent on a file. There may be several slips for a file in one day, and sometimes one slip is used for several days. This is a very popular method because it allows flexible input in automated systems and easy bill preparation in manual systems. The major drawback is that the slips tend to be small and easily misplaced. In medium-sized firms that specialize in a certain field of practice, it is cost-effective to have custom-printed time slips with standard service descriptions. Figure 3–2 illustrates a completed and posted time slip.

Carpenter & Cook

TIME SHEET

LAWYER (INIT.): __L.M.__ DATE: _Nov. 5,_ 19 _98_

Client Number	Client Name	Description	hr	1/10
1073.6	Northwest Machinery	Dft. SOC, TTC, LTC,		
		MTF, CW C Weaver	1	2
2143.6	" "	TF Bowman, LT Bowman		4
2246.7	Dr. Milton	RL, CW staff		5
1513.1	Wood	attend mtg. of creditors		6
1156.9	Prairie Wheel	TFC, LT IRS		8
1844.0	Century Textiles	RL Re: Cr remedies, TTC	2	1
2409.1	United Investment	R dft. S/H agree		3
2111.3	Georgian Manor Inn	CWC; interview emp'ee		5
1844.0	Century Textiles	TF Bank		1
2479.4	Central Environment	RF, CW McPhee	2	7
		TOTAL WORK FOR DAY	7	8

This is one of Lee's time sheets. Everyone else uses time slips. We record parts of hours to the nearest tenth. M.

FIGURE 3–1   Completed Time Sheet

FIGURE 3–2
Completed
Time Slip

12/22/98	S.C.	Sawyer	2277.2	2	30
DATE	**INITIAL**	**CLIENT**	**FILE NO.**	**TIME**	
DESCRIPTION: *Rev Material Re: S/H agree't (1.2); LTC (0.3);*					
TF Ms. North (0.5); MTF (0.3)					
			POSTED:	*L.S./Dec 23*	

Sandy's time slips are usually quite easy to read. Leslie enters them directly onto the client ledgers and I summarize them weekly for reports. M.

- In pegboard systems separate slips are mounted like shingles on a backing sheet, which may be used as a posting control. As each slip is written, summary information (date, file identification, lawyer identification, time logged) is duplicated automatically onto the backing sheet, as illustrated in Figure 3–3.

- *Other written records* such as photocopies of lawyer's desk diaries and appointment calendars. These have the advantage of being flexible and always available to the lawyer and do not require anyone to make a time entry in addition to the appointment notation. However, many diaries do not have sufficient space to note lengthy service descriptions.

- *Direct entry into automated systems,* usually by the lawyer or secretary. The time entry may go into a stand-alone time recording routine in nonintegrated accounting systems or directly into the client's accounting records in integrated systems. The secretary enters time directly either from written notes in the lawyer's calendar or from dictation tapes. This method has the advantage of prompt recording and accuracy of spelling, as the secretary is more familiar with the lawyer's handwriting and the file and is likely to spell proper names correctly. A major disadvantage of direct entry is that the notes and tapes are not usually kept, and errors are difficult to investigate.

As technology advances, more user-friendly time-keeping methods are gaining popularity. Large firms may invest in a bar-code system that enters file, date, lawyer, and description information by passing a light-pen over a printed list of choices. Computer-literate lawyers may keep a background on-line time log by entering symbols as they work at their desks while the system tracks how long a task takes. Such systems may also be integrated with the telephone system to record the telephone number called, length of call, and any long-distance charges.

TIME CONTROL SHEET

TIME CONVERSION – 1/100 UNITS

1 - 6 MINUTES = 10	31 - 36 MINUTES = 60
7 - 12 " = 20	37 - 42 " = 70
13 - 18 " = 30	43 - 48 " = 80
19 - 24 " = 40	49 - 54 " = 90
25 - 30 " = 50	55 - 60 " = 100

DATE	INITIAL	CLIENT	FILE NO.	TIME	
12/22/98	S.C.	Milton	2246.7	1	70
12/22/98	S.C.	Central Environ.	2479.4	1	40
12/22/98	S.C.	Sawyer	2277.2	2	30

DATE	INITIAL	CLIENT	FILE NO.	TIME

DESCRIPTION: *Rev Material Re: S/H agree't (1.2); LTC (0.3);*

TF Ms. North (0.5); MTF (0.3)

	POSTED:	
	POSTED:	
	POSTED:	
	POSTED:	
	POSTED:	
	POSTED:	
	POSTED:	
	POSTED:	
	POSTED:	
	POSTED:	
	POSTED:	
	POSTED:	

FIGURE 3–3 Pegboard Time Slips

Time Entry Details

Time records are generally kept only for time spent by lawyers, although the secretary may actually generate the records. Legal assistants (paralegals) also often record time spent on client files. In discussions of time and billing records in this book, paralegals are included with lawyers. Time entries include the following information:

- *Identification of lawyer* performing services (initials and/or number).

- *Date* that services were performed.

- *Client and matter identification* (number, name, and description) or identification of a nonbillable task.

- *Brief description* of services (abbreviations are common), often called the narrative.

- *Amount of time* spent, usually in tenths of hours, but sometimes in quarters or hundredths of hours.

- *Special instructions* regarding billing rates or fees. Sometimes service descriptions are added to the file records even though the time is not added into the total.

Although the secretary may produce the entries, the lawyer should at some point review and approve them.

Practical Application 3–2

Daphne: I'm the busiest associate in the whole firm. I'm always here before eight and I'm usually still finishing up on the computer when the six o'clock news comes on. Scot is really getting to me about this file number business on my timesheets. I'm not a numbers type like he has to be in data entry. I always put the name and matter reference. Can't he just look up the number? Even when I do put the file number down, he wants it for each and every entry for that file. If there are ten entries for a file on one timesheet, he expects me to write in the number ten times! Something is wrong here.

What is wrong? How would you go about trying to fix it if you were Scot? If you were the administrator?

Service Description Abbreviations

Firms adopt standard letter abbreviations in time recording systems so that lawyers' time is not wasted writing commonly used terms in longhand. They are usually tailored to the field of practice and vary significantly in length. Standard number codes are used by some firms, but lawyers find them awkward to use, as it is hard to make such codes meaningful. Figure 3–4 illustrates a selection of service description abbreviations.

Some automated systems "read" the abbreviation code and substitute a standard phrase (character string) when the time is entered, and the phrase becomes a permanent part of the record. Most systems substitute the phrase only when the ledger is printed, so if the phrase is changed in the master profile for the time code, existing time entries using the code may print out incorrectly. Therefore, it is usually best to add an abbreviation if more are needed rather than change one, unless it contains a spelling or similar error.

FIGURE 3–4

Time Recording
Abbreviations

Examples of Time Recording Abbreviations

C; Cl	Client (usually used with other abbreviations)
Crt; Crt of App	Court; Court of Appeal
CW	Conference with
Dft	Draft (either verb, adjective, or noun, as in a document)
Doc; Docs	Document; Documents
F	File
IME	Independent medical examination
LT; LF; LFC; LFOC	Letter to; Letter from; Letter from client; Letter from opposing counsel
MT; MTF; MTC	Memo to; Memo to file; Memo to client
Mtg; Mtge	Meeting; Mortgage
NoM	Notice of motion
OC	Opposing counsel
OCW	Office conference with
R; Rev; RL; RF	Review; Review; Review law, Review file
SoC; SoCC; SoD	Statement of claim; Statement of counterclaim; Statement of defense
TT;TF;TCW	Telephone call to; Telephone call from; Telephone conference with
WoS	Writ of summons
XFD	Examination for Discovery
Δ	Defendant/Defense
π	Plaintiff/Claim

Here is a list of time recording abbreviations that most of the lawyers use. M.

Revenue Recognition

Law firms earn revenue by providing clients with the services of lawyers, so technically speaking, revenue is earned at the time the services are rendered, and billable WIP time represents an asset. From an accounting perspective, the income patterns of many firms would justify revenue recognition at the time the services are rendered, using the full *accrual method* of revenue accounting. For some types of legal service fee arrangements (discussed in detail in Chapter 5), such as contingency cases and fixed-fee agreements, revenue cannot be known until the service is complete and the final bill has been presented to the client. Because so much of WIP time is adjusted upon billing, recognizing the revenue as the time is posted to the WIP ledger may not accurately reflect the firm's profitability.

Most firms do not record unbilled fees as either assets or revenue in the general ledger at the point the time is entered, even if the time is posted to a client WIP time ledger. Instead, the revenue is recognized as illustrated in Figure 3–5. Management information requirements, accounting system configurations, and (especially) tax rules and the desire to keep only one set of books combine to encourage most firms to recognize revenue at the time it is *billed* to the client. This is the **modified accrual method** for recognizing revenue.

A year-end adjustment recording the estimated value of unbilled fees is sometimes made, often for income distribution or tax purposes, but firms rarely have any record of WIP time in the general ledger.

<table>
<tr><td>

Practical Application 3–3

</td><td>

Michael: Most of the successful information systems I've seen aren't dependent on the type of accounting method used. Really good systems will give you the pertinent information in some form or other.

Clair: But you can't look at just one thing in isolation. If the financial information doesn't match your management information, how do you know where the differences are without going to accounting school for six years?

Michael: You either get a feel for it eventually or ask the accounting staff to explain it to you. Partners should not be so concerned with the mechanics of accounting—they need the big pictures to make sound decisions.

Discuss both Michael's and Clair's viewpoints. What types of reports could they both use?

</td></tr>
</table>

─────────────────────── TERMS ───────────────────────

modified accrual method   A hybrid accounting method that recognizes revenue when it is billed, instead of when it is worked (full accrual) or collected (cash method).

FIGURE 3–5
Accounting
Methods and
Revenue
Recognition

Event	Cash		Modified Accrual		Full Accrual	
	Debit	**Credit**	**Debit**	**Credit**	**Debit**	**Credit**
Time Recorded	WIP Ledger		WIP Ledger		**Unbilled Fees** WIP Ledger	**Fee Revenue**
Time Billed	A/R Ledger	WIP Ledger	**Accounts Receivable** A/R Ledger	**Fee Revenue** Wip Ledger	**Accounts Receivable** A/R Ledger	**Unbilled Fees** WIP Ledger
Client Pays Bill	**Bank Account**	**Fee Revenue** A/R Ledger	**Bank Account**	**Accounts Receivable** A/R Ledger	**Bank Account**	**Accounts Receivable** A/R Ledger

Boldface indicates entries to the general ledger.

Billing Rates

If WIP time is presented in the general ledger or supplementary reports in dollar amounts, a value is calculated by multiplying the number of hours by a **billing rate**. Sometimes a standard rate is used for each lawyer, and an adjustment is made at the time of billing if a different rate is charged to the client. Billing rates are governed by:

- Seniority of the lawyer (years in practice, expertise in a certain field of practice).

- Agreements with individual clients to charge a certain rate per hour for all lawyers.

- Agreements with clients to charge certain lawyers at certain rates.

- Special challenges presented by certain types of cases.

Rate structures can be very complicated and are subject to confusion and error in manual recording systems, especially if more than one lawyer works on a file. Most automated systems can charge the correct rates, but caution is needed when setting up the client file if the file information controls the billing rate. Figure 3–6 illustrates two types of billing rate criteria used in combination. Billing rates that are not realistic for a lawyer or field of practice should be avoided.

Case 3–2

Found: **Skill required to perform legal tasks was not extraordinary.**

Ordered: Less than 50% of requested fees awarded to firm.

———————————————— TERMS ————————————————

billing rate   A value attached to lawyers' services, usually an hourly rate.

FIGURE 3–6
Billing Rates

Carpenter & Cook
Billing Rates
Effective: November 1, 1998

Init.	Name	Title	Premium	Standard	Discount	Cost
P.C.	Pat Carpenter	Partner	240.00	210.00	180.00	140.00
S.C.	Sandy Cook	Partner	230.00	200.00	180.00	125.00
T.B.	Terry Baker	Associate	180.00	160.00	140.00	90.00
L.M.	Lee Mason	of Counsel	195.00	180.00	165.00	100.00
K.G.	Kim Gardener	Paralegal	60.00	60.00	45.00	35.00
M.F.	Marty Fisher	Paralegal	75.00	50.00	40.00	30.00

This is the most recent billing rate schedule. The "cost" figure is based on the break-even point for a "slow" month (about 70 billable hours). M.

Sometimes WIP time is recorded not according to hours spent but by the nature of the task, as with court appointments or other assignments where the total amount to be billed is determined by statute. Some systems permit task codes to be set up and automatically apply the correct fee. However, this method is not helpful in determining whether the work is lucrative at the lawyer's standard rate and is not used in systems where performance evaluation is a major objective.

Practical Application 3–4

Dan: I always encourage associates to use a billing rate that is a little on the high side. That way, if you reduce the bill, you feel good about it and so does the client. It gives you what you might call maneuvering room—a bit of slack so you can make an equitable decision about billing without losing your shirt.

What are the pros and cons of Dan's philosophy? How would you react as an associate? As a client, if you knew about his perspective?

Entering Time Data

There are many ways to distribute the time recording procedure. Whether the accounting, clerical, or secretarial staff make the original time entry, the responsibility for *controlling* the procedure usually rests with the accounting staff, who are ultimately responsible for the completeness and quality of the records and supplementary reports for the whole firm. Lawyers and secretaries are still responsible for their assigned duties and must cooperate with the accounting staff to ensure the system runs smoothly.

Time records are entered promptly, as recent events are likely to be remembered by the lawyer if questions arise in the recording process. Whether using a manual or automated system, the procedure requires the following controls:

- When accessing the client ledger, the client name and file reference are checked to the time data source document.

- The total of each batch of time entries is compared to an edit or control total.

- Each entered document is clearly marked, identifying the individual who entered it and the *entry* date.

- After entry, the source documents are filed in a way that permits easy retrieval of *incorrectly* recorded items. The best method will depend on the recording process, the form of the document, and the type of WIP ledgers used. Timesheets are usually filed chronologically by lawyer in separate binders, or under separate lawyer tabs in monthly binders. Time slips allow more flexibility in filing after input. They are filed chronologically and/or by lawyer, as timesheets are, or by client. However, if they are filed by client, misfiled or incorrectly entered slips are harder to trace.

Practical Application 3–5

Rosemary: I wait until I get all of the timesheets for one day before I enter any of them. That way, I know I have them all. When I go into the computer, I always work on the same date so that there is no confusion. Mr. Rook is always the last to give me his timesheet, but lately he's only been about two weeks late. Some of the other lawyers are complaining that the time isn't up to date, and I tell them to go and talk to Mr. Rook. I'm a time entry clerk, and I'm not paid to handle complaints that lawyers basically have about each other. The buck doesn't stop here.

What can the other lawyers do to resolve the situation if Mr. Rook is a partner? A senior associate? Of counsel?

Time Journals

Time journals can be memorandum journals, used for management reporting and data organization, as opposed to journals recording financial transactions in the general and client ledgers. In automated systems the journal may be simply the list of posted transactions, often called the batch or edit list.

In automated systems, the time journals are created when the time is entered. However, if the revenue is not recognized until the WIP time is billed, there is no entry into the general ledger. Entries are made only to the client time ledger and to memo records, which are used to generate reports for each lawyer or by other criteria. Many firms that use manual time recording systems either do not require reports on logged time or require only a total of hours logged per lawyer each month.

Client Time Ledgers

Almost all time recording systems are designed to provide a basic chronological record of services the firm provides to individual clients. There may be no service description but simply a summary of hours spent on the file each week. The level of detail in posting time to the client ledger depends on the firm's needs and the system's capabilities. In a manual ledger, such as the one illustrated in Figure 3–7, usually only the date, lawyer identification, hours logged, and dollar value are recorded. These manual ledgers may be difficult to summarize if many lawyers work on the same file at different billing rates. If an itemized bill is required, the time records are kept until the bill is typed or the service descriptions are entered into a word-processing document.

In automated systems, time data are entered as received, and the client ledger contains all the details until the time is billed. In many automated systems the time details are purged after billing and are no longer available for review. In these situations, a copy of the time details (before purging) must be retained in the client and/or accounting records.

In the simplest time recording systems, no time journal or formal client WIP time ledger is created in the accounting sense, and the source time data are not recorded in any other accounting records. Such systems include:

- *Billing details in a word-processing document* used to create itemized bills, entered by the secretary from timesheets or time slips.

- *Collections of time slips* filed by client file until billing when they are summarized as necessary.

- *Client time logs* or sheets of paper kept for each client file in the front of a client folder. These are not submitted to the accounting staff, although they must be referred to if itemized bills are to be produced. This system may be adequate for billing and diary purposes but is not useful in assessing the performance of individual lawyers or the value of the firm's unbilled time. Lawyers usually remember to document time if the folder is handy but may forget to make entries if it is not. As time is billed, the log is ruled off and the running total starts at nil. Figure 3–8 illustrates such a log.

Carpenter & Cook

CLIENT WIP TIME LEDGER

Re: *Fraud Claim: Ladies' Best Bet*   Client Name: *Century Textiles Inc.*

Responsible Lawyer: *S.C.*   Notes: *use "discount" billing rates*

Week Ending	Lawyer	Hours	Rate	Amount	Total
10/7/98	LM	2.3	150.00	345.00	
" "	SC	1.6	180.00	288.00	633.00
10/14/98	SC	4.2	180.00	756.00	1,389.00
10/28/98	LM	0.6	150.00	90.00	
" "	SC	12.7	180.00	2,286.00	3,765.00
11/5/98	LM	2.3	165.00	379.50	
" "	SC	0.4	210.00	84.00	4,228.50
11/19/98	LM	15.3	165.00	2,524.50	
" "	SC	14.6	210.00	3,066.00	9,819.00

Sandy's team uses time ledgers for all files to be billed on an hourly basis. There was a billing rate increase for some lawyers at the beginning of November. M.

FIGURE 3–7   Client WIP Time Ledger

Carpenter & Cook

CLIENT TIME LOG

Lawyer: _T.B._   Client Name: _Top Dog Drycleaning_

File Number: _2276.4_   Re: _Corporate (General)_   Page _1_

Date	Initial	Description	Hours	Bal(hrs)
10/6/98	TB	Init. interview	1.2	1.2
10/10/98	KG	TTC, Dft Agrmnt	2.4	3.6
10/13/98	KG	MT T.B. re: Law	1.1	4.7
10/20/98	TB	CWC, Execute Agreement	.6	5.3
10/31/98	TB	TFC, RF, RL, TTC	1.3	6.6
10/31/98	KG	RL, MTF, LTC	.9	7.5
10/31/98	Bill # 164	Acct. Rend.	(7.5)	0
11/06/98	KG	TFC, LT Bank	1.7	1.7
11/10/98	TB	CWC, MTF re: mtg	2.6	4.3

Pat's team uses time logs for files billed on an hourly basis. M.

FIGURE 3–8   Client Time Log

These systems are obviously limited in the management information they provide, but they are uncomplicated and inexpensive and are popular in very small practices that do not have automated accounting systems.

Randy: We have a new associate who will be bringing in some insurance defense work from a large company, and we'll have to start a time-keeping system. I don't like it myself, but this is a good client and they demand detailed bills. Yes sir, life in six-minute intervals. I'm worried we'll all get to be clock watchers and uptight all the time.

What are some ways to ensure that the new system doesn't completely change the atmosphere of the firm, and also that there are not too many different systems?

Policies and Controls

In firms using time recording to its full potential, time records are often the most numerous of all accounting-related records in the firm. Because they are generated internally and there are no outside checks to help detect errors (until the bill is reviewed by the client, when it is often too late to correct errors properly) as there are with other accounting records, internal controls must be rigorous, and overlapping where possible. However, the volume and variety of time entries makes strong controls especially difficult to design, administer, and implement, and lawyers may begin to feel that the time recording system is a master instead of a servant. Although they recognize the need for quality time records, many lawyers find the process tedious and have difficulty following strict routines. Figure 3–9 illustrates an example of the complete time recording and reporting function in a medium-sized firm.

Policies regarding time recording should be established at the management or partnership level, preferably in writing. At a minimum, well-designed policies specify that the original time data is to be prepared:

- *Promptly:* lawyers may forget to record small segments of time after several hours.

- *Accurately:* time amounts, file numbers, and client names must be recorded correctly.

- *Thoroughly:* all of the required information is completed so that others who are less familiar with the file will not have to guess at incomplete information.

- *Legibly:* illegible records cannot be accurate or complete.

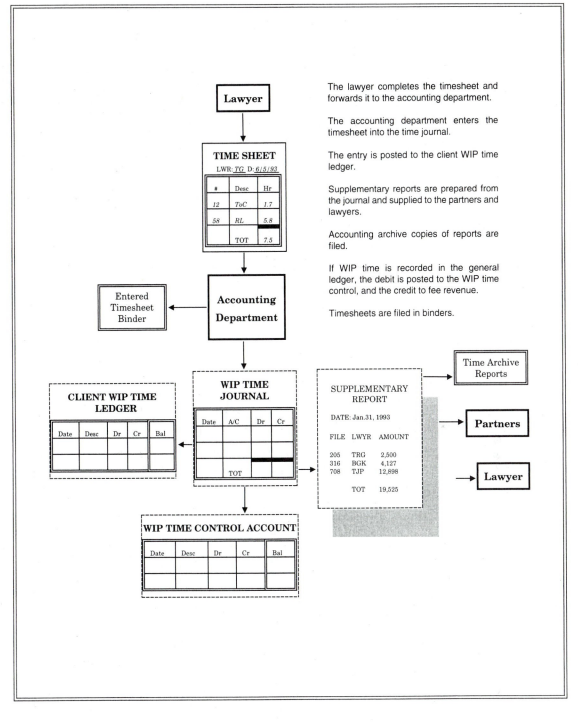

FIGURE 3–9 Time Recording Process

Because most people within the firm are involved in some phase of time recording, special care should be taken to ensure that *all* components contribute to a smooth-running system. Concerns that all effective time recording systems address are:

- Identifying missing and delinquent entry documents.

- Potential for recording errors, especially incorrect client numbers, amounts, and lawyers.

- Entries out of order that cannot be sorted or isolated from the other records.

- Flexibility of reporting options, which is an essential feature of usefulness in reporting.

<table>
<tr><td>**Practical Application 3–7**</td><td>Fay:</td><td>I understand that completing time slips is not the most exciting task in the world, but it's important in our firm. We bill all through the month and need to be up to date at all times. But Kirk is always at least a week late with his slips, and he makes a scene if I nag him. He even calls me Fuss-budget Fay and that annoys me. I'm just doing my job as data entry clerk, why can't he do his bit?</td></tr>
</table>

What should Fay do?

WIP Time Reports and Summaries

The time data that have been entered into the system are used to create a variety of information reports, which are used for specific purposes such as determining which files are to be billed. Some reports identify missing or incorrectly recorded time data, and frequent review of time reports is essential in locating and correcting errors at the earliest possible opportunity.

Many WIP time reports and summaries are produced at regular intervals, monthly or annually, and form part of the standard accounting archives. Reports and summaries, such as the budget summary illustrated in Figure 3–10, are also produced to provide budgetary control. Although most productivity reports in law firms are generated from *billing* records, WIP time reports can also be very useful if they are understood and interpreted properly.

Sometimes a report that would normally be generated from billing records is compiled from the WIP records because files are not yet billable (for example, incomplete matters or those billed on a contingency basis) and an estimate of the ultimate bill amount is required. Also, partners' profit distribution ratios may be calculated partially on WIP as an estimate of the realizable value of fees.

FIGURE 3–10
Budget Report:
Time Logged

MONTHLY LOGGED TIME SUMMARY BY LAWYER

MONTH: Nov. 1998

LAWYER	HOURS	DOLLARS	BUDGET	(UND)/OVR
P.C.	125.6	21,875.00	23,000.00	(1,125.00)
S.C.	136.7	24,606.00	25,000.00	(394.00)
T.B.	154.4	18,655.50	15,000.00	3,655.50
L.M.	147.0	22,785.00	23,250.00	(465.00)
TOTALS	**563.7**	**87,921.50**	**86,250.00**	**1,671.50**

Pat does not have a high budget because of all the time administration takes. This report is distributed to partners only. M.

Reports are produced using various criteria, often in combination. Even in advanced automated systems, some reports may require extra calculations, either manually or through a spreadsheet program, to produce information needed to support management decisions such as human resource allocation. Figure 3–11 illustrates examples of both common and unusual reports produced from the WIP records.

WIP Time Adjustments

Adequate internal controls limit WIP time adjustments due to omission, duplication, and misallocation. However, errors do occur and should be corrected promptly, with a description of the nature of the adjustment. Many firms do not adjust the WIP ledger at all, or adjust it only at billing time, especially if the only error is in the billing rate. The effect on lawyers' performance reports, however, is important, especially where there is a duplication or omission and where logged time is an issue in lawyers' remuneration.

Errors often come to the lawyer's attention through a review of a summary client WIP list, and the lawyer requests a copy of the client's WIP time details. Adjustments noted on this copy are used as the adjusting entry data source, or a separate entry document may be required.

Purpose	**Recipient(s)**	**• Report/Frequency**	**Criteria Options • (1) : (2) : (3)**
Billing decision and/or Trust transfer	Responsible lawyer	• WIP time by file/monthly • WIP time and trust by file/weekly	• (own files) : (numerically) • (own files over threshold $) : (alpha) • (select area) : (over threshold $)
File housekeeping and/or Inactive file report	Secretary Lawyer Accounting staff	• date of last time entry/monthly	• (120+ days) : (lawyer) : (numerically) • (firm files) : (alpha) : (last entry date) • (under threshold $) : (file start date)
Marketing focus	Marketing committee	• firm hours logged/annually	• (select area) : (zip code) : (lawyer)
Responsibility level	Management committee	• firm hours logged on own files ÷ total firm hours logged/monthly	• (lawyer) : (seniority) : (area)
Supervisory burden	Management committee	• total firm hours on own files ÷ own hours on own files/annually	• (lawyer) : (# of hours)
Referral capacity	Marketing committee	• firm hours on referred files ÷ total firm files/annually	• (lawyer) : (area) : ($ value of hours)
Performance measurement (associates)	Each associate Compensation committee	• hours logged vs. budget/monthly • billable hours ÷ total hours/monthly	• (lawyer)
Volume growth (firm or lawyer)	Lawyer Management	• logged this period vs. logged last period/quarterly	• (hours) • ($ value of hours)
Partners' profit distribution	Distribution committee Partner	• own (responsible) WIP amount ÷ firm WIP amount/annually	• (partner)
Change in WIP investment	Finance committee	• WIP value this period vs. WIP value last period/ monthly	• (area) : (lawyer) • (lawyer) : (WIP age)

FIGURE 3–11 Time Reports: Uses and Selection Criteria

There are two types of WIP time adjustments: corrections and deletions. Many types of corrections and deletions should be made only by accounting staff who are familiar with all of the ramifications of making an adjusting entry. In almost all cases, complete removal of a transaction from the system should be avoided, especially where the original entry affected reports that have already been distributed.

WIP Time Corrections

Corrections are often made out of date order. Most automated systems will not allow any entries to a closed period, especially if it affects client ledgers. In any system, back-dating entries to a closed period is avoided because it often creates more problems than it solves. The date the adjustment was *made* should be used, with a description of the adjustment and a notation of the original date.

If a time entry was simply not recorded when it should have been, the adjusting entry will be similar to what the correct entry would have been. If the time was not to have been recorded or was recorded twice, an entry is made to all ledgers originally affected, often in the form of a reverse time entry. If the original entry was recorded in the wrong amount (hours and/or billing rate), then the original should be reversed and the correct one entered. Some firms with manual ledgers simply strike out the wrong entry and adjust the total, but this method provides insufficient information to trace the reason and/or authorization for the change if questions arise later.

Time entries that are merely posted to the wrong file can sometimes be corrected by making entries in both client WIP time ledgers and cross-referencing the file numbers without affecting the other journals or ledgers. Some automated systems will not allow this, and so reversing and correcting entries must be made. Automated systems that use or emulate database-type records may permit simply changing the client file field, but this method should be avoided unless an audit trail to the original entry can be generated.

Practical Application 3–8

Sheila:	I think it's always best to have the time records as perfect as possible even if it means making lots of corrections. You save time when you have to do the client's bill.
Jade:	That's not really how I see it. The time records are just the basis for preparing the bill; they aren't the last word. If you bill on schedule, you have lots of time to make any adjustments then.
Sheila:	But you don't know if you'll have lots of time then. What if some emergency comes up, or the printer crashes, or . . . ?

How do people's working and personal styles affect the efficiency of a system? Do these traits need to be considered when deciding about system changes? To what degree?

WIP Time Deletions

WIP time is usually deleted (often called "written off," although this term is normally applied only to items that have been billed) when:

- The file was charged with an incorrect time entry and an ordinary adjustment would be pointless (if the correct file has been closed or cannot be billed for the item).

- The firm has agreed to reduce or remove a correctly recorded time charge.

- The firm cannot bill the time because the client lost on a contingency matter (discussed in Chapter 5).

Firms develop an in-house form for **WIP time deletions**, as illustrated in Figure 3–12, or use a copy of the client's WIP time ledger. Deletions from summary reports are discouraged because the "deletion" might actually be a recording error.

The proper authorization must be provided, and the supporting document is filed chronologically, by file number, or in another logical order after the deletion has been done. Usually, policies of firms require that any WIP deletion be authorized by the lawyer responsible for the file, the lawyer whose time is being deleted (if different), and/or a partner.

If the general ledger is affected, the debit is posted to either a time variance account or directly against a fee revenue account, with the credit to the WIP time asset. Some automated systems require that a "zero bill" be entered in order to correct the WIP time ledger or permanently remove entries that net to zero.

Practical Application 3–9

Simon: I've been here less than two weeks and already I think my job's in jeopardy—and I was only trying to help and do thorough work and show some initiative! Ms. Wells was in court and I had no immediate assignments, so I went through the WIP report we got today. Some of the time had already been billed or the file was closed and it obviously could not be billed again, so I sent in some WIP deletion forms. That was part of my job at Mr. Cairns' office—to keep the WIP report nice and clean, with only time that could be expected to be billed so that he knew exactly where he stood with unbilled fees. Not the same here, though! Ms. Wells had a fit about what I'd done. She said I was overstepping the bounds and doing things I had no authority to do. How was I to know things are so different in this office? Now the bookkeeper has put through the deletions and they have to be reversed and she's mad at me, too. Why didn't she

--------------------------------- TERMS ---------------------------------

WIP time deletion   The removal of a time record from a client ledger before the record is billed.

tell me that she couldn't put them through on my authority? Is she trying to get me in trouble?

What would you do if you were Simon, given the current situation? What would you have done differently if you were Simon? What do you think Ms. Wells should do? What should the bookkeeper do?

FIGURE 3–12
WIP Time
Deletion Form

WIP TIME DELETION FORM

Date: _Nov. 30, 1998_   Client: _Pleasant Hills Mortuary_

File Number: _1289.8_   Re: _Deadbeat Collection Agency Inc._

Cut-off Date: _Nov. 15, 1998_   Authorized: _S Cook_

LAWYER	HOURS	VALUE
TB	4.5	495.00
SC	1.6	240.00
PC	1.1	192.50
TOTAL	7.2	927.50

Reason: _Opposing party ultimately prevailing. Final bill sent Sept. 30, 1998. This was more for clean-up and goodwill--Miles Hall will bring in more work in the new year._

We use these forms to delete "leftover" time. For time deletions that are single entries, use a copy of the WIP time ledger. M.

Comprehensive Exercises

1. Using the procedural flowchart in Figure 3–9, design a control system integrating the following features:

   a. Assurance that any missing timesheets are identified within three working days.

   b. Review by the lawyer of time entries each week.

   c. A monthly report of how many billable hours each lawyer worked each day.

2. Design a time entry and reporting checklist for a new law office staff person following the example table. There should be at least thirty items to complete.

3. Choose a field of practice and design at least twenty service description abbreviations that cover common services. Describe what criteria you used in designing the abbreviations (such as a string that is not used in English or extra characters). Is a numeric system easier than an alphabetic one? Why or why not?

4. Discuss the relative merits of the three main alternatives of revenue recognition. What is the impact of the field of practice? Level of automation in the firm? Types of clients?

▌▌▌▌

CHAPTER 4

DISBURSEMENT RECORDS

In most client matters, the firm not only provides the legal services of its lawyers but also incurs certain costs incidental to conducting the matter, called *disbursements* or advance costs. In the context of disbursements, "incidental" does not mean "insignificant" or "negligible," and certainly not "free to the firm." It refers generally to goods and services purchased by the firm in its role as the client's *agent* (or fiduciary) in handling the client's affairs. ABA Model Rule 1.8(e) enumerates situations where a lawyer is permitted to advance costs to or on behalf of a client.

ABA Model Rule 1.8(e)

(e) A lawyer shall not provide financial assistance to a client in connection with pending or contemplated litigation, except that:

(1) a lawyer may advance court costs and expenses of litigation, the repayment of which may be contingent on the outcome of the matter; and

(2) a lawyer representing an indigent client may pay court costs and expenses of litigation on behalf of the client.

Therefore, lawyers must be careful, especially in litigation matters, that disbursements relate to the client-lawyer relationship. It is not acceptable in most jurisdictions for lawyers to lend money to or otherwise support clients, except as required in the conduct of the legal services being rendered.

Case 4–1

Found: **Lawyer advanced money to client for automobile insurance premiums and mortgage payments.**

Ordered: Lawyer disqualified from representation.

In fields of practice such as criminal defense or in fixed-fee billing arrangements, firms may choose not to record or charge any disbursements. In fields like real property, anticipated disbursements might be billed to clients before they have been entered into the accounting system. Because estimating disbursements can cause more problems than the increase in monetary recovery is worth and because lawyers have been disciplined for billing unsupported "estimated disbursements," many firms prefer quoting a fixed fee that includes small, predictable disbursements to avoid both the costly recording procedure and the risk of overbilling the client. If the firm will be applying for court-awarded costs on behalf of the client, however, it has a clear obligation to ensure that records of disbursements are complete, supportable, and reasonable. A properly established and maintained system not only reduces the need to estimate disbursements but improves overall recovery.

Some disbursements are paid from clients' funds in trust (escrow) rather than from the firm's own funds. These are discussed in Chapter 7.

Disbursement Source Documents

Internal disbursements, sometimes referred to as allocated overhead costs or noncash disbursements, occur solely within the firm. These are also called service disbursements, implying that built into the charge for an item is an element of internal cost recovery to the firm. For example, photocopying charges may include costs related to paper and other consumables and the photocopier lease and service contract. Internal disbursements include:

- photocopies made on the office photocopier;

- fax charges, incoming and outgoing charges on a per-page or per-minute basis;

- postage through a mail machine;

- on-line connection fees for searches or legal research;

- file opening fees to recover the firm's cost of stationery and file folders; and

- secretarial fees for special transcriptions and nonroutine services.

If firms intend to charge the latter two, the client fee agreement makes specific mention of this type of charge.

Case 4–2   Found: Lawyer charged client for secretarial fees in addition to agreed flat hourly fee. **This constituted an excessive fee if such fees were not part of the agreed compensation.**

Ordered: (for this and other issues) Two-year suspension.

Other disbursements are invoiced to the firm by the supplier on a **summary invoice**, or statement, which often includes some costs that the firm itself incurs as overhead such as:

- long-distance telephone and fax charges;

- courier charges;

- on-line title searches;

- taxi fares;

-- TERMS --

internal disbursements   Disbursements arising from a combination of goods and services that are generated within the firm on behalf of a client.

summary invoice   An invoice from a supplier of client disbursements, normally listing disbursements for several files.

- filing fees (on account with court registries);

- agents' fees charged by agents in filing, serving, and searching;

- case law from a research company; and

- travel-related disbursements and other costs charged to a firm credit card.

Direct disbursements are paid separately by check directly to the supplier, especially where it is not practical to have a running account with the supplier, such as for a medical report. Direct disbursements include:

- filing fees paid directly to court registries;

- document service;

- doctors' and clinical reports;

- expert witness fees;

- evidence photography and videotaping services;

- specific stationery costs such as corporate records books and seals;

- documents from government offices and police departments;

- printing and binding charges for legal documents when a printing company is used; and

- photocopies billed by other law firms, usually the opposing side in litigation where copies of documents are supplied.

Some suppliers request advance payment, especially for doctors' reports and information from government offices.

Internal Disbursements

Internal disbursements are recorded on small all-purpose forms (illustrated in Figure 4–1) or on a condensed manual log (see Figure 4–2). Firms also use recording devices to ensure that equipment cannot be used unless a valid client or nonbillable activity or department code is entered into a control device. With some equipment such as fax machines, activity printouts are a regular part of the machine's functions. The device dispenses a printout as a source document (shown in Figure 4–3). With some equipment such as fax machines, activity printouts are a regular part of the machine's functions. Some devices can produce electronic records that are transferred directly into the accounting system and no additional input

───────────────── **TERMS** ─────────────────

direct disbursement   Separate disbursements paid by individual check and often in advance of receiving the item or service.

labor is required. The data input, however, should still be supported by a printout kept permanently in the accounting records.

FIGURE 4–1
Multipurpose
Disbursement
Form

Date	File #	Description	Code	Amount
11/12/98	2409.1	Postage	16	38.50
		Fax L/D	13	
11/12/98	2015.6	On-line	19	19.53
11/12/98	2277.2	Corp Binder	42	36.00
Posted: M.F. Nov. 14, 1998			Total	94.03

We don't have a separate log for some types of disbursements so we use these slips to record them. M.

FIGURE 4–2
Manual Log: Long
Distance Charges

Carpenter & Cook

LONG DISTANCE PHONE CALL SUMMARY

Date of Phone Invoice: _Nov. 30, 1998_   Journal Number: _LD/1198_

File #	Client Name	#	P	Charges
1512.3	Hunter, M.	2	P	6.79
1289.8	Pleasant Hills	5	P	45.65
1156.9	Prairie Twine	3	P	13.33
2111.3	Georgian Manor	2	P	28.67
2409.1	United Investment	8	P	109.22
2277.2	Sawyer	14	P	266.54
2377.0	Hall, M.	9	P	76.45
TOTALS		43		546.65

We call the operator to get a quote on time and charges for all long-distance calls for client files. Leslie keeps the log at the reception desk and takes all of the operator call-backs and produces this monthly summary which indicates the number of calls included in the total charges. M.

FIGURE 4–3
Device-Generated
Log: Fax Records

TRANSMISSION AND PAGE COUNT
11/01/98 - 11/07/98

DATE	REF #	TO	FROM	# PGS	MESSAGE
11/01/98	1073.6		488-1020	03	REC OK
11/01/98	1073.6	488-1020		16	TRAN OK
11/03/98	1087.6		487-9111	04	REC OK
11/04/98	2479.4	485-4375		09	TRAN ERR
11/04/98	2479.4	485-4375		18	TRAN OK
11/05/98	2479.4		485-4375	05	REC ERR
11/05/98	2479.4		485-4375	17	REC OK
11/05/98	2409.1		488-7917	02	REC ERR
11/05/98	2409.1		488-7917	14	REC OK

```
REC   OK  = 38
REC   ERR = 07
TRAN OK   = 34
TRAN ERR  = 09

ACTIVITY  = 88
```

END REPORT

Leslie makes a list of all of the client fax numbers and completes this weekly printout from the machine with the file numbers for faxes received. We charge $1.00/page, but not for the "ERR" transmissions. M.

Some disbursements can only practically be paid by cash, either directly from the accounting staff to someone who comes to the office (such as a delivery person) or by other staff who pay for something outside of the office. These disbursements are reimbursed from petty cash, using a voucher, and include:

- special delivery charges that must be paid at the post office;

- courthouse or university library photocopies and copy cards; and

- local bus, rail, and taxi fares.

The disbursements are entered as they occur or they are entered from the petty cash journal when petty cash is reconciled (see Chapter 2). The vouchers are attached to the petty cash reconciliation or kept in envelopes in the accounting area.

Staff members also personally incur larger disbursements using their own cash or a personal credit card. These are summarized on an expense report (see Chapter 2) and usually relate to travel, such as:

- hotel accommodations;

- air, ferry, taxi, rail, and bus fares;

- meals, accommodation, and subsistence allowances; and

- mileage charges for business use of a personal automobile.

The expenses are reimbursed to staff by check after the disbursements have been approved by the lawyer(s) responsible for the file(s). The expense reports are filed in separate binders by individual and date after the reimbursement check has been issued.

Case 4–3	Found:	Lawyer charged client illegal, inappropriate, and excessive fees and expenses, **including a personal vacation taken ostensibly to take a witness's statement when the lawyer knew the witness would be locally available soon thereafter.**
	Ordered:	(for this and other issues) Three-month suspension.

Summary Invoice Disbursements

Summary invoice disbursements could be recorded in the same manner as internal disbursements (in a log or using forms) at the time the disbursement is incurred. For example, long-distance "time and charges" requested from the operator are kept in a log by the receptionist and are entered into the accounting system before the telephone bill is received by the firm because the amount and file reference are known at the time the disbursement is incurred.

Some firms wait until the summary invoice is received before entering these disbursements into the system, especially if the supplier provides the firm's own file reference names or numbers on the invoice and/or attached supporting documents, as illustrated in Figure 4–4.

Direct Payment Disbursements

A check request form, such as the one illustrated in Figure 4–5, serves both as an authorization to make an advance payment and as a source document. It specifies the details of the payment, including:

- full *identification of the file* to which the disbursement is to be charged;

- *bank account* if the firm draws disbursement checks on more than one account;

FIGURE 4–4
Summary Invoice:
Agent

S *undown*
earch
&
ervice

1700 Eastern Way
Sundown, ST 10100

Carpenter & Cook
Attorneys at Law
2400 - 555 North Ocean Street
Fielding, ST 10001

Statement Date:
December 31, 1998

Invoice Date	Invoice Number	Your File Reference	Filing Disb.	Agents Fees/Disb.	Invoice Total
12/17/98	546789	2409.1	100.00	19.00	119.00
12/19/98	546782	1673.3	150.00	62.00	212.00
12/20/98	546133	2186.5	125.00	32.00	157.00
12/27/98	54512	2186.5	50.00	15.00	65.00
				Statement Total	553.00

This is one of the invoices we accrued at the end of December. M.

- full and correct *name of the payee*;

- *nature of the disbursement* and the code where one is used; and

- *total amount of the check* and the currency if it is for a foreign supplier such as a government providing documents.

Other details that help to trace transactions and improve efficiency include:

- *date the request was prepared*;

- *date the check is to be available*;

- *person who prepared the form* in case the person preparing the check has questions;

- *person to whom the check should be forwarded* for handling if it is not mailed directly by the accounting staff;

- any necessary *internal authorization*; and

- *specific instructions*.

These forms are prepared by the lawyer or secretary and forwarded to designated accounting staff for preparation of the check.

Carpenter & Cook

DISBURSEMENT CHECK REQUEST

Request date _Nov 26, 1998_	Date Required _Nov. 29, 1998_
Approved by _____S.C._____	at: _____noon_____
	Forward to _____C.W._____

File #: _2409.1_   Name: _____United Investment Corp._____

Re: _____Cross Town Towing_____

Drawee Bank: _____State Eastern - Disbursements_____

Amount: _$678.00_ To: _Dean Business Consultants_

Description/Code: _valuation of Cross Town_

Other instructions _____

Check number	1416
Check date	Nov 28, 1998
Check prepared by	L.S.
Check entered by	M.F.

Here is an example of our disbursement check request. Usually, the secretaries complete them, the lawyer approves them, and Leslie or I prepare the checks. M.

FIGURE 4–5 Check Request Form: Direct Disbursement

Basil: I always ask the administrator to approve my disbursement check requests. After all, he knows the firm's policy on issuing checks. As a legal
secretary, I can't approve them, and the lawyer I work for is usually too
busy to approve forms and do in-office paperwork. Requests sometimes
sit in his in-tray for days, and some checks need to go out right away.

What problems might arise from this method? What can Basil do?

Disbursement Journals

Technically, a file disbursement is created when it is *incurred,* irre-
spective of when it is paid, but in practice different types of disbursement journals affect how (or if) it is recorded in the general ledger and
client WIP disbursement ledgers and how it is treated upon billing.

Automated systems organize many small transactions well, but in
manual client accounting systems, recording small frequent disbursements is so time-consuming and awkward that it is often considered
more an obstacle to efficiency than an aid to it.

Shelly: Each Monday morning, I get a tape from our copy-recording device and
enter the number of copies and dollar amount on the client ledger. It can
take up a lot of room on the card, but the immediate recovery is worth it.

Mona: Is the improved recovery really worth all that time? You not only have to
record the copies each week, but you then have to summarize them
when you prepare the bill. If you take into consideration your hourly rate
of pay, I'd bet you actually lose money on the time it takes, compared to
making a conservative estimate and billing that amount.

Discuss the merits of both approaches. Under what conditions would Shelly's method
work best? Which method would you recommend for a small firm? For a large one?

Most automated systems provide a disbursement code, similar to a
time recording code, that helps the system group similar disbursements. Even manual systems are easier to work with if there is some
standard abbreviation for each type of disbursement. Figure 4–6 illustrates a disbursement coding system.

—————————————————————— TERMS ——————————————————————

client WIP disbursement ledger   A subsidiary ledger listing unbilled disbursements
on a client file.

FIGURE 4–6
Disbursement
Codes

DISBURSEMENT CODES

11	Photocopies
12	Long-distance calls
13	Long-distance faxes
14	Incoming faxes
15	Outgoing faxes
16	Postage
17	Computer legal research
18	Computer registry search
19	On-line fees
22	Courier
23	Agent's fees & disbursements
25	Filing fees
27	Search fees
28	Document service
31	Police report
32	Expert report
33	Doctor's report
34	Clinical records
35	Expert evidence
36	Video evidence
40	Case law
42	Corporate records book
52	Conduct money
53	Local travel
54	Long distance travel

We use disbursement codes to summarize disbursements on the client bills and to reduce writing time. M.

The data required to create disbursements journals are:

- *A date,* preferably the date incurred for direct disbursements or the last day of the summary period for disbursements posted from internal records as a period total.

- *Description of disbursement* that will be printed on the client bill, often a code.

- *Client file reference,* number and/or name of client and matter.

- *Posting source reference,* either the journal number or the check number.

- *Amount of the disbursement.* Some disbursement data are entered as quantities, such as the number of photocopies, and the system converts each quantity to an amount by applying a predefined rate.

After the journals have been posted to the ledgers, they are filed separately in disbursement journal binders or chronologically with the firm's other journals.

Accounting Methods

General ledger treatment of WIP disbursements varies considerably between firms and is determined by the firm's accounting method (cash or accrual, as discussed in Chapter 1) and system and by its financial information requirements.

The *cash* method is common in both manual and nonintegrated automated systems, especially where there are no client WIP ledgers. Disbursements are directly expensed when paid to third parties and either lumped into one general ledger expense account or separated into several accounts according to type.

In *accrual* systems, unbilled disbursements are recognized as assets. If the total of all client WIP disbursement ledgers is expected to equal the asset, then the asset account is a *control account*. This configuration is common only in integrated automated systems, where the software will not allow unbalanced entries and the client ledger is posted simultaneously with the general ledger. Internal disbursements must also be recorded in the asset account, with the credit posted to either a disbursement revenue or an expense recovery account. When the disbursements are billed, the same asset is credited so that the control is always in balance with the client ledgers. If a controlling asset account is used in the general ledger, the sum of the client ledger balances is compared to it at least monthly.

Sometimes a WIP disbursement asset account is not a control account because no effort is made to ensure that the client WIP disbursement ledgers total to the net asset. These accounts are common only in nonintegrated automated systems where the firm does not use the cash method. The WIP asset account is simply a convenient place to post the debit side of a disbursement paid to a third party, and no entries are made for internal disbursements.

Practical Application 4–3

Rosemary: I don't see how unbilled disbursements can be assets. They're a cost of doing business on behalf of our clients, and those types of costs are expenses.

Chester: Yes, but they're different from the *firm's* cost of doing business, which would be the same whether or not we incurred any disbursement costs on behalf of clients.

Rosemary: That may be but until we bill them, we may not get them back from the client.

Chester: In certain cases, though, we are quite certain to receive them with the fee award.

What are some of the assumptions that Rosemary and Chester make to support their opinions. Does the validity of these assumptions vary between fields of practice?

Internal Disbursement Journals

Internal disbursement logs and forms are totaled daily, weekly, or monthly, with the total serving as an input control in systems with a controlling WIP asset account. They are entered in batches and identified in the journal by a single reference, as illustrated in Figure 4–7.

FIGURE 4–7

Copier Tracking Tape

	End Date: 11/30/98	
1073.6	3	.45
1087.6	20	3.00
1289.8	83	12.45
1489.4	268	40.20
1512.3	12	1.80
1514.9	1	.15
1673.3	7	1.05
2015.6	22	3.30
2111.3	43	6.45
2143.6	62	9.30
2479.4	<u>39</u>	<u>5.85</u>
***	560	84.00
Journal # C/1198		
9997.8	14	.70
9998.6	135	6.75
9999.4	877	43.85

Every month, Leslie prints this list from our copier tracking device. The 9000 series codes are nonbillable, such as administration, accounting, and professional development. M.

In automated accrual systems, the client ledger entries are made when the batch is posted. In manual cost systems, there is no entry to the general ledger, only to client ledgers or other less formal records. Figure 4–8 compares the entries for the most common methods.

After the disbursements are entered, logs for each type of disbursement are filed chronologically in binders or bundles. If there are supporting forms for a log, they are filed by client in envelopes or boxes. If there is no summary log, however, filing the forms by client may mean that they cannot be located if they have been posted to the wrong client file.

FIGURE 4–8
Recording Internal
Disbursements in
Ledgers

Event	Cash		Modified Accrual		Full Accrual	
	Debit	Credit	Debit	Credit	Debit	Credit
Disbursement Incurred	WIP Ledger		WIP Ledger		**Unbilled Disbursements** WIP Ledger	**Cost Recovery**
Disbursement Billed	A/R Ledger	WIP Ledger	**Accounts Receivable** A/R Ledger	**Cost Recovery** WIP Ledger	**Accounts Receivable** A/R Ledger	**Unbilled Disbursements** WIP Ledger
Bill Paid by Client	**Bank Account**	Disbursement Revenue A/R Ledger	**Bank Account**	**Accounts Receivable** A/R Ledger	**Bank Account**	**Accounts Receivable** A/R Ledger

Boldface indicates entries to the general ledger.

Summary Invoice Journals

There are two ways to record summary invoice disbursements in the client ledgers:

- *At the time the disbursement is incurred,* providing that the amount is known—for example, time and charges received from the operator for long-distance calls.

- *At the time the summary invoice is received* and the supporting documents are compared to the invoice—for example, when the telephone bill is received and the log or individual slips are compared to the charges on the bill.

Procedures vary not only between firms, accounting methods, and systems, but also between types of disbursements within a firm. If the firm is not concerned about cost recovery or regards elaborate cost-recovery procedures as not ultimately cost-effective, the disbursements recorded may never be compared with the invoice to ensure that all recoverable disbursements have been recorded. Other firms simply compare the recovered amounts to the invoices over a period of time or perform periodic spot-checks. In these situations, the firm regards the potential forfeiture of monetary recovery as less important than the time and effort required to identify and enter small amounts. Figure 4–9 shows a number of ways that firms record summary invoice disbursements.

From a control and recovery perspective, the best method is to:

1. Record the disbursements in the client ledgers as soon as all of the information is available. Batch totals posted to accounts payable improve control, especially when internal forms are used.

2. When the invoice is received, carefully compare the recorded slips or logs with the invoice to ensure that all recoverable disbursements have been recorded.

FIGURE 4–9
Recording
Summary Invoice
Disbursements in
Ledgers

Event	Cash		Modified Accrual		Full Accrual	
	Debit	Credit	Debit	Credit	Debit	Credit
Disbursement Incurred	WIP Ledger		WIP Ledger		Unbilled Disbursements WIP Ledger	Accounts Payable
Disbursement Paid to Third Party	Disbursement Cost	Bank Account	Disbursement Cost	Bank Account	Accounts Payable	Bank Account
Disbursement Billed	A/R Ledger	WIP Ledger	Accounts Receivable A/R Ledger	Disbursement Revenue WIP Ledger	Accounts Receivable A/R Ledger	Unbilled Disbursements WIP Ledger
Bill Paid by Client	Bank Account	Disbursement Revenue A/R Ledger	Bank Account	Accounts Receivable A/R Ledger	Bank Account	Accounts Receivable A/R Ledger

Boldface indicates entries to the general ledger.

3. Immediately investigate any discrepancies between the records.

If logs and internal forms are used as source documents, they are filed like internal disbursement source documents, either by disbursement type or by client file. If invoices are used as source documents, they are filed in the same manner as the firm's general expense invoices or chronologically by supplier name or disbursement type.

Direct Payment Checks

Disbursement checks must be carefully prepared, with all elements (see Chapter 1) complete and correct. The check date is usually the date the check is prepared, as there are few situations where it is appropriate to postdate disbursement checks.

Details including the check date and number are completed on the request form once the check has been issued. After the check has been entered, the check request form is completed with the journal or batch number and identification of the person who made the entry. Disbursement checks are entered into the system either in a separate client disbursements check journal or in the same journal as the firm's operating expenses and other checks, using the check register (or check stub) and/or check request form as source data.

In automated systems, direct disbursements are posted to the client WIP disbursements ledger when the check journal is updated. In manual systems, they are usually posted as they are issued, with a small mark in the synoptic indicating that the client ledger has been updated. The reference in the client ledger is the check number. Figure 4–10 illustrates various methods of recording disbursement checks.

FIGURE 4–10
Recording Direct
Disbursements in
Ledgers

Event	Cash		Modified Accrual		Full Accrual	
	Debit	Credit	Debit	Credit	Debit	Credit
Disbursement Paid to Third Party	Disbursement Cost WIP Ledger	Bank Account	Disbursement Cost WIP Ledger	Bank Account	Unbilled Disbursements WIP Ledger	Bank Account
Disbursement Billed	A/R Ledger	WIP Ledger	Accounts Receivable A/R Ledger	Disbursement Revenue WIP Ledger	Accounts Receivable A/R Ledger	Unbilled Disbursements WIP Ledger
Bill Paid by Client	Bank Account	Disbursement Revenue A/R Ledger	Bank Account	Accounts Receivable A/R Ledger	Bank Account	Accounts Receivable A/R Ledger

Boldface indicates entries to the general ledger.

Some firms assign a separate bank account or group of checks for direct disbursements so that nonaccounting staff can issue routine disbursement checks without gaining access to the firm's general operating information.

Check request forms and other supporting documents such as original invoices and copies of letters enclosing advance payments are filed by either file number or check number. Invoice *copies* are also often kept by the secretary in the client folders.

Client Disbursement Ledgers

Disbursements are normally posted to the client's ledger only if the firm intends to bill them to the client. Posting frequency depends on firm policy, the type of source document, and billing cycles.

In addition to the standard client information, the client ledger (see Figure 4–11) should provide space to enter:

- *date of disbursement,* preferably the date incurred for direct disbursements or the last day of the summary period for disbursements posted from internal records as a period total;

- *description of disbursement,* or payee if paid by check;

- *posting source* (journal or check number);

- *amount of disbursement;*

- *billing notation area* to indicate whether the disbursement has been billed; and

- *total* of unbilled disbursements.

When the disbursements are billed or adjusted, the WIP ledger is credited for the net amount.

FIGURE 4–11

Client WIP
Disbursement
Ledger

Carpenter & Cook

CLIENT WIP DISBURSEMENT LEDGER   Pg. # _2_

Client: _United Investment Corp._   File No.: _2409.1_

Re: _Cross Town Towing/Acquisition_   Date Opened: _10/9/98_

Date	Description	Code	B	Source	Amount	Balance
10/29/98	Balance Forward		B			39.54
10/31	Copies	11	B	C1098	16.00	55.54
11/07	Fax 14 pgs in	14	B	F11A98	14.00	69.54
11/12	Postage (internal)	16	B	M12996	38.50	108.04
11/28	Dean Business Consult's	35	B	BS11/98	678.00	786.04
11/30	Long Distance (8 calls)	12	B	LD/1198	109.22	895.26
"	Train to/from Sundown	54		XS1198	62.00	957.26
12/10	Postage/Special Delivery	16	B	PC/1298	13.38	970.64
12/31	Sundown S & S	25	B	AP/1298	100.00	1,070.64
"	"	23	B	"	19.00	1,089.64
12/31/98	Billed (bill #205)				1,027.64	62.00

We use WIP disbursement ledgers to keep track of unbilled disbursements. M.

If there is no formal client WIP disbursement ledger, copies of forms and invoices or informal logs are kept in an envelope by file name or in a special client folder. At the time the bill is prepared they are summarized, then bundled by client file for permanent storage.

Policies and Controls

When the firm directs a supplier to provide services, the firm, *not the client,* accepts the liability for payment to the supplier. For this reason, firms may have strict limits on the authority of staff members to incur large client disbursements. Client fee agreements should address even routine disbursements and make specific mention of large or unusual ones.

Disbursements that are recorded only internally require special controls because, as with time records, there is no reliable external check on the accuracy of the original data or the resulting information. Some firms require only minimal controls, such as monitoring the photocopier counter to ensure that there is a minimum rate of recovery. Even small disbursements, however, can add up over time or on a major matter and represent a significant loss to the firm if not recovered.

Practical Application 4–4

Sheila: Normally I just count the photocopies that I know I've made when I prepare the bill for a file. I know how many copies I sent out of the office and how many I made for the file and other people in the office. Why add them up any more often than that? It's more work to tally them every week or month and it just takes up a lot of space on a ledger card or in a computer system.

Sheila makes some good points, but in some situations her method may not be ideal. Discuss her viewpoint with reference to accounting principles and concepts and internal controls. Under what conditions is her method not appropriate? When might it be appropriate?

Relying on verbal instructions to record disbursements causes control problems, especially if the disbursement could be identified again through another source and perhaps entered twice.

Each stage of the disbursement recording process, as illustrated in Figure 4–12, is important in ensuring optimal disbursement recovery. Proper procedures throughout the recording process ensure that disbursement data is:

- *exhaustive,* with all recoverable disbursements recorded;

- *complete,* with full identification of the file and posting reference; and

- *unique,* with each disbursement recorded in only one journal.

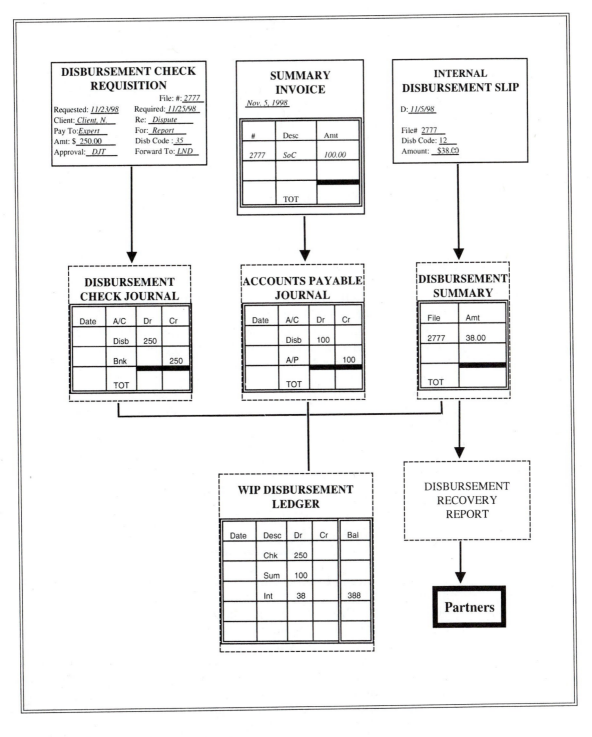

FIGURE 4–12 Disbursement Recording Process

WIP Disbursement Summaries

Firms may carry significant client disbursements for considerable periods of time and be especially concerned about the investment they represent. Billing large disbursements as soon as possible improves both the ultimate recovery rate and the firm's cash flow. Proper and timely reporting helps to locate errors that, if undetected, could result in lost disbursement recovery or problems with clients.

<table>
<tr><td>

Practical Application 4–5

</td><td>

Alma:
</td><td>

I never review the unbilled disbursements on a file ledger until I'm ready to bill. The amounts are always small and there are few errors. If I find an error, I phone down to the accounting department and ask them to just get rid of it. There have never been any problems with doing it that way.
</td></tr>
</table>

Comment on Alma's methods.

Disbursement summaries are usually quite simple. The most common is a list of all WIP disbursement ledger balances, either for the firm or by individual responsible lawyer. Often the WIP time, accounts receivable, and trust balances are on the same report.

Other summaries like the one illustrated in Figure 4–13 are common in firms that are anxious to monitor recovery rates for internal disbursements. These summaries are usually not prepared by individual client but rather by week or month in which the disbursements were recorded. Sometimes a list of all WIP disbursement balances exceeding a threshold amount is produced to monitor large disbursement balances or an aging list is prepared to monitor uncollectible disbursement balances that should be removed from the system.

WIP Disbursement Adjustments

Procedures and internal control issues for WIP disbursement adjustments are similar to those for WIP time except that the general ledger is often affected. Disbursement corrections should be made by reversing incorrect entries and re-entering them, especially if recording errors cause an automated reconciliation program to work improperly.

Substantive errors are usually checks that should never have been issued at all, that must be re-issued, or that were issued twice. These corrections involve reversing and voiding the check and re-issuing one if necessary. All supporting documents are referenced with both the original check number and the new one.

FIGURE 4–13
Disbursement
Recovery Report

Carpenter & Cook

Disbursement Recovery Report

November 1998

Disbursement	Code	Units	Value	Appr.
Photocopies	11	560 copies	84.00	M.F.
Faxes In	14	167 pages	167.00	M.F.
Faxes Out	15	87 pages	87.00	M.F.
Postage	16		71.71	L.S.
On-line	19	28.7 min.	43.05	C.W.
Binders	42	2	72.00	C.W.

Each month I give each partner a copy of the disbursement recovery report so that they know how much we make on the fax machine, copier, etc. M.

WIP disbursement deletions are similar to WIP time deletions except the procedure is more formal if the general ledger is affected. Deletions do not involve adjusting performance reports where disbursements are not attributed to separate lawyers.

Debits are usually posted to a disbursements variance account, with the credit to the WIP asset if one is used. There is no general ledger adjustment in the cash method. Unrecovered disbursements are not eligible as a tax-deductible expense in some jurisdictions.

Case 4–4

Found: Five-partner law firm deducted from its taxable income charges incidental to clients' cases. State bar rules assert that client is responsible for litigation costs, therefore **disbursements paid constitute a loan to the client, not a necessary business expense of the firm.**

Ordered: Firm to pay assessed late taxes and interest to Internal Revenue Service.

——————— TERMS ———————

WIP disbursement deletion   Removal of an unbilled disbursement from the client disbursement ledger.

It is often necessary to delete small disbursements incurred after the main work on a file is concluded and billed. Although some firms allow secretaries and accounting staff to prepare deletion requests for small amounts, the lawyer should approve all deletions when signing the file closing request. Otherwise a form such as the one illustrated in Figure 4–14 is used.

FIGURE 4–14

WIP Disbursement
Deletion Form

Carpenter & Cook

WIP DISBURSEMENT DELETION FORM

Date: _Nov. 30, 1998_   Client: _Pleasant Hills Mortuary_

File Number: _1289.8_   Re: _Deadbeat Collection Agency Inc._

Cut-off Date: _Nov. 15, 1998_   Authorized: _S Cook_

DATE	DESCRIPTION	SOURCE	CODE	AMOUNT
11/30/98	Long Distance	LD/1198	12	45.65
11/30/98	Copies	C/1198	11	12.45
		TOTAL		58.10

Reason: _Disbursements too late for final bill._

_____

Disbursement deletions are usually authorized by the partner for the file, but Terry and Lee can authorize deletions up to $100 and Kim and I can authorize deletions up to $50. M.

Comprehensive Exercises

1. Design a checklist for the handling of disbursement records. Cover each of the three main types of source documents. The list should have at least sixty items.

2. Describe the control problems for each type of disbursement source. Design a procedure consistent with the firm of Carpenter & Cook. Recommend and support changes to current procedures.

3. For each disbursement source, discuss the relative merits of the main ways to record each in the general ledger. (Use Figures 4–8, 4–9, and 4–10.)

4. How does the control of disbursement records impact on cash management? On professional responsibility?

IIII

CHAPTER 5

CLIENT BILLS

CHAPTER OUTLINE   Fee Agreements

Types of Bills

Billing Procedures

Bill Calculation

WIP Adjustments

Billing Journals

Client billing requires dedicated teamwork within the law office more than any other accounting-related function. Efforts expended to produce high quality time and disbursement information are more than recouped during the billing process.

Significant financial and management information is generated from law firm billing records, and the firm's managers and creditors take great interest in the monthly "billing figures." Billing records that do not accurately reflect the firm's productivity obscure both its problems and its opportunities and are poor planning guides. Billing is the central function in providing the cash flow necessary to maintain a law practice, and procedures to ensure prompt and complete billing are essential. Billing also requires strict attention to accuracy and form, as the bill is an important document representing the firm to the client.

Most states' regulation of the practice of law include standards and restrictions on billing practices similar to those found in ABA Model Rule 1.5, and all legal staff should be familiar with the state rules. The critical concept of reasonableness in billing legal clients is explained in Model Rule 1.5(a).

RULE 1.5

(a) A lawyer's fee shall be reasonable. The factors to be considered in determining the reasonableness of a fee include the following:
> (1) the time and labor required, the novelty and difficulty of the questions involved, and the skill requisite to perform the legal service properly;
> (2) the likelihood, if apparent to the client, that the acceptance of the particular employment will preclude other employment by the lawyer;
> (3) the fee customarily charged in the locality for similar legal services;
> (4) the amount involved and the results obtained;
> (5) the time limitations imposed by the client or by the circumstances;
> (6) the nature and length of the professional relationship with the client;
> (7) the experience, reputation, and ability of the lawyer or lawyers performing the services; and
> (8) whether the fee is fixed or contingent.

There are many steps in billing clients, but there are two factors that must be considered before a bill can even be drafted:

- Client bills must conform to the *fee agreement* (basis of billing), which establishes and confirms the expectations of both lawyer and client concerning the services to be performed.

- The *type of bill* must be consistent not only with the fee agreement but also with the firm's systems and with changing circumstances.

Case 5-1	Found:	**Lawyer entered into contract to represent client in domestic suit for $70 an hour, subsequently billed $25,000 for work involving at most 38.8 hours,** and falsely represented to client that fee would be calculated on quantum meruit basis.
	Ordered:	One-year suspension.

Fee Agreements

ABA Model Rule 1.5(b) requires that lawyers communicate rates and basis of billing to new clients promptly.

> (b) When the lawyer has not regularly represented the client, the basis or rate of the fee shall be communicated to the client, preferably in writing, before or within a reasonable time after commencing the representation.

If the client has an ongoing or "master" fee agreement with the firm (such as insurance companies and large corporations), the fee agreement is implicit when an individual file is accepted by the firm. Nonetheless, many lawyers consider it prudent to obtain a separate agreement for all new files. Arrangements for the payment of fees are also discussed with the client before the firm accepts the file and are preferably included in the written fee agreement. The agreement covers:

- the scope of services the lawyer expects and is expected to perform,

- the basis for charging fees,

- whether a fee advance will be required and how much,

- expected billing and payment schedules and interest to be charged if in default,

- whether incidental disbursements will be charged,

- provision for advance or immediate payment of large disbursements, and

- how the agreement can be terminated by either the lawyer or the client.

The first two are very important in averting misunderstandings between lawyer and client, especially if a client has asked for an estimate before the start of the work. Lawyers who find that the client makes escalating requests for advice and services, perhaps not even directly related to the file, can then refer to the section of the agreement dealing with the scope as an explanation of bills in excess of the estimate.

State rules may also restrict the payments that lawyers may receive from clients, most commonly with respect to contingency fee agreements.

Any fee agreement exceeding statutory limits is not likely to be enforced by the courts.

Case 5–2	Found: **Fee agreement waiving state statutory limit on contingency fee percentage was not enforceable.** Ordered: Firm awarded statutory limit.

Practical Application 5–1	Gowan: In our firm, we don't have a set policy about fee agreements. Each lawyer decides what to do. Some clients are scared away if you want to talk about money first thing. We try to get their confidence and get a feel for the case before we even try to make an estimate of fees. If you make an estimate before you know much about the case, you will tend to give a high estimate to cover all your bases. The result is that either the client is alarmed at the large amount or you end up billing to the limit of the estimate, even if it took less time.

What are Gowan's concerns? What kinds of policies might be flexible enough to accommodate the peculiarities of each file yet provide some guidelines to all legal staff?

Fixed Fees

Many fee agreements are for a **fixed fee**, where a specific amount is agreed upon before the file work starts. These are common in:

- *criminal defense,* where fee advances must be obtained to ensure ultimate payment of the full contemplated amount of the fees;

- *corporate office and records,* where a small corporation is charged a fixed amount for the firm to file statutory corporate reports and act as principal corporate office for the following year; and

- *routine short-term services,* such as incorporations, conveyancing, will preparation, document notarization, certificates of independent legal advice, and other services where competition between firms demands that the client be assured of the fee in advance.

Small and incidental disbursements often are not charged, although lawyers take this into account when negotiating fee agreements. Common problems with these fee agreements are that the client's demands may exceed the scope of agreed services and that the lawyer underestimates the time required to properly serve the client if unforeseen complications arise.

—————————————— TERMS ——————————————

fixed fee An agreement for a client to pay a determined amount for a specified legal service.

Contingency Fees

Because of the potential for conflicts between lawyer and client in contingency (or contingent) fee agreements, these agreements are subject to more and stricter regulation than most other fee agreements. Most states' regulations are similar to ABA Model Rule 1.5(c).

> (c) A fee may be contingent on the outcome of the matter for which the service is rendered, except in a matter in which a contingent fee is prohibited by paragraph (d) or other law. A contingent fee agreement shall be in writing and shall state the method by which the fee is to be determined, including the percentage or percentages that shall accrue to the lawyer in the even of settlement, trial or appeal, litigation and other expenses to be deducted from the recovery, and whether such expenses are to be deducted before or after the contingent fee is calculated. Upon conclusion of a contingent fee matter, the lawyer shall provide the client with a written statement stating the outcome of the matter and, if there is a recovery, showing the remittance to the client and the method of its determination.

Contingency fee agreements are often used for collections, personal injury, product liability, and medical malpractice claims. Although lawyers may enter into contingency fee agreements for a large variety of files, in most states certain family matters and criminal defense are expressly excluded, as illustrated in Model Rule 1.5(d):

> (d) A lawyer shall not enter into an arrangement for, charge, or collect:
>
> (1) any fee in a domestic relations matter, the payment or amount of which is contingent upon the securing of a divorce or upon the amount of alimony or support, or property settlement in lieu thereof; or
>
> (2) a contingent fee for representing a defendant in a criminal case.

Contingency fee agreements describe the basis of calculation for the *maximum* of the firm's fees, often on a percentage scale that increases as the matter progresses. Where large amounts are recovered, it is not unusual for the lawyer to reduce the fee or unilaterally "cap" it.

Except as provided for in state rules, there is no limit on the *amount* (either percentage or fixed fee) that the lawyer may charge except that, like all legal fees, it must be reasonable. If reasonableness cannot be agreed on by lawyer and client, the courts will determine what is reasonable.

TERMS

---

contingency fee An amount payable (usually but not necessarily a percentage of an award or settlement) by a clnent subject to a desired outcome of a legal matter.

Case 5–3   Found: Lawyer representing client in divorce case agreed to accept house that was subject of representation, deeded to brother-in-law, in return for representation. **Arrangement constituted "illegal and void" one-hundred-percent contingency fee arrangement in divorce case.**

Ordered: Costs assessed against lawyer.

Hourly Rate

Hourly rate agreements specify that the client will be billed for the actual time spent at various lawyers' hourly billing rates and are often found in:

- contract litigation (claims and defense),

- tort defense,

- securities and other complex long-term nonlitigation work,

- estate administration, and

- most areas of law involving nonroutine litigation where a contingency fee agreement is not desirable or not permitted.

Large organizations that bring many files to the firm, such as insurance companies and unions, have a blanket fee agreement specifying the rates for various lawyers on all files. The agreement is updated periodically as the firm and client agree.

Retainer Fees

There is often confusion between terms referring to fee advances and retainer fees. **Fee advances** (also called *fee retainers* or simply *advances*) are basically down payments on future services that the lawyer has agreed to perform or payments for large anticipated file disbursements. The fee advance is deposited into the firm's trust account and remains there until the services are performed or the disbursements are paid. Chapter 7 discusses the handling of fee advances. **Retainer fees** (or *retainers, advance fees,* or *general retainers*), on the other hand, are paid by a client for the assurance that a particular lawyer will be available to perform services during a specific period. While some retainer fee agreements

---------- TERMS ----------

fee advance   An amount paid in advance to the firm and kept in its trust account for future expenses of the matter.

retainer fees   An amount paid by a client to secure the availability of a lawyer, regardless of whether legal services are actually performed.

provide that if services are performed, the retainer fee will be credited against the lawyer's bill, normally the retainer belongs to the lawyer whether or not any legal services are actually performed.

Case 5–4

Found: **Lawyer did not violate rule requiring placement of advance fees in trust account, as fee was a "retainer" (paid by client to secure lawyer's availability over a given period of time,** such a fee being earned when paid, since lawyer is entitled to money regardless of whether he actually performs any services for client), and not an "advance fee payment."

Ordered: Lower court's finding of violation reversed.

Retainer agreements are not common but do occur where:

- a client of means wishes to deal only with one specific lawyer in a firm,

- the lawyer retained has specialized knowledge or renown in a field of practice of particular sensitivity to the client, or

- the lawyer must be available to travel to another jurisdiction to assist as advisor to the responsible lawyer in the trial jurisdiction.

Retainer agreements do not per se prohibit lawyers from performing legal services for other clients during the term of the retainer, although they may make it practically impossible to set court dates during the retainer period.

Practical Application 5–2

Peggy: I'm really pleased and flattered that the Dare Family want to put me on a large monthly retainer. It's strange, because they own a lot of rental apartment buildings in town, and I'm known as being about the only lawyer around who will take on residential tenancy problems for tenants. That doesn't pay much, I can tell you, and this new retainer will help with the cash flow. Frankly, I'm flattered to have landed such a plum of a client. I have to call them right after lunch and finalize the retainer agreement. Hmm . . . I think I'll have the broccoli crepe.

Joy: Are you sure that's what you want?

Peggy: Why not? I love broccoli. . .

Joy: No, I mean the retainer. Maybe they're trying to make sure you can't take on any of their tenants' claims. Conflict of interest, you know? Chicken pot pie with caesar salad, please.

What are the real dilemmas facing Peggy?

Court Appointments

Lawyers may be appointed by a court to represent a client who cannot afford legal counsel. Because court appointments do not pay well, lawyers may be less eager to accept them than they are to take private paying clients. Once an appointment is made and accepted, however, the lawyer owes the client the same duties as for any other client. ABA Model Rule 6.2 outlines the reasons why a lawyer may reasonably decline an appointment.

RULE 6.2

Accepting Appointments
A lawyer shall not seek to avoid appointment by a tribunal to represent a person except for good cause, such as:

(a) representing the client is likely to result in violation of the Rules of Professional Conduct or other law;
(b) representing the client is likely to result in an unreasonable financial burden on the lawyer; or
(c) the client or the cause is so repugnant to the lawyer as to be likely to impair the client-lawyer relationship or the lawyer's ability to represent the client.

Not all states have rules that essentially require lawyers to accept reasonable appointments. It is generally accepted, however, that all lawyers should make some moderate contribution to their communities and the service of justice through providing uncompensated or minimally compensated legal services to indigent clients and public causes.

Case 5–5	Found:	Lawyer appointed by court to criminal cases where **rates for fees and limits on expenses were so low that they failed to meet constitutional standards. Involuntary appointments exceeding ten percent of lawyer's normal work year was unconstitutional taking of property from lawyer.**
	Ordered:	Respondent circuit court judge prohibited from appointing lawyer to cases exceeding ten percent of normal work year.

Pro Bono Representations

Pro bono publico representations, as described in ABA Model Rule 6.1, are undertaken by lawyers as a public service. Although no fees are paid by the client, all other aspects of the client-lawyer relationship remain.

RULE 6.1

Voluntary Pro Bono Publico Service
A lawyer should aspire to render at least (50) hours of pro bono publico legal services per year. In fulfilling this responsibility, the lawyer should:

(a) provide a substantial majority of the (50) hours of legal services without fee or expectation of fee to:

(1) persons of limited means or

(2) charitable, religious, civic, community, governmental and educational organizations in matters which are designed primarily to address the needs of persons of limited means; and

(b) provide any additional services through:

(1) delivery of legal services at no fee or substantially reduced fee to individuals, groups or organizations seeking to secure or protect civil rights, civil liberties or public rights, or charitable, religious, civic, community, governmental and educational organizations in matters in furtherance of their organizational purposes, where the payment of standard legal fees would significantly deplete the organization's economic resources or would be otherwise inappropriate;

(2) delivery of legal services at a substantially reduced fee to persons of limited means; or

(3) participation in activities for improving the law, the legal system or the legal profession.

In addition, a lawyer should voluntary contribute financial support to organizations that provide legal services to persons of limited means.

Besides providing legal services directly to clients, lawyers participate in public education and legal reform activities.

Agreements with Third Parties

Under certain circumstances, third parties—often family (parents paying for a minor's defense) or friends of the client—may agree to pay for the client's representation. Such payments are like loans or gifts to the client, and the lawyer makes no disclosure to the third party regarding the representation. Sometimes, the third party agrees to pay for other reasons. For example, an employer may pay for an employee's defense where a finding of any liability would render the employer also (vicariously) liable.

Types of Bills

The type of bill determines how and when the bill is prepared by the secretary or accounting staff. In some areas of law, only certain types of bills are produced. For example, interim bills are not common in personal injury files because such cases are usually taken on a contingency fee basis.

The use of standard formats for different types of bills makes the billing process quicker and simpler for everyone involved and ensures uniform style and content for the firm's bills.

Interim Bills

Interim bills (progress billings) are rendered to clients before the conclusion of the file work. They represent periodic charges for fees and often disbursements where the firm is not financing the client's matter up to its conclusion. They are usually for:

- contingency fees where part of the client's award or settlement is known but the matter is not concluded or is under appeal, or

- ongoing work on an hourly rate file.

The latter is very common, and in such cases the billing process normally starts when:

- it is the normal billing time for the whole firm (usually the end or beginning of the month), for a group of lawyers, or for an established set of client files;

- the lawyer, often through the secretary, has requested that an interim bill be produced; or

- the unbilled fee amount has reached its billing threshold, which is determined by firm policy for all files or on an individual file basis.

The main purpose of interim billing is to provide cash flow during the course of the file work. Although client ledgers should always be as up-to-date as possible, it may be more important to prepare interim bills promptly or regularly than to ensure that all of the WIP information is complete to a certain date. In some systems, *no* WIP entries should be posted between the time the draft is prepared and the bill is posted, as these entries may be deleted in the bill posting routine. Drafts, therefore, should be reviewed promptly. Figure 5–1 illustrates a typical interim bill format for an hourly rate file.

Sometimes interim bills are rendered when clients are not expected to pay promptly but the firm wishes to remind clients of the cost of the ongoing work and the eventual payments that will be required.

Partial Bills

Partial bills are common in large matters where a specific area of service has been concluded and will be billed as a separate total, although other areas remain unconcluded and unbilled. Where possible, it is better to open separate file ledgers to avoid confusion between dates of service and because some automated systems cannot distinguish billed from unbilled open-item (individual) WIP records properly.

---- TERMS ----

interim bill A bill rendered by the firm before the client's matter is concluded and the file closed.

Carpenter & Cook
Attorneys at Law
2400 - 555 North Ocean Street, Fielding, ST 10001

Telephone: 488-1111
Fax: 488-6666

Pat Carpenter
Sandy Cook
Terry Baker
Lee Mason (Associated)

December 27, 1998

United Investment Corp.
1798 14th Avenue
Seaside, ST 10002

INVOICE #205

Re: Cross Town Towing (Acquisition)
      Our File Number 2409.1 - Interim Bill

DATE	LWYR	DESCRIPTION	HRS
11/05/98	LM	Review draft Shareholders' Agreement	0.3
12/12/98	SC	Letter to Cross Town shareholders	0.7
	LM	Review law re: rights of minority shareholders; reporting letter to client	1.6
12/14/98	LM	Telephone call from Mr. West; letter to accountants; draft formal offer	3.8
12/15/98	SC	Meeting with clients and Mr. West	2.3
12/23/98	LM	Telephone call from Mr. West; office conference with accountants	1.4
12/24/98	SC	Telephone conference with accountants and Dean Business Consultants	0.8
	LM	Telephone call from Mr. West	0.7

FEE SUMMARY:

SC	3.8 hrs @ 230.00	874.00	
LM	7.8 hrs @ 195.00	1,521.00	
	11.6 hrs		$ 2,395.00

DISBURSEMENTS:

Photocopies	26.00	
Faxes (in)	33.00	
Postage	51.88	
Long distance	119.76	
Business valuation	678.00	
Filing and service	119.00	
		1,027.64

STATE TAXES: (on fees only) 3%   71.85

THIS IS OUR ACCOUNT: $ 3,494.49

Sandy Cook

E. & O.E.

This is an example of an interim bill that we sent out at the end of December. M.

FIGURE 5-1   Interim Bill: Hourly Rate

A firm may finance the fee portion of a matter but require the client to pay disbursements either periodically or when large direct disbursements are incurred, through a transfer from the trust account against a fee advance. Opposing counsel request copies of pertinent documents from the firm, and they are billed for the photocopies, or in the instance of medical reports in personal injury files, for the total cost of the document, as illustrated in Figure 5–2. As with partial fee billings, some automated systems do not allow open-item disbursement billing.

Final Bills

Final bills are produced when:

- The file work has been concluded and the client is receiving the final (and perhaps only) bill.

- The client or lawyer is terminating the firm's services and a final bill is being prepared before the file is closed or leaves the office. Sometimes the bills are sent to the new lawyer to be paid at the conclusion of the file.

Because the firm generally does not want to present further charges to a client who has already been "final billed" and because lawyers and secretaries are often unaware that posting may not be up-to-date, extra attention should be given by accounting staff to ensure that all WIP entries for the file are posted before the draft for a final bill is prepared.

A complicated type of final bill is a "designated total" bill, where the lawyer specifies the *total* dollar value to bill but not the items. These bills are common where the file WIP charges and necessary taxes exceed an amount quoted or the advance fee balance and the firm wishes to conclude the matter with its final bill. They are also used in contingency fee agreements where the client will agree to an early settlement offer only on the condition of receiving a minimum *net* amount (which is in excess of the amount stipulated in the agreement) and the firm is satisfied with receiving the balance. Figure 5–3 illustrates a final bill on a contingency matter.

Court-Awarded Fees

Fee awards (or costs) may be provided to prevailing parties in litigation as a contribution toward the expense of the action. Supporting documents filed with the motion could be thought of as bills the firm *prepares* for the client to present to the opposing party in support of a claim for costs. **Court-awarded fees** belong to the client, not the lawyer.

───────────────── TERMS ─────────────────

court-awarded fees   An amount awarded by a court to a prevailing party to be paid by the defeated party as a contribution toward the expense of litigation.

Carpenter & Cook
Attorneys at Law
2400 - 555 North Ocean Street, Fielding, ST 10001

Telephone: 488-1111
Fax: 488-6666

Pat Carpenter
Sandy Cook
Terry Baker
Lee Mason (Associated)

December 3, 1998

Plowman & Planter
Attorneys at Law
1000 - 1208 Commerce Street
Fielding, ST 10003

Attn: Clay Potter

INVOICE #194

Re: M.V.A. November 26, 199_
      Your File: #C-09-76_2; Martin Stone
      Our File : #1489.4; Daisy L. Carpenter

Enclosed as per your request:

Photocopies of the recovery diary of Ms. Daisy Carpenter

117 pages @ $0.15/page:

THIS IS OUR ACCOUNT: **$17.55**

C. Weaver

Secretary to S. Cook

E. & O.E.

When we supply copies of documents to opposing counsel, we send out a bill like this. Usually the secretary or I sign them. M.

FIGURE 5–2   Partial Bill: Disbursements to Opposing Party

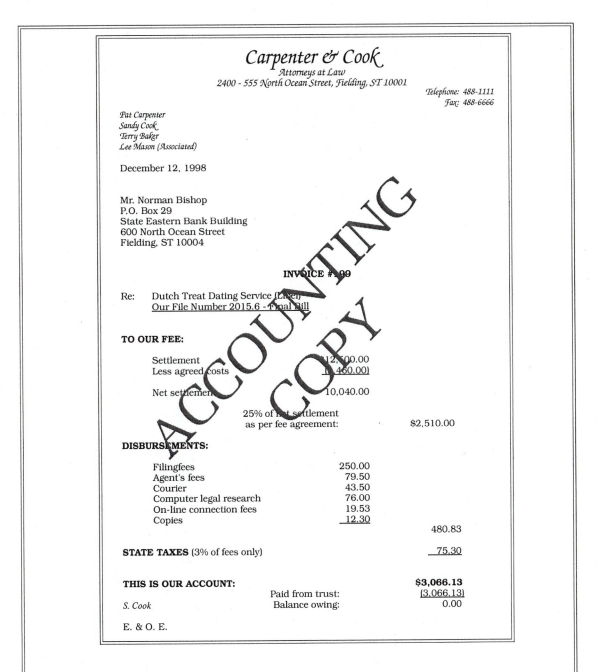

Carpenter & Cook
Attorneys at Law
2400 - 555 North Ocean Street, Fielding, ST 10001

Telephone: 488-1111
Fax: 488-6666

Pat Carpenter
Sandy Cook
Terry Baker
Lee Mason (Associated)

December 12, 1998

Mr. Norman Bishop
P.O. Box 29
State Eastern Bank Building
600 North Ocean Street
Fielding, ST 10004

INVOICE # 99

Re: Dutch Treat Dating Service (Libel)
      Our File Number 2015.6 - Final Bill

TO OUR FEE:

Settlement	12,500.00	
Less agreed costs	(2,460.00)	
Net settlement	10,040.00	
25% of net settlement as per fee agreement:		$2,510.00

DISBURSEMENTS:

Filingfees	250.00	
Agent's fees	79.50	
Courier	43.50	
Computer legal research	76.00	
On-line connection fees	19.53	
Copies	12.30	
		480.83

STATE TAXES (3% of fees only)   75.30

THIS IS OUR ACCOUNT: **$3,066.13**

Paid from trust: (3,066.13)

S. Cook   Balance owing: 0.00

E. & O. E.

We do some contingency files. Agreed costs have to be subtracted from the settlement, because the costs always belong to the client, not to C & C. M.

FIGURE 5–3   Final Bill: Contingency

Case 5–6	Found:	**Lower court fee award of $2,000 to client who successfully challenged ordinance banning nude dancing, who was required to seek immediate relief within a few days, and whose case could be considered undesirable was inadequate.**
	Ordered:	Reversed and remanded.

Although the court has a considerable degree of discretion in awarding fees, most awards are not equal to the actual costs of litigation.

Case 5–7	Found:	Notwithstanding that lawyer fee clause in contract allowing for compensation on either hourly or contingency rate (whichever was higher) bordered on the unreasonable, **lower court fee award of $5,000 was not excessive, regardless of whether it exceeded amount of recovery.**
	Ordered:	Award affirmed.

Fee awards create some problems in dealing with contingency fees. When costs are received in a *judgment,* all of the costs are excluded from the calculation base of the contingency fee. Any disbursements recovered are simply included in the bill to the client. In calculating contingency fees on a *settlement* amount, any amount received for costs must be subtracted from the settlement amount in calculating the fees. The lawyer should always be consulted about the effect of costs in both judgments and settlements when calculating the amount of contingency fees.

Billing Procedures

A firm's billing procedures depend on the type of system in place, the field of practice, and firm policies. Because the billing process has a considerable impact on the profitability of the firm, policy is usually set by the partners or management committee. In a well-designed system it is easier to produce useful information than it is to circumvent proper methods.

In small firms where a bookkeeper attends the office infrequently, it is not unusual for the secretary to prepare the bill and submit only internal copies for the accounting staff.

Like all other law office accounting processes, efficient billing requires well-communicated procedures. All individuals including lawyers, paralegals, secretaries, and accounting staff should be aware of the distribution of duties, particularly the responsibility for:

- *Initiating billing,* usually by requesting draft bills, or at the established billing time such as the end of the month, or at the conclusion of the matter.

- *Producing the draft bill,* which *includes* ensuring that the information is up-to-date and complete. In networked systems, the secretary may produce a draft from the accounting system, but especially in the case of a final bill based on hours spent, the accounting staff should be consulted to ensure that all entries are up-to-date.

- *Reviewing, editing, and adjusting the draft.* The lawyer specifies changes in amounts or service descriptions.

- *Recalculating the draft.* If any amounts have changed, subtotals and taxes will require adjustment.

- *Producing final-form bills,* on letterhead or other high quality paper, and often including a standard cover letter.

- *Approving and signing bills.* Usually the lawyer responsible for the file does this, but some firms require that all bills be signed by a partner.

- *Issuing the bill to the client,* including making copies and attaching relevant information required by the accounting system.

- *Determining the* **fee allocation**, where the allocation is not obvious or determined by firm policy.

The division of these responsibilities varies greatly between firms, and even within firms to accommodate certain fields of practice. For example, in a firm that handles both defense and claims in personal injury actions, the accounting staff may be responsible for monitoring the threshold amount for billing defense files, but the secretary requests a draft bill at the conclusion of a claim (plaintiff's matter).

Practical Application 5–3

Tom: We partners have to do something about the billing procedures. This morning I had a call from an important client who was, quite understandably, upset about a bill we sent out. This is a client we bill our highest rate to, but they somehow got a bill with everyone's "charity case" rate on it. They're concerned that they've been overcharged for years and want an answer from me. What can I tell them?

Dick: How did this happen? Who is responsible for checking these things? Make the bookkeeper explain it to them—it's his error! Send them some flowers, tickets to the game. . . .

Harry: I think it goes a little deeper than that, Dick, For example, I don't even know who is responsible for double-checking that the right rates have been used. We never had these problems before we got that computer

---

——————————————— TERMS ———————————————

fee allocation   The apportionment of a firm's billed fees between its lawyers.

system. Now our old procedures don't work any more and we haven't got a decent new structure.

Dick: . . . I think it's the Blue Jays.

If the partners asked you to make *general* recommendations, what would be your priorities in the new procedures? How would you go about formulating the plan? Who would you ask to help and provide input? Who would you ask for approval?

Initiating Billing

In small- and medium-sized firms where most files are billed on an hourly basis, the billing cycle begins with the monthly review of WIP time and disbursement summaries. Automated systems usually produce these easily by lawyer, field of practice, WIP age and threshold amount, or other criteria and include trust balances to remind lawyers to bill up to the remaining fee advance if possible. These selected reports are useful for streamlining the billing process, but a *complete* WIP listing should be produced at least once a month to assist in identifying incorrect entries, forgotten files, and other anomalies that require attention. Figure 5–4 illustrates a WIP report.

FIGURE 5–4
WIP Report

```
                        WIP REPORT

                                        DATE: NOV 12/98

     CRITERIA: TIME ≥ 1,000 AND DISBURSEMENTS ≥ 150
     SEQUENCE: TIME—DESCENDING

     FILE        CLIENT NAME        LWYR      TIME        DISB

     1861.4      SUNRISE/SUNSET      PC     5,273.50     723.99
     2162.6      TEAL, W.            PC     5,199.00     152.00
     1844.0      CENTURY TEXTILES    SC     4,228.50     215.68
     1489.4      CARPENTER, DAISY    SC     2,516.50     318.88
     2302.8      PEEL, D.            TB     1,562.00     635.73
     2276.4      TOP DOG DRYCLEANING TB     1,181.00     481.12

                 TOTAL FOR REPORT          19,960.50   2,527.40
```

I do these reports in a spreadsheet program. The partners like a weekly list of all unbilled fees over $1,000 and unbilled disbursements over $150. M.

To avoid overloading the accounting system, large firms designate certain lawyers' files or certain file sequences for billing at regular alternating intervals during the month. Alternatively, secretaries may request or produce draft bills at the conclusion of a matter, or the accounting staff may be required to monitor fee advances that are available for transfer. Figure 5–5 illustrates staggered billing cycles.

Drafting Bills

Bills are drafted and reviewed before being produced in final form on letterhead or other high quality paper. The draft bill (or pre-bill, or statement draft) is reviewed by a lawyer, preferably the one responsible for the file, although it is not unusual for secretaries to review the draft, make changes, and submit the final copy to the lawyer for signature.

If lists are issued, the lawyer or secretary reviews the list and either produces a draft bill from the system, or requests that the accounting staff do so, by marking on the list the files for which drafts are required. In firms where there is no set time for billing, lawyers and secretaries request draft bills from the accounting system as needed, using a standard form, as illustrated in Figure 5–6. Some firms have the accounting staff briefly review the draft bills for spelling, accuracy, and consistency with billing instructions before forwarding the draft to the lawyer or secretary. A copy of the fee agreement or a summary of the terms is useful for the accounting staff who are preparing draft bills. The terms are often included on the file opening form.

FIGURE 5–5
Billing Cycles

Carpenter & Cook

Billing Cycles

Lawyer	Hourly	Fixed Fee	Contingency	Other	Trust Trans
P.C.	3 / 14	5 / 16	7 / 18	9 / 12 / 17	9 / 18
S.C.	4 / 15	6 / 17	8 / 19	5 / 13 / 16	11 / 18
T.B.	3	7	10	11 / 19	14

These are the billing and review cycles for each lawyer. The day is the working day in the month. M.

FIGURE 5–6
Draft Bill Request
Form

DRAFT BILL REQUEST

File Number: _2049.1_   Client Name: ___United Investment___

Forward to: _C.W._

                                                              Urgent [ ]

Bill Type: Interim   [✓] Final   [ ] Disb. only [ ]

Fee Detail: Description [✓] Lawyer [✓] Date [✓]

Fee Summary: Lawyer   [✓] Hours [✓] Total [✓]

Fee Amount: As per WIP [✓] To (date) _Dec. 27, 1998_

                    Contingency [ ] __ % of _____ = $ _____

                    Quoted Fee [ ] $ _____

Disbursements: To (date)   _Dec. 27, 1998_

                     Selected: _Summary_

Other instructions _special fee rate?? look up fee agreement_

Request Date _Dec. 27, 1998_   Required Date _Dec. 28, 1998_

We always do a draft bill and supply a WIP report, even on fixed-fee bills, because we catch a lot of mistakes with that method. M.

In many automated systems, producing a draft automatically labels WIP items as billed. If a draft is produced and the lawyer subsequently decides not to issue the bill, the draft should be clearly marked and returned to the accounting staff to restore the WIP items as unbilled. As a control, the accounting staff record all of the draft bills that have been produced and question the lawyer or secretary if they do not receive a copy of the issued bill within a certain period of time. This also ensures that out-of-date drafts are not used to produce bills.

Service Descriptions

The fee portion of the bill usually provides some description of the services rendered. Firms have standard descriptions for routine fixed-fee services, although many firms give clients a detailed description of services, even though the fee was agreed upon at the commencement of the work, so that clients are aware of the work done on their behalf. This awareness operates at two levels:

- Clients are made aware of the progress of the file, which is often slower than they anticipate.

- Clients are informed of all of the activities they never see, such as drafting documents and researching law, and those that seem trivial but are nonetheless time-consuming (telephone calls, reading letters received).

Most automated systems allow the services description to be permanently altered within the accounting program and/or permit the draft bill to be exported from the accounting program into a word-processing document for editing. Special attention should be given to abbreviations the client may not understand and the spelling of proper names, especially the client's.

Practical Application 5–4

Carol: Detailed interim billing is not a good idea. Instead, the client should just be given a bill saying "For Services Rendered" and an amount. If you send them a list of everything a lawyer did, they will probably ask pointless questions. When we used to send out detailed interim bills, one client called and asked why she should pay for legal research. She wanted to know why she should pay for research time when the lawyer was supposted to know the law already.

What client relations issues does Carol's statement raise? What professional issues? Under what circumstances would her points be valid? Under what circumstances would they not be valid?

Adjusting Client WIP Ledgers

Reviewing draft bills brings errors in the WIP ledgers to the lawyer's attention. Many are recording errors that should be corrected using the appropriate procedure. As they might affect other WIP ledgers that are also being billed, corrections are made promptly. It is best to produce another draft bill if the WIP ledger has been changed extensively. Figure 5–7 illustrates a WIP ledger change.

Some adjustments do not require changing the WIP ledgers and the adjustment is simply recorded at the time the bill is posted. Such adjustments are usually:

- changes in billing rates,

- deletions of charges for and/or descriptions of correctly recorded time,

Carpenter & Cook

CLIENT WIP TIME LEDGER

Re: *Fraud Claim: Ladies' Best Bet*   Client Name: *Century Textiles, Inc.*

Responsible Lawyer: *S.C.*   Notes: *use "discount" billing rates*

Week Ending	Lawyer	Hours	Rate	Amount	Total
10/7/98	LM	2.3	150.00	345.00	
" "	SC	1.6	180.00	288.00	633.00
10/14/98	SC	4.2	180.00	756.00	1,389.00
10/28/98	LM	0.6	150.00	90.00	
" "	SC	12.7	180.00	2,286.00	3,765.00
11/5/98	LM	2.3	165.00	379.50	
" "	SC	0.4	210.00	84.00	4,228.50
11/19/98	LM	15.3	165.00	2,524.50	
" "	SC	14.6	210.00	3,066.00	9,819.00
12/4/98	SC corr	15.0	(30.00)	(450.00)	9,369.00
12/5/98	LM adj			(339.00)	
" "	SC adj			(670.00)	8,360.00
" Billed	SC	195	(5,360.00)		
" "	LM	195	(3,000.00)		0.00

I forgot to use the "discount" rate for Sandy, so this WIP ledger had to be adjusted. Also, both Sandy and Lee agreed to reduce their fees by about 11%. M.

FIGURE 5–7   Adjusted WIP Ledger

- adjustments of fee amounts to conform to a fixed-fee or contingency fee agreement, and

- adjustments to disbursements, perhaps adding anticipated disbursements.

Approval and Issue to Client

Even the most advanced automated systems are no substitute for careful review of the bill before it is submitted to the client. Although many firms state "E. & O.E." (errors and omissions excepted) on the face of each client bill in case errors in the bill come to light later, it is difficult to collect additional amounts from clients.

Some firms number bills when they go out to the client, although often a number is assigned only to internal copies for identification purposes or because a number is required to record the bill in an automated system.

Bills are approved and signed by the lawyer responsible for the file or by the supervising partner if the firm's policy dictates that only a partner may sign bills. At least two copies of the *signed* bill are made before the bill is sent to the client: one for the client folder and one for accounting staff to use as a source document. The original should not be copied before it is signed because if changes are made to the original, it could be unclear which bill actually went to the client.

Most firms send the client a cover letter and a running statement of the trust ledger and/or accounts receivable ledger with the bill. In the interest of client relations and to encourage clients to discuss fee disputes as they arise, the cover letters of many firms specifically invite clients to bring up any questions they have regarding bills (see Figure 5–8). It is also standard practice to include a sentence saying how pleased the firm is to provide its services to the client. Some firms send an extra remittance copy of the bill to help identify the payment when the copy and check for payment are received by the firm.

Criminal defense and family law clients may prefer that bills not be sent to their homes. A bill is prepared in any event and the original is kept for future reference.

Bill Calculation

There are established guidelines for the calculation and presentation for many types of bills. They must be calculated accurately and presented in a form the client can understand.

FIGURE 5–8

Cover Letter

Carpenter & Cook
Attorneys At Law
2400 - 555 North Ocean Street, Fielding, St 10001

Telephone: 488-1111
Fax: 488-6666

Pat Carpenter
Sandy Cook
Terry Baker
Lee Mason (Associated)

Month #, 1999

Client Name
Street Address
City, St 00000

Attn: contact

Dear Name:

Re: File Description
     Our File #

We enclose our account dated Month #, 1999 in the amount of $X,XXX.XX, which we trust you will find to be in order. Our terms are net 15 days.

Paragraph about the progress of the file if the lawyer wants to include one.

As always, we consider it a privilege to serve your legal needs. If you have any questions, please do not hesitate to call me.

Yours truly,

(signed)
Lawyer

LWYR/sec

encl.

We send a cover letter like this with each client bill. M.

If the amount of the bill has been changed from the draft, the bill must be recalculated by either the secretary or the accounting staff. Because recalculations often affect supplementary reports, many firms prefer that relevant WIP ledgers be adjusted before the bill is recorded.

Many automated systems can recalculate billing rate changes but cannot charge the appropriate taxes if many changes have occurred during the billing period.

Fee Adjustments and Allocations

When the firm bills fees at any value other than that recorded in the WIP time ledger, there will be adjustments, often referred to as revenue variances. If WIP time is not recorded in the general ledger or not summarized in supporting schedules, there is no accounting effect of any adjustment.

A firm's policies often dictate that partners and/or staff lawyers bill and collect a minimum fee amount in a period (month or year) or that their compensation is directly related to their fees. Allocation of the fee amount is very important in these cases, although it usually applies only to files that more than one lawyer works on. Subject to individual firm policy, hourly fee bills are usually allocated as follows, unless otherwise specified on the accounting copy of the bill:

- Where there is no adjustment of WIP time in the billing, fees allocated as recorded to each lawyer.

- Where there is an attributable adjustment, to the lawyer in question.

- Where there has been an unattributable adjustment or courtesy discount, the adjustment to the responsible lawyer and the WIP amount to all other lawyers.

Variances between recorded WIP time and fees billed are inevitable in fixed-fee and contingency fee bills, although the allocation is usually much less obvious. In contingency cases where the client commenced an action with a lawyer outside the firm and subsequently brought the file to the firm, the other lawyer usually must be paid first. Adjustments are allocated as follows:

- Where the lawyer responsible is a partner or senior lawyer and the only other lawyers are junior staff lawyers, to the responsible lawyer.

- Where the lawyers are about the same seniority, proportionately according to the dollar value of the WIP time.

- Where the conduct of the file has been sequential, according to instructions.

The responsible lawyer is consulted before the bill is recorded if there is any question regarding the allocation of fees.

Penny: I'm sure that George makes more on bonuses than I do. My hourly billing rate might be higher, but my hours are always cut by Mr. Fell, who is the senior partner on most of the files I work on. I'm sure that even though I work just as hard as George, my total annual billings are lower, and so is my bonus. Of course, I have no say on what time gets cut on the bill to the client, but it sort of comes out of my pocket when it is my time that gets cut, doesn't it?

What are some human resource issues surrounding fee adjustments? What would you advise Penny to do? What are some other options for calculating bonuses?

Fee-Splitting

Complex client matters may require specialized legal expertise that is not available through the firm and must be obtained through another firm. Compensation to the subcontracting lawyer or firm is referred to as fee-splitting, or fee-sharing, as explained in ABA Model Rule 1.5(e).

> (e) A division of a fee between lawyers who are not in the same firm may be made only if:
> (1) the division is in proportion to the services performed by each lawyer or, by written agreement with the client, each lawyer assumes joint responsibility for the representation;
> (2) the client is advised of and does not object to the participation of all the lawyers involved; and
> (3) the total fee is reasonable.

The fiduciary nature of the client-lawyer relationship dictates that clients must be informed if their lawyers intend to share fees with a lawyer from another firm. In any fee-splitting arrangement, all lawyers must assume some level of professional responsibility, not merely giving advice to the client's primary counsel.

Case 5–8

Found: **Referral agreement between unassociated lawyers is unenforceable as being against public policy where client was never informed of and never agreed to fee-splitting agreement.**

Ordered: Referring lawyer to receive no fees.

Disbursements

Disbursements are usually not adjusted upon billing, although some are not charged to the client at all. Estimates of disbursements should be avoided, but if an estimate is required, it should be clearly identified as such to the client.

Some automated systems automatically purge billed disbursements, so if records are needed for an application for a fee award, they should be printed before the bill is posted and kept in a separate client "Accounting" folder.

Disbursements are itemized and subtotaled separately from fees.

Taxes on Bills

In the few jurisdictions that impose sales taxes on lawyers' fees and/or disbursements, accurate tax calculation is an important step in determining the total bill because the tax due is paid by the firm, regardless of whether it has properly charged the client.

Business and institutional clients who can recover taxes or at least record them as expenses against revenue for income tax purposes may be somewhat indifferent to the taxes they pay on lawyers' bills. Personal clients, on the other hand, are often unable to recover any portion of taxes, so all taxes collected by the firm are true financial burdens. Special care must be exercised in calculating any tax-exempt portion of the fees.

Some clients, including governments of various levels and government-related agencies, may be exempt from taxes and usually must provide the firm with an exemption number for audit purposes.

WIP Adjustments

In some firms and fields of practice, the WIP time and disbursements are billed exactly as recorded. However, adjustments are common even when the WIP has been recorded properly.

Bills are reviewed by accounting staff before they are recorded because if the WIP ledgers require adjustment *before* the billing journal is created, a separate WIP adjustments journal must be created and posted first. In systems where the WIP ledgers are adjusted at the same time as the journal is created, an initial review of the WIP identifying the changes will expedite the data entry process.

Certain WIP adjustments are easier to make after the bill has been recorded. These may be "zero bills" required by a system to remove incorrect and/or reversing entries, or they may be simple deletions.

Staff must consider the possibility that additional WIP entries have been made since the draft bill was produced unless the firm suspends posting of new WIP entries during the bill preparation process. Adjustments may have already been made if the draft bill required extensive revision of the WIP before the final bill was produced. In systems that do not sort WIP transactions by date order, adjustments may appear after new entries and must therefore be credited out of order.

Most fee adjustments made when recording bills are to correct billing rates for hourly rate bills or to allocate over- or under-realizations on the WIP time for contingency or fixed-fee bills. Figure 5–9 illustrates effects of WIP adjustments.

If the WIP amount is adjusted substantially or the fee allocation is not obvious, a copy of the WIP details used to produce the draft is attached to the accounting copy or the allocation and adjustments are noted on the face of it. Many firms require that fee adjustments exceeding a certain value be approved by a partner or the responsible lawyer.

Practical Application 5–6

George: Penny's billing rate is higher than mine even though I was a qualified lawyer two years before she was. The administrator says it's because in her field of estates, acceptable rates are higher than what our major insurance client, International Casualty, will accept as my hourly rate. My salary is a bit bigger than hers, but we get substantial bonuses based on what we bill, so I'm sure I end up making less, even if I bill up to ten percent more *hours* than she does. The administrator is sympathetic but says there's nothing I can do about it except change fields. Mr. Gault thinks I'm pretty good at what I do. He says that the reason he can bill International Casualty more than his usual rate is that I keep the client very happy with my reporting letters to them. I like working for Mr. Gault and I like insurance defense. What can I do?

What are some of the possible positive and negative effects of the firm's remuneration policy? What advice would you give George?

FIGURE 5–9

Recording WIP Adjustments in Ledgers

Event	Cash		Modified Accrual		Full Accrual	
	Debit	Credit	Debit	Credit	Debit	Credit
WIP Time Increased	WIP Ledger		WIP Ledger		Unbilled Fees WIP Ledger	Fee Revenue OR Fee Variance
WIP Time Decreased		WIP Ledger		WIP Ledger	Fee Revenue OR Fee Variance	Unbilled Fees WIP Ledger
Disbursements Increased	WIP Ledger		WIP Ledger		Unbilled Disbursements WIP Ledger	Disbursement Recovery OR Variance
Disbursements Decreased		WIP Ledger		WIP Ledger	Disbursement Recovery OR Variance	Unbilled Disbursements WIP Ledger

Billing Journals

Bills are entered into the billing journal from a copy provided to the accounting staff by the secretary. Each bill is actually a separate journal, but most firms use some sort of special journal (see Figure 5–10) or posting batch.

Billing journals are often complex where the lawyers' fee allocations are tracked for performance reports. A separate billing journal may be kept for each lawyer each month, although this is awkward in a manual system if more than one lawyer works on a file. Many automated systems, however, deal with this easily by producing supplementary reports each month.

General Ledger Entries

There are no entries to the general ledger from the billing journal if the cash method is used. If the modified accrual method is used and the firm records neither WIP time nor disbursements assets in the general ledger, the entire amount of the bill is debited to accounts receivable (and recorded in the client accounts receivable subledger), with credits:

- for fees, to fees revenue (small firms may have separate general ledger fee revenue accounts for each lawyer);

- for disbursements, to disbursements revenue (usually not separated by lawyer, but often by type of disbursement) or to the original expense (cost recovery); and

- for taxes, to the appropriate tax liability accounts.

If either WIP time or disbursements are recorded in the general ledger, the assets must be adjusted to reflect the bill. Small firms using manual systems may also maintain separate WIP and/or accounts receivable assets by lawyer in the *general ledger,* and extra care is needed to ensure that the proper asset account is credited and that it is credited for the correct amount. Figure 5–11 illustrates the most common combinations of entries. Any differences between the WIP asset amount recorded and the corresponding amount billed must also appear in the general ledger, usually in a variance or billing adjustment account in the revenue section.

Client WIP Ledger Entries

If the time and disbursements being billed were previously recorded in the client WIP ledger, these amounts must be relieved from (credited to) the ledger. If there is no controlling asset account in the general ledger, the WIP ledger is simply ruled off and the WIP balances begin

Carpenter & Cook

BILLING JOURNAL   Month _December 1998_

Date	File #	File Name	Lwyr	Bill #	Fees	Disb.	Taxes	P	Total
12/03/98	1489.4	Carpenter, D.	SC	194	0.00	17.55	0.00	P	17.55
12/05/98	1844.0	Century Textiles	SC / LM	195	5,360.00 / 3,000.00	215.68	250.80	P	8,826.48
12/07/98	1861.4	Sunrise/Sunset	PC / TB / KG	196	365.00 / 4,650.00 / 775.00	877.76	173.70	P	6,841.46
12/10/98	1087.6	Parsons	SC	197	400.00	4.00	12.00	P	416.00
12/10/98	2302.8	Peel, Don	TB / SC	198	1,100.00 / 562.00	635.73	46.86	P	2,344.59
12/12/98	2015.6	Bishop, N.	SC / LM	199	1,960.00 / 550.00	480.83	75.30	P	3,066.13
12/18/98	2162.6	Teal, W.	PC	200	6,950.00	1279.34	208.50	P	8,437.84
12/19/98	1073.6	Northwest Mach.	SC / LM	201	430.00 / 240.00	0.00	20.10	P	690.10
12/20/98	2111.3	Georgian Manor	SC	202	0.00	2,355.25	0.00	P	2,355.25
12/21/98	2276.4	Top Dog Dryclean.	TB / KG	203	1,250.00 / 680.00	559.20	57.90	P	2,547.10
12/21/98	2479.4	Central Envir.	SC / LM	204	(550.00) / 1,550.00	28.50	EXEMPT	P	1,028.50
12/27/98	2409.1	United Inv.	SC / LM	205	874.00 / 1,521.00	1,027.64	71.85	P	3,494.49
12/31/98		Totals	PC SC TB LM KG		7,315.00 9,036.00 7,000.00 6,861.00 1,455.00 / 31,667.00	7,481.48	917.01		40,065.49

I do the billing journal each month and summarize it like this. M.

FIGURE 5–10   Billing Journal

Event	Cash		Modified Accrual		Full Accrual	
	Debit	Credit	Debit	Credit	Debit	Credit
Time Billed	A/R Ledger	WIP Ledger	Accounts Receivable A/R Ledger	Fee Revenue WIP Ledger	Accounts Receivable A/R Ledger	Unbilled Fees WIP Ledger
Disbursements Billed		WIP Ledger		Disbursement Revenue OR Cost Recovery WIP Ledger		Unbilled Disbursements WIP Ledger

Time (fees) and disbursements are normally consolidated in the accounts receivable.

FIGURE 5–11   Recording Client Bills in Ledgers

again at zero. If WIP items are not billed in sequence, as in partial fee or disbursements-only bills, then the billed items are flagged (marked), with the new balance totaling all unmarked items.

Client Accounts Receivable Ledger Entries

The **client accounts receivable ledger** is set up like other client ledgers except that it is often combined with the trust ledger in simple manual systems and may show only the *total* of each bill and the offsetting payments. A more complete ledger showing a breakdown of fees and disbursements for each bill is helpful in recording receipts if the full amount of each bill is not paid. The complete bill recording process is illustrated in Figure 5–12.

─────────────────────── TERMS ───────────────────────

client accounts receivable ledger   A subsidiary ledger listing bills and payments on a client file.

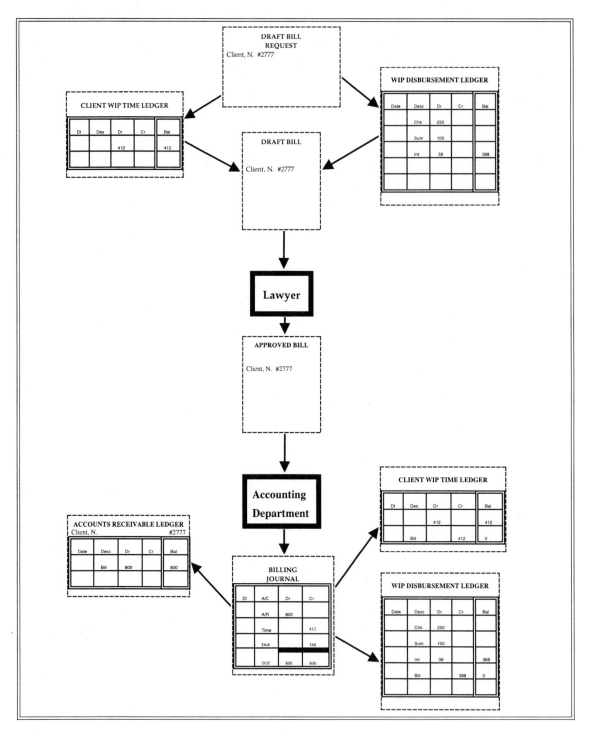

Figure 5-12   Complete Billing Process

Comprehensive Exercises

1. Design a billing procedure checklist for a new person entering a law firm. The list should be consistent with former lists and all steps exhaustive and mutually exclusive (i.e., no overlaps and no gaps). There should be at least fifty items.

2. Describe the special challenges in designing controls for billing procedures. In particular, address the positive and negative personnel and motivational impact of controls.

3. Billing procedures are often necessarily a compromise between promptness and accuracy. Draft a set of policies that would serve as billing guidelines for Carpenter & Cook.

IIII
CHAPTER 6

ACCOUNTS RECEIVABLE

Law firms generate virtually all revenue by receiving money in exchange for providing legal services, a process comprising three major steps:

- determining the fees to be charged,

- billing clients, and

- collecting bills.

In other words, if a client bill is never collected, there is ultimately no revenue for the related work. Although not desirable from the firm's point of view, it is not unusual for a client to successfully dispute bills, even after having voluntarily entered into a fee agreement accurately used to calculate the bill.

Case 6–1	Found:	Contingent fee agreement for defense of defamation suit **based on a percentage of the difference between the prayer in the petition and the amount awarded was against public policy and void.**
	Ordered:	Lower court award of contingency fees reversed and remanded for law firm to seek fees on quantum merit basis.

Client Payments

Money received by the firm for deposit into its general bank account (the firm's operating checking account) is mostly from clients paying bills already sent to them, although other monies such as supplier reimbursements are also deposited into the general account. For some clients, the firm transfers fee advances from funds held in trust into its general account to pay these bills, as discussed in Chapter 7.

Client payments (**general receipts**) received in the mail are forwarded to the secretary for the lawyer responsible for the file or to the accounting staff by the receptionist or mail-room clerk. If clients give checks and cash directly to lawyers during an appointment, the lawyer gives the payment to the secretary to produce the proper documentation. Clients are given receipts for cash payments, and many firms issue numbered receipts for all payments as an added internal control. If the firm does not issue a bill for services such as notarial fees, a receipt like the one illustrated in Figure 6–1 must be issued.

--------------------------- TERMS ---------------------------

general receipt Payment for deposit into the firm's general account, usually payment for a client bill.

FIGURE 6–1
Receipt for Cash
Payment

Carpenter & Cook

41028

December 29, 1998

RECEIVED FROM: ___*Warren & Flora Parsons*___ $ *416.00*

THE SUM OF: --------------*four hundred sixteen*------------*00*/100 Dollars

RE: *Bill #197/File #1087.6*   ___*Leslie Steward*___

We always give a receipt like this for any cash payments. Leslie gives the original to the client, and I get this copy. The second copy stays in the receipt book. M.

Cash receipts present particular concerns, especially when the amounts are large and nonaccounting staff are nervous about handling them. Specific written procedures are followed, including:

- verification by the lawyer of the cash amount and denominations, and delivery of the cash by the lawyer to the person responsible for banking;

- immediate signed verification of the receipt and immediate delivery to the bank; and

- verification directly to the lawyer that the funds were deposited, with a copy of the bank deposit slip.

Practical Application 6–1

Simon: I think I might be in trouble this time. Ms. Wells asked me to take a large cash deposit to the bank instead of asking the accounting clerk to do it. I'm not sure if she doesn't trust the clerk or whether she thought I had the spare time. Anyway, she prepared the deposit slip and put it in an envelope and told me to take it to the bank. When I got to the bank, I took the deposit out, threw away the envelope, and gave the deposit to the teller. There were all these thousand dollar bills! I've never seen so much cash in my life. The teller said the deposit was a thousand dollars short, and I counted the bills and sure enough it was. I was very shaken because I didn't know how much cash I'd been carrying, so I didn't know if I'd been given the right amount. The only thing I could think of was that it might be in the envelope, so the bank manager came and unlocked the waste paper container. There was the thousand dollars still in the envelope! What a relief. I just hope the bank manager doesn't call Ms. Wells and complain about the trouble the bank went through because of me.

How could this problem have been prevented? Draft a brief list of procedures that Ms. Wells should have followed.

Documenting Payments

Before preparing the documentation for the payment, the secretary or accounting staff member must ensure that the funds are to be deposited to the firm's general account by verifying that the funds are due to the firm. An accounts receivable listing or other reliable document is consulted to verify the amount and client to whom the payment should be credited. Funds not belonging to the firm should not be deposited in the general account, as discussed in Chapter 7.

Practical Application 6–2

Ruby: We use the cash method, so we don't have a billing journal. All of the unpaid client bills are kept in a binder in alphabetical order. We always know who owes what by just looking in the binder. We don't need client ledgers either. The system is very simple, effective, and accurate.

What types of potentially valuable information cannot be produced using Ruby's system?

Each check is proofed (see Chapter 1) before depositing it, and potential problems are brought to the attention of the responsible lawyer *before* the deposit is made. Special attention should be given to checks that may be for payment on more than one file.

To ensure that payments are credited properly, firms use a general receipt form such as the one illustrated in Figure 6–2. It provides space to photocopy the check and form together for the client folder and should specify at a minimum:

- *identification of the client file(s) to be credited* (sometimes one check is received to pay on several files);

- *date* the payment was received by the firm;

- *amount* of the payment;

- *form of the payment* (cash, check, money order);

- *whether the payment is on account* or for a specific bill, including identification of the bill by bill number or date;

- the *identity of the payer,* who may not be the client; and

- the *staff member* who prepared the form.

Forms can also provide space for recording details of nonstandard allocations or payments for several bills for one client as illustrated in Figure 6–3.

FIGURE 6–2

General Receipt
Form with Check
Copy

Carpenter & Cook
GENERAL RECEIPT

Prepared by _L.S._

File	_1844.0_	_Century Textiles_
Date	_11/10/98_	_Ladies' Best Bet_
Amount	_$840.34_	Bill number _141_

Deposited by	L.S.
Receipt entered by	M.F.

Century Textiles Inc.   **455**
2545 Eastern Way
Sundown, ST 10010

Nov. 8 19 _98_

PAY TO THE
ORDER OF _____Carpenter & Cook_____ $____840.34___

--------------*eight hundred forty*----------------------------------*34* /100 DOLLARS

RE   _Fees - Ladies' Best Bet_

The Bank of the East
149 - 240 John Street
Fielding, ST 10101

Don Peel

000100   29873 10 456 123

Leslie or the senior secretaries usually fill out the general receipt form and copy the check at the bottom. They also make a copy for the client file. M.

Banking Procedures

Checks are photocopied before they are deposited into the general account, and a photocopy is filed with the receipt form in the accounting records and/or in the client folder. If a problem arises later and the check has been negotiated, the firm must have access to the pertinent information on the check.

Although firms might hesitate to write the client's name on the bank deposit slip, some identification (such as the number) of the file to be credited must be clear on the slip, as illustrated in Figure 6–4.

FIGURE 6–3
Client Payment
Form: Multiple
Files

Carpenter & Cook

CLIENT PAYMENT FORM

Date: _Nov. 12, 1998_   Cash $_____

Received from: _Northwest Machinery_   Check $ _5,422.59_

Received by: _C.W._   _____ $_____

File #	Re:	Date	Bill	Lyr	Fees	Disb	Tax	Total
1073.6	Sundown	09/12	108	SC	350.00	12.92	10.50	373.42
1073.6	"	10/03	127	SC	400.00	40.82	49.50	
"	"	"	"	LM	1,250.00			1,740.32
1073.6	"	11/03	162	SC	1,850.00	376.50	55.50	2,282.00
2143.6	Bowman	11/03	163	SC	985.00	12.30	29.55	1,026.85
TOTALS				SC	3,585.00	442.54	145.05	5,422.59
				LM	1,250.00			

Special Instructions: _____

Posted:

Initial	Date
M.F.	11/14

Photocopy Check Here

If clients give us one check to pay for several bills and/or files, I use this form to break the payment down so that it can be posted to the client ledgers and general ledger. M.

Recording Receipts

General receipts are entered in the general receipts special journal, using the supporting documentation. In pegboard systems, combination journals are used.

The general receipt form and/or check photocopy and/or validated deposit slip are used make the entry to the receipts journal. A unique reference number for each deposit helps to trace the entry if necessary. Many firms make only one general deposit per day, in which case the date is sufficient. The client ledger entries are posted from the journal, often with the added description of the form of the funds received (cash or check) and the reference number of the bill being paid. This will be simultaneous in pegboard systems and many automated systems.

FIGURE 6–4
Bank Deposit Slip

Account Number: 18872-2		Account Name: Carpenter & Cook - General			
Checks		Cash	(1087.6)		
		1	X	1 =	1.00
1489.4	17.55	1	X	5 =	5.00
2276.4	1,000.00	1	X	10 =	10.00
2162.6	8,437.84	5	X	20 =	100.00
		4	X	50 =	200.00
STATE EASTERN BANK		1	X	100 =	100.00
600 North Ocean Street Fielding, ST 10004			X	=	
5 DEC 29 1998 5		COIN		=	
17004-01		TOTAL CASH			416.00
		TOTAL CHECKS			9,455.39
		TOTAL DEPOSIT			9,871.39
Deposited by:	L.S.	Teller:		J.G.	

This is how the bank likes the deposit slips to be made out. M.

To facilitate bank reconciliations, entries to the bank ledger show the *total* of the deposit, regardless of the number of client entries the deposit slip represents.

Entering Receipts

In the cash method, fee revenue for a client bill is recorded in the general ledger only after the payment has been received. The credits in the journal are for the fee revenue, disbursement revenue, and/or sales tax liability accounts. Debits are to the general bank.

Accrual method receipt journals may be even simpler—the credit is to accounts receivable and the debit is to the bank.

Both the cash and accrual methods often have supporting schedules indicating the **receipt allocation** between lawyers whose fees are being collected. In automated systems, entries to these schedules are created when the journal is posted. Figure 6–5 shows a journal with supplementary information columns.

--------- TERMS ---------

receipt allocation   The apportionment of a firm's collected fees between its lawyers.

Carpenter & Cook

GENERAL RECEIPTS JOURNAL Month December 1998

Date	File #	File Name	Lwyr	Bill #	Fees	Disb.	Taxes	P	Total
12/05/98	1289.8	Pleasant Hills	SC	109	1,551.00	0.00	46.53	P	1,597.53
"	1156.9	Prairie Twine	SC LM	139	1,564.00 235.00	1,867.92	53.97	P	3,720.89
12/12/98	2015.6	Bishop, N.	SC LM	199	1,960.00 550.00	480.83	75.30	P	3,066.13
"	1861.4	Sunrise/Sunset	PC TB KG	196	365.00 4,650.00 775.00	877.76	173.70	P	6,841.46
12/29/98	1489.4	Carpenter, D.	SC	194	0.00	17.55	0.00	P	17.55
"	2276.4	Top Dog Dryclean	KG	203	427.96	559.20	12.84	P	1,000.00
"	2162.6	Teal, W.	PC	200	6,950.00	1279.34	208.50	P	8,437.84
"	1087.6	Parsons	SC	197	400.00	4.00	12.00	P	416.00
12/31/98	2302.8	Peel, Don	TB SC	198	1,100.00 562.00	635.73	46.86	P	2,344.59
12/31/98		Totals	PC SC TB LM KG		7,315.00 6,037.00 5,750.00 785.00 1,202.96 21,089.96	5,722.33	629.70		27,441.99

The receipts journal is like the billing journal. The total deposits are in the general bank synoptic. M.

FIGURE 6–5 Receipt Journal with Fee Allocation

When the journal is posted to a manual client accounts receivable ledger, only the total received is entered, and the running balance is updated. In automated systems, the entry often shows separate amounts for the fees, disbursements, and taxes collected, as illustrated in Figure 6–6.

FIGURE 6–6
Accounts
Receivable Ledger

Carpenter & Cook

ACCOUNTS RECEIVABLE LEDGER

Client: _Top Dog Drycleaning_   File #: _2276.4_

Lawyer: _T.B._   Opened: _Oct. 6, 1998_

Date	Lwyr	Bill #	Fees	Disb.	Taxes	Total	Balance
10/31/98	TB KG	164	465.00 220.00	269.50	20.55	975.05	975.05
11/24/98	TB KG	164	(465.00) (220.00)	(269.50)	(20.55)	(975.05)	0.00
12/21/98	TB KG	203	1,250.00 680.00	559.20	57.90		2,547.10
12/29/98	KG	203	(427.96)	(59.20)	(12.84)	(1,000.00)	1,527.10

Accounts receivable ledgers are especially useful when the client pays only part of a bill. M.

After the receipts are entered, the receipt forms are filed chronologically, alphabetically by client name, or numerically by bill number in binders or folders. The validated deposit slips are kept in a temporary file until the bank account is reconciled, and then filed permanently with the bank records. Figure 6–7 illustrates the receipt entry process.

Receipt Allocation

Firms hope that clients will pay their bills in total as they are rendered, which creates no problem in preparing lawyers' fee collection reports because the allocation is the same as for the bill. However, a client who cannot pay the full amount of a bill renders payments *on account,* where the money received is to be applied to that client's accounts

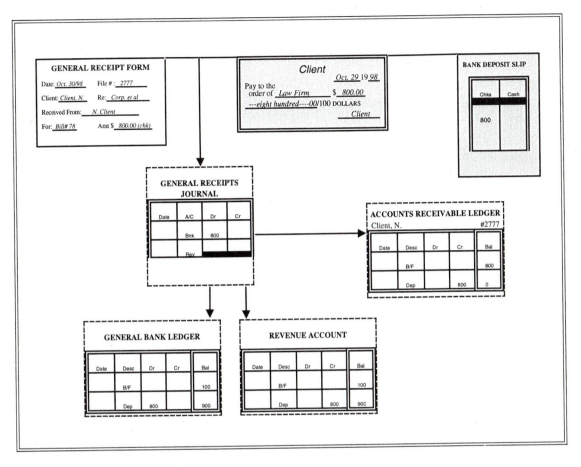

FIGURE 6–7   General Receipts Process

receivable generally as opposed to an individual bill. These situations lead to questions about the allocation of receipts because it is not known when or if the balance will be paid. Policies for allocating payments on account include:

- allocating the payment first to disbursements and taxes thereon, then to fees and taxes thereon;

- allocating fee payments first to the most junior lawyers, then to the senior or responsible lawyers, or allocating all fees proportionally; and

- allocating payments to the oldest bills first.

Some automated systems handle the allocation of partial receipts quite well, either by allowing specific bills to be credited exactly as posted or by automatically applying payments on account to taxes and disbursements first, and the balance proportionally to the fees for each lawyer. Sometimes, however, this allocation is not appropriate, and supplementary reports require manual adjustment.

Practical Application 6–3

Pearl: My client Western Steel is not very happy about some of the bills they've received. I'm senior counsel on the file, and they don't mind paying for my time, but they don't want to pay for Dirk's time, who was junior counsel and did an excellent job. Dirk's well-publicized defense of an alleged brutally violent criminal has many local citizens questioning the firm's judgment in representing such a person. Of course, this should not be an issue with Western Steel, but I'm in a very difficult position. Western's case could also get a lot of media attention, and quite soon. They don't want to be tainted by associated as having anything to do with someone who would defend a "nefarious criminal." It's not fair for Dirk not to get credit for the time, but I don't think I can collect for it, and I don't see that I should absorb it. The partners have asked for my suggestions on handling the receipt allocation.

What should Pearl suggest to the partners? What is the practical effect on the firm of public reaction?

Dishonored Checks

Although most people are familiar with checks being dishonored because of nonsufficient funds (NSF), many do not realize that there are several other reasons why drawees do not accept checks for payment, some of which are not the fault of the drawer. From a public relations perspective, therefore, some caution is advisable when approaching clients about dishonored checks.

Because records of client payments are often used to compile management reports in automated systems, the method for recording dishonored client payments depends on how the system handles entry reversals. Examples are:

- entering a reverse bill using the same allocation used to record the receipt, and a reverse deposit to correct the bank ledger;

- entering a reverse bill using a standard allocation policy, such as reversing the total deposit against the responsible lawyer's fees, and entering a reverse bank deposit; and

- charging the reverse bank deposit to the general ledger account for bad debts and using a separate entry to correct the accounts receivable.

Unfortunately, even advanced automated systems seldom handle client payment reversals well.

Collection Activity

Bill collection is a complicated issue in law firms and a source of discomfort that many professionals prefer to avoid. Lawyers recognize that an unpaid bill is revenue uncollected and a potential bad debt. Despite this awareness, many are hesitant to approach clients about overdue accounts for fear of alienating them, particularly when:

- The file is ongoing and there are more bills to be rendered in the future—although if these, too, are uncollectible, the firm will have lost even more revenue.

- The client has other matters in the firm. If one file is not being paid but all others are, there may be a good reason, such as the client waiting for a particular event before paying.

- The client is expected to introduce more and better files in the future. However, a client with old outstanding bills may be too embarrassed to approach the firm again.

Consideration is given to the field of practice and difficulties certain clients face. For example, it is not unusual for bills in family matters to be long outstanding, especially if family assets can be sold only pursuant to a court order.

There are also professional responsibility issues in collections. Some collection methods necessarily expose confidential material regarding either the legal matter or the client's personal circumstances. Certain methods simply are not permitted, such as any that prejudice a client's matter in progress, and under no circumstances should a nonlawyer do or say anything to anyone that might be construed as the firm's abandonment of the client for nonpayment of a bill.

Case 6–2	Found:	Subsequent to fee dispute with clients, **lawyer intentionally and unjustifiably attempted to injure clients (prospective adoptive parents) in adoption case by suggesting to social worker that clients might be in financial difficulty.**
	Ordered:	Three-month suspension.

Firms benefit from proper written policies and procedures for collections, including:

- All collection activity is approved first by the responsible lawyer. This ensures that the lawyer has fully considered the client's ability to pay, which may be confidential knowledge not shared with support staff, and the effects on future relationships. However, contention may arise between lawyers when collection performance is a major element of their remuneration formulas. Lawyers who work on another lawyer's file may not be permitted to contact the client and could thereby lose income if collection is delayed.

- Collection activity is undertaken by one particular lawyer or senior staff person who has a special aptitude for or training in collections. Lawyers may prefer not to be involved with collecting from their clients, but many clients prefer that their own lawyers contact them to maintain confidentiality.

- The accounting and/or secretarial staff maintains records of all collection activity by file, possibly on a special form or in a word processing document. Lawyers are notified immediately when a payment on an overdue account is received.

- The firm maintains standard letters approved by the partners to ensure that the presentation is consistent and courteous. Alternatively, a set of approved paragraphs or phrases is available to lawyers so they can adapt correspondence to the individual situation.

- The firm requires fee advances before continuing work for clients with a poor payment history.

- Secretaries prepare collection letters and records and obtain copies of bills and other materials to assist lawyers and minimize lawyer time spent on collections.

- The partners monitor all collection activity and require that certain conditions be met before dealing with the clients themselves.

- Monthly standard computerized statements that do not appear to target the client but appear to simply "come out of the computer" are sent only to overdue clients.

- Individual lawyers are permitted, under clear guidelines, to negotiate reasonable payment schedules with their clients.

Firms that charge interest on client accounts receivable must ensure that the fee agreement makes specific provision for interest charges. Many automated systems produce reminders each month and calculate interest at the same time, usually without posting it to the client's accounts receivable ledger. In some systems, however, this is not an option, and the interest becomes part of the receivable in the general ledger.

Collection time is usually reduced by sending self-addressed envelopes and remittance copies with client bills or bill reminders. For corporate and institutional clients, timing the bills to coincide with the client's accounts payable cycle can also reduce payment time.

<table>
<tr><td>

Practical Application 6–4

</td><td>

Herb: The partners have decided to do something about the huge number of overdue accounts we are carrying for our clients. It's a step in the right direction, I'm sure, but I kind of wish they hadn't picked me to be in charge of it. I guess as junior associate, they feel I'm the best person because my time is less valuable in billing. I really do have enough real work to do, and I don't hold out much hope for many of these collections. I want to maximize my time but still do a thorough job. Frankly, I'm not sure of the best place to start.

Can you help Herb? What general guidelines and preliminary procedures would you recommend?

</td></tr>
</table>

Accounts Receivable Adjustments

There are two types of adjustments to the accounts receivable records: billing amendments, which are sent to clients, and internal adjustments, which affect only the firm's accounts.

Proper documentation of both types of adjustments is required to support tax remittances and income tax calculations. Proper authorization ensures the firm's profitability is not adversely affected by inappropriate modifications to client billing records.

Billing Amendments

Billing amendments are made to:

- *Correct WIP recording errors.* Firms correct the error in the WIP ledger and then generate a modified bill.

- *Correct the calculation of an amount.* If contingency fees, hourly rates, internal disbursements, or other charges subject to a fee agreement are calculated incorrectly, the bill must be modified.

- *Restore deleted (relieved) WIP items.* Sometimes an entire bill that has already been recorded is canceled (not written off). The relieved WIP must be restored to be billed either at a later date or under a separate file number.

- *Discount correct items permanently.* In the interest of goodwill or to maintain client relationships, firms often reduce bills when a client

---

TERMS

billing amendment   A change or addition to a bill that has been issued.

disagrees with a specific charge or the total bill. Bills are sometimes reduced if the client is a friend or relative of someone in the firm.

Billing amendments, except perhaps small calculation errors, are approved in the same manner as the original bill and supported by documentation detailing the purpose of the amendment and any reports that must be revised. Figure 6–8 illustrates a billing amendment that affects partners' productivity reports.

Authorizing amendments usually does not require a special form, although information similar to that attached to a regular bill is required to enter amendments into the journal. Amendments are recorded in a separate billing amendments journal or are included in the regular billing journal. Taxes are treated consistently with the original calculation method, assuming it was correct. Billing amendments are documented to clients as follows:

- *Modified bills* are used when the firm has billed an item in error, duplicated or omitted a charge, or made an incorrect calculation. The original bill is reversed and the modified bill entered if it is issued in the same month as the original. If the system does not allow the billing details to be corrected and generated again, the bill is simply retyped. Modified bills usually must be used if the items were correctly recorded in the WIP but are being restored.

- *Additional bills* are simpler than modified bills, especially if the client was merely not charged for an item. These may be given a number that shows they are related to the original bill if this reference is important, but usually it is not. Clients who will not accept additional bills require a modified one instead.

- *Credit notes* are used to reverse only those charges that are removed or reduced with the firm's agreement when the original charge was not made in error. If the charge was made in error, a modified bill is preferred. Credit notes issued in firms that use WIP asset accounts in the general ledger are recorded in a separate journal, not simply as a reverse bill, because this would cause the debit to go back into the WIP account. Some software manuals advocate that credit notes be entered into the general receipts journal, but this method should be avoided if it will cause inconsistencies in performance reports. A better method is to enter a negative total bill amount to the accounts receivable, with the debit to the revenue or recovery or variance accounts, with no effect on the WIP ledger. A credit note allocation calculation is illustrated in Figure 6–9.

FIGURE 6–8
Credit Note

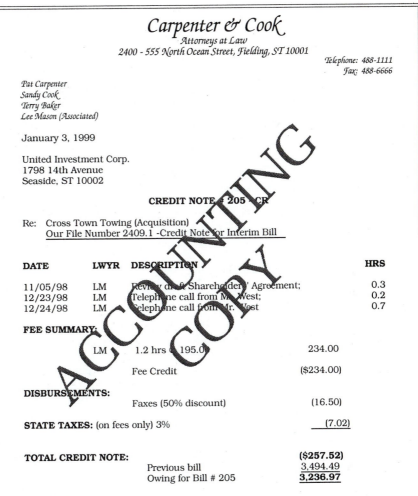

Carpenter & Cook
Attorneys at Law
2400 - 555 North Ocean Street, Fielding, ST 10001

Telephone: 488-1111
Fax: 488-6666

Pat Carpenter
Sandy Cook
Terry Baker
Lee Mason (Associated)

January 3, 1999

United Investment Corp.
1798 14th Avenue
Seaside, ST 10002

CREDIT NOTE # 205 CR

Re: Cross Town Towing (Acquisition)
     Our File Number 2409.1 - Credit Note for Interim Bill

DATE	LWYR	DESCRIPTION	HRS
11/05/98	LM	Review draft Shareholders' Agreement;	0.3
12/23/98	LM	Telephone call from Mr. West;	0.2
12/24/98	LM	Telephone call from Mr. West	0.7

FEE SUMMARY:

LM   1.2 hrs @ 195.00   234.00

Fee Credit   ($234.00)

DISBURSEMENTS:

Faxes (50% discount)   (16.50)

STATE TAXES: (on fees only) 3%   (7.02)

TOTAL CREDIT NOTE: **($257.52)**
Previous bill   3,494.49
Owing for Bill # 205   **3,236.97**

Sandy Cook

E. & O.E.

The client complained about the original bill #205 because of Lee's time. The November time had been posted to the wrong file, and Ms. Cantor felt that it should not be charged. It will be charged to Sandy's time. The two calls from Mr. West were taken after Ms. Cantor had said (after the meeting on Dec. 15) not to take calls from him, but we had a temporary receptionist that week (Leslie was sick) who didn't know not to put these calls through. Lee should not have taken them anyway, so the time will be charged to Lee. Ms. Cantor feels that $1.00/page for faxes is too much, so we reduced them by 50%. M.

Carpenter & Cook

BILLING JOURNAL   Month *December 1998*

Date	File #	File Name	Lwy	Bill #	Fees	Disb.	Taxes	P	Total
01/03/99	2409.1	United Investment	SC LM	505CR	(58.50) (175.50)	(16.50)	(7.02)	P	(257.52)

This is the way to post the credit note for bill #205 in the billing journal. M.

FIGURE 6–9   Billing Amendment Allocations

Practical Application 6–5

Liz: I've had a lot of trouble with Atlantic Produce about some February time that we had entered incorrectly and finally billed on their July bill. We've agreed on the amount of the reduction, but not on how to present it. I want to issue a credit note dated at the end of last month, September. They want an amended bill back-dated to July, so that it will look better on their books, which they closed at the end of August. Because of the seasonal cycles of my billings, my performance will look better if I send the credit note dated September.

What should Liz do? What are the effects on the client? On Liz?

Bad Debts

Nonaccounting staff are often confused about "write-offs." Theoretically, the term relates only to **bad debts**—amounts that are owed to the firm but that it accepts as basically uncollectible. If the firm sued the client on the bill, it would receive a favorable judgment but would probably not be able to collect on it. In some firms, write-offs include all accounts receivable adjustments that result in a nil balance, even if the write-off is "negative." Some of these write-offs are actually billing amendments made by agreement with the client or unilaterally by the firm.

TERMS
---

bad debts   Amounts billed that are considered to be uncollectible and are removed permanently from the accounts receivable balance.

Bad debts are identified by lawyers on a file-by-file basis where collection is considered to be virtually hopeless and often require the approval of a partner before they are officially recorded. Lawyers should be aware that bad debts will no longer appear on accounts receivable reports. If a lawyer wishes to continue collection action, however, a reminder can be incorporated into the bring-forward or calendaring system.

Recording bad debts involves eliminating unpaid bills permanently from the firm's accounts where the firm will not be pursuing active collection measures. Revenues and recoveries previously recognized are reversed because the client is unwilling or unable to pay. Bad debts can be recorded at any time during the year, although most smaller firms with few bad debts record them only at year-end to ensure that income tax is not paid on uncollectible revenue. Bad debt write-offs during the year are more common in:

- firms with automated systems, where a file cannot be closed in the accounting system if any client balances remain, and holding the file open until year-end would mean excessive system storage;

- firms with limited filing space in the office, where the file must be closed to be removed to an off-site storage facility; and

- firms that require precise interim reports on the collectability of bills (cash flow planning), the collection performance of lawyers (remuneration and staff planning), and realizable income (partners' tax planning).

As with WIP deletions, bad debts must be authorized by the appropriate lawyer and must include adequate allocation instructions. In large firms or in firms that record bad debts throughout the year, a standard form such as that illustrated in Figure 6–10 is used.

Full documentation relating to each bad debt bill is kept in a permanent file in the accounting records in the event the bill is eventually recovered or if it is needed for tax purposes. If an entire bill is unpaid, it is simply credited to the accounts receivable and debited to the bad debt expense account and the tax liabilities. Some firms debit the fee revenue and disbursements recovery accounts instead of bad debts.

Bills that have been partially paid may require adjustments to allocate the payment correctly. The usual allocation policy is to apply the payment:

- *First to disbursements and the taxes on disbursements.* If the payment does not cover all disbursements, the tax is prorated to the disbursements paid.

- *Second to fees, with the tax prorated,* using the appropriate fee allocation.

Carpenter & Cook

ACCOUNTS RECEIVABLE WRITE-OFF AUTHORIZATION

Date: _Dec. 31, 1998_   File: _1783.0_

Bill Number: _103_   Client: _Pizza Pie Co._

Bill Date: _Sept. 10, 1998_   Re: _Crusty's Bakery_

FEES

LAWYER	VALUE	TAX
TB	698.21	20.95
TOTAL	698.21	20.95

DISBURSEMENTS

TYPE	CODE	VALUE
Copies	11	24.15
TOTAL		24.15

Authorized: _T.B. P.C._   Total W/O: _743.31_

Reason: _Company bankrupt - cannot collect._

Any write-off over $100 has to be authorized by a partner. M.

FIGURE 6–10 Bad Debt Write-off Form

Firms keep a list of their bad-debt clients, so that work will not inadvertently be taken on by another lawyer in the firm. One way to do this is to build a notation into the conflict system.

Recovery on bills previously recorded as bad debts does occur. In law firms it is important to allocate taxes correctly to recovered amounts, and depending on the level of detail of the firm's records, it may be best to record the bill again as an account receivable and record the receipt as a regular payment to avoid problems with the ancillary records and collection reports.

Practical Application 6–6	Herb: My collection efforts are going surprisingly well! I've managed to get payment on some really old bills—some so old they had been written off as bad debts. In order to make everything tie in, we need to allocate the receipts to someone in the firm, and some of the original lawyers have left. I think I should get the credit for their time, since the time I spend on collections necessarily reduces my other billings.

What are some options for Herb's firm? What fee receipt allocation makes the most sense? Why?

Accounts Receivable Allowances

There is also some confusion about the differences between a bad debt and an **allowance for doubtful accounts** (or allowance for bad debts). The income tax effects are approximately equivalent, but the accounting and reporting treatments are quite different. Although nonaccounting staff are not generally involved in determining or recording allowances, they must understand the concept if they deal with any doubtful client accounts receivable and subsequent client payments. There are no allowances for doubtful accounts in cash method systems.

Firms often prefer that amounts that are "borderline" bad debts, where collection is doubtful but not hopeless, be included in the allowance instead of recorded as bad debts. Allowances are recorded only at year-end (for income tax purposes) except where more precise interim financial information is required. For example, if the firm is negotiating a loan or admitting or removing partners, interim financial statements are prepared by the accounting firm. The accounting firm may recommend that a standard limit be used to determine the allowance

─────────────────── TERMS ───────────────────

accounts receivable allowances   Amounts recorded as being possibly uncollectible, which are recorded only as a temporary amount and are not permanently removed from the accounts receivable balance.

allowance for doubtful accounts   The accepted account title for an accounts receivable allowance.

amounts. One of the simplest standards is to record all receivables over a certain age, often 120 but sometimes 90 days, depending on the field of practice and the firm's collection history.

Doubtful accounts amounts remain on the clients' ledgers so that they are not ignored in the accounts receivable reports and to ensure that lawyers are consistently reminded through the reports to attempt collection or monitor the client's financial status.

Practical Application 6–7

Lira: We all do our best to minimize bad debts, but they still happen sometimes. The best thing to do is get them off the books and concentrate on better prospects. No one needs old papers lying around, and besides, old receivables look bad to the bank and reduce office morale.

Wade: I think you've got that backwards. We need to keep questionable accounts on the books as a constant reminder to keep up collection efforts. If we just sweep them under the rug, people will not think carefully about making efforts to minimize bad debts. Morale is reduced when you admit failure, not when you keep trying.

Discuss Lira's and Wade's viewpoints. What are some governing principles that they may be able to agree on and adopt?

If the allowance appears only in the general ledger, it is supported by a schedule referencing the files. The credit is posted to a contra account (to avoid problems with the control account) titled "Allowance for Doubtful Accounts" directly following accounts receivable in the general ledger. The debits are usually posted to the bad debt expense or to the respective fee revenue and disbursement recovery accounts. Taxes, however, are not debited to the tax liability accounts; they are either charged to bad debt expense or are excluded from the allowance total. Allowances are not posted to any client ledgers, although some notation is usually made on ledger cards in a manual system.

Billing and Productivity

The most reliable and significant performance information is generated from the firm's billing and collection records. Although some useful information is generated from time records, the more important productivity information is accessible only from the billing and cash receipt summaries, which identify what time is spent profitably, by whom, and in what field of practice. All of this information helps the firm's management to plan and make decisions.

The primary purpose of billing is to provide money to the firm in return for its having provided services to clients. The following tenets guide the billing process:

- The sooner the firm receives the money for the services provided, the stronger its cash position and the higher its profitability generally.

- The longer bills are unpaid, the less likely they will ever be paid.

- Any method or control that necessarily complicates or delays billing will negatively affect efficiency and profitability.

Managing the Billing Process

In firms where lawyers are responsible for few files, the billing cycle is initiated by the secretary and responsible lawyer. In firms where lawyers are responsible for many files and lawyers work on each other's files, the billing process is initiated by accounting staff because the volume of files is too large for the lawyers' secretaries to monitor file amounts regularly. Proper management of the billing process:

- *Promotes prompt billing* by providing as much support as possible. Accounting staff routinely produce drafts that require minimal involvement from the lawyer and secretary.

- *Clearly indicates the other uses of billing information* so that lawyers who alter billing data do not inadvertently compromise report integrity in the process.

- *Incorporates reasonable deadlines* for billing decisions. The importance of these deadlines is communicated clearly by the partners and/or management committee.

- *Conforms to accepted conventions* in various fields of practice and the requirements of particular clients.

- *Encourages reliance upon the system's* strengths while recognizing its weaknesses. No system is perfect, but any weaknesses should not be obscure. They should be identified and communicated so that lawyers understand the items that must be reviewed in the greatest depth. For example, advanced automated systems allow editing of the services description within the accounting program. Others require that the details be transferred into a word processing system and edited there. This can create problems if staff not familiar with the accounting software think that changes made in the word processing system somehow find their way back into the accounting system.

Manual systems do not easily create lists and reports to help control the billing process. Any reliable automated system that records WIP time and disbursements provides more accurate, efficient, and timely billing when used properly.

Information Reporting

Reports related to billing and collections carry much more weight than WIP reports in the evaluation of the performance of both individual lawyers and the firm as a whole. Common monthly billing and receivables reports include:

- *Realization rates.* These are usually expressed as percentages of the time recorded or billed. Rates are commonly calculated for:

  — billing realization: the billed amount divided by the associated WIP amount originally recorded. Alternatively, the billed amount is divided by the associated number of hours at the standard billing rate.

  — collection realization: the percentage of billed fees collected within a reasonable period.

  — overall realization: fees collected within a reasonable period of time from when the time was originally recorded, usually at a standard rate. This figure is useful only in certain fields of practice.

- *Total of billed fees by lawyer,* often including the amount of WIP relieved and the billing variance. Credit notes and adjustments may be presented separately; sometimes the value of disbursements billed is included.

- *Fees collected and written off.* The allocated fees collected for the month is an important report where there are concerns that some lawyers do not provide adequate cash flow from their file work. Write-offs may be on a separate schedule.

- *Outstanding accounts receivable by client,* produced from the client accounts receivable ledgers. This is also often *aged,* meaning that the amounts are presented by the length of time they have been outstanding, which is important in determining if individual lawyers are following collection policies or are reluctant to write off bad debts for fear of adverse performance reports.

- *Total accounts receivable by lawyer,* often presented as percentages of the firm's total accounts receivable.

--- TERMS ---

realization rate   The percentage of time logged or billed in relation to the corresponding amount collected.

- *Turnover ratios,* either of WIP or accounts receivable. These are expressed in the number of days (or times per year) that the total revenue of a lawyer or the firm is billed or collected.

Automated systems are capable of producing many reports for performance evaluation purposes. Systems with advanced report generators allow firms to select a combination of report criteria and frequencies to suit their needs and make it especially easy to accumulate comparative information in formats that would be very time-consuming even with the aid of a spreadsheet. Popular reporting options include:

- current month and year-to-date;

- current month compared to the same month in the previous year;

- current year-to-date and previous year-to-date; and

- current year or month to budget, including variances by percentage.

Figure 6–11 illustrates types of productivity and realization reports.

Practical Application 6–8	Steven: For some reason, these accounts receivable reports don't seem consistent. We have very good realization rates—over 100% in fact! But our aged receivables listing shows that there are a lot of bills outstanding for over 120 days, even though our average turnover is only 60 days. The average for our field of practice is about 90 days, so we must be doing something right, but why all the over 120 days bills? Why don't the reports support each other?

Give some reasons for the apparent inconsistency. What does this illustrate about reports in general? About the supplementary information to be provided? About the number and variety of reports that provide the most valuable information?

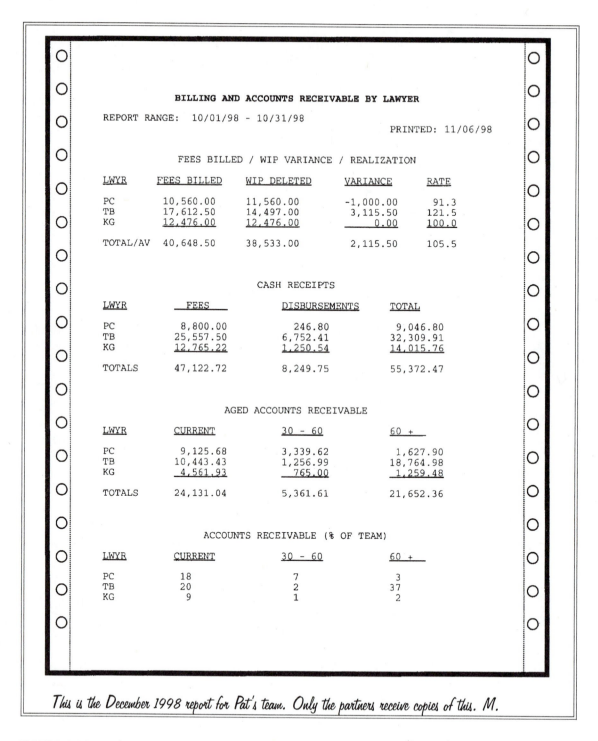

BILLING AND ACCOUNTS RECEIVABLE BY LAWYER

REPORT RANGE: 10/01/98 - 10/31/98

                                                  PRINTED: 11/06/98

FEES BILLED / WIP VARIANCE / REALIZATION

LWYR	FEES BILLED	WIP DELETED	VARIANCE	RATE
PC	10,560.00	11,560.00	-1,000.00	91.3
TB	17,612.50	14,497.00	3,115.50	121.5
KG	12,476.00	12,476.00	0.00	100.0
TOTAL/AV	40,648.50	38,533.00	2,115.50	105.5

CASH RECEIPTS

LWYR	FEES	DISBURSEMENTS	TOTAL
PC	8,800.00	246.80	9,046.80
TB	25,557.50	6,752.41	32,309.91
KG	12,765.22	1,250.54	14,015.76
TOTALS	47,122.72	8,249.75	55,372.47

AGED ACCOUNTS RECEIVABLE

LWYR	CURRENT	30 - 60	60 +
PC	9,125.68	3,339.62	1,627.90
TB	10,443.43	1,256.99	18,764.98
KG	4,561.93	765.00	1,259.48
TOTALS	24,131.04	5,361.61	21,652.36

ACCOUNTS RECEIVABLE (% OF TEAM)

LWYR	CURRENT	30 - 60	60 +
PC	18	7	3
TB	20	2	37
KG	9	1	2

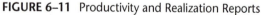

This is the December 1998 report for Pat's team. Only the partners receive copies of this. M.

FIGURE 6–11 Productivity and Realization Reports

Comprehensive Exercises

1. Design a checklist for payment procedures for a person new to a law firm. It should have at least forty items.

2. Design a comprehensive set of collection procedures for each lawyer in the firm of Carpenter & Cook.

    a. Incorporate some sample collection letters:

        i.   a "friendly reminder" at 30 days,

        ii. a follow-up to the above letter at 60 days, and

        iii. a strong but professional "request for immediate payment" at 90 days.

    b. Summarize the control, client relations, and motivational issues your procedures address.

3. Draft a sample letter to Norman Bishop describing the following problem with the bill in Figure 5–3:

    > Due to a calculation error and misunderstanding, the firm under-billed the client. The agreed costs should have been only $1,460.

    Recalculate the bill. What steps would you follow from the point you were asked to draft the letter to the time it is issued?

IIII

CHAPTER 7

CLIENT-LAWYER TRUST ACCOUNTING

A **trust** is a legally binding arrangement in which a **trustee** holds legal title to property for the benefit of the trust's beneficiaries who have the **equitable title** in the property. The trust is established by the **settlor** (also called the donor, trustor, or grantor) through a trust instrument, such as a will or deed of trust.

In the context of the client-lawyer relationship, trust accounting is the management and record-keeping of property that the lawyer, as trustee, holds for a beneficiary in the role of the client's fiduciary. The beneficiary of the trust may be the client and/or other parties. This type of trust accounting is different from accounting for a trust for which the lawyer is not the sole trustee, as addressed in Chapter 8.

There are situations where the lawyer will be deemed to be a trustee even when not acting as a lawyer per se.

Case 7–1

Found: **Lawyer who accepts position as fiduciary is held to the high standards of the legal profession, whether or not he acts in his capacity of lawyer,** and must maintain proper books of account and records of transactions and may not commingle client funds or use them for personal purposes.

Ordered: (for this and other breach of fiduciary duty) Three-year suspension on condition of probation, including one-year actual suspension.

The duties of a trustee are demanding and complex and are ultimately governed by statute and common law.

> Trustees have a fiduciary relationship with their beneficiaries. This is a relationship of trust and confidence requiring the exercise of a high degree of honesty and good faith. Trustees must be loyal to their trust at all times: they cannot profit personally from the trust property; they cannot commingle trust property with their own property; they must treat their beneficiaries fairly; they cannot delegate the management of the trust to others. Trustees must also keep accurate accounts, showing receipts and disbursements of principal and income. In addition, trustees must exercise reasonable care and prudence in the management of the trust property.
>
> *Source:* Brown, *Administration of Wills, Trusts and Estates* (Delmar LCP).

TERMS
---

trust† A fiduciary relationship involving a trustee who holds trust property for the benefit or use of a beneficiary.

trustee† The person who holds the legal title to trust property for the benefit of the beneficiary of the trust, with such powers and subject to such duties as are imposed by the terms of the trust and the law.

equitable title† Title recognized as ownership in equity, even though it is not legal title or marketable title.

settlor† The creator of a trust; the person who conveys or transfers property to another (the trustee) to hold in trust for a third person (the beneficiary).

Basic Rules and Concepts

Lawyers receive property for safekeeping *in trust,* meaning that the property, while managed by the law firm and in its title, cannot benefit the firm in either principal or income.

Trust property is held on a lawyer's undertaking, which may be explicit but is always at least implicit, pending some event that permits the release of the property. Any property to which a lawyer obtains title as a result of such an undertaking is automatically subject to a trust, regardless of where the property is situated or how portable or liquid it is.

Client-lawyer trust relationships are subject to state regulations, which basically follow ABA Model Rule 1.15.

RULE 1.15
Safekeeping Property

(a) A lawyer shall hold property of clients or third persons that is in a lawyer's possession in connection with a representation separate from the lawyer's own property. Funds shall be kept in a separate account maintained in the state where the lawyer's office is situated, or elsewhere with the consent of the client or third person. Other property shall be identified as such and appropriately safeguarded. Complete records of such account funds and other property shall be kept by the lawyer and shall be preserved for a period of (five years) after termination of the representation.

(b) Upon receiving funds or other property in which a client or third person has an interest, a lawyer shall promptly notify the client or third person. Except as stated in this rule or otherwise permitted by law or by agreement with the client, a lawyer shall promptly deliver to the client or third person any funds or other property that the client or third person is entitled to receive and, upon request by the client or third person, shall promptly render a full accounting regarding such property.

(c) When in the course of representation a lawyer is in possessio of property in which both the lawyer and another person claim interests, the property shall be kept separate by the lawyer until there is an accounting and severance of their interests. If a dispute arises concerning their respective interests, the portion in dispute shall be kept separate by the lawyer until the dispute is resolved.

This rule is really a codification of sound fiduciary conduct. It clarifies certain obligations but does not alone provide guidelines for the day-to-day handling of trust property. Firms must institute procedures and controls to ensure that trust property is protected from risk to both lawyer and client. Even if no loss befalls the beneficiary, a lawyer can still be held responsible for failing to act properly as a trustee.

Case 7–2	Found:	**Lawyer knowingly misappropriated clients' trust funds, notwithstanding absence of subjective intent to steal and absence of client losses as a result of conduct** (as illustrated in lawyer's own statement):

I was aware that what I was doing was wrong, and I was also aware that no one was being hurt by what I was doing. And what I was doing, especially by keeping lists [of "borrowings" from and repayments to trust account], was making sure that nobody would get hurt by what I was doing.

Ordered: Disbarred.

The types of trusts common in the client-lawyer relationship are:

- **Express trusts** that arise from verbal or written agreements between the trustee (lawyer) and the settlor (client or other party). Most client-lawyer trusts are express trusts.

- **Resulting trusts** that are implied trusts created by operation of law where there has been no stated intention to form a trust, but it is only equitable to assert that a trust has been formed. For example, a firm that receives a check for a client that should have gone directly to the client deposits it innocently into its trust account before the error is discovered.

- **Constructive trusts** that arise only to remedy a fraud or other wrongdoing, or unjust enrichment. For example, a client offers a large fee advance to the lawyer, knowing that the amount is excessive, to conceal assets from judgment creditors. This creates a constructive trust between the lawyer (trustee) and the client's creditor (beneficiary). Fortunately, constructive trusts are rare in most law firms.

Practical Application 7–1	Kirk:	This client has me a little concerned. She's very high-powered in the business community and is known for her very scrupulous dealings in business, even though she's quite tough. Now we're getting involved with some of her divorce matters, especially regarding assets. Right now, I have some bonds in the office vault that I see she hasn't claimed on the statement of assets in her divorce matter. These are "bearer bonds," meaning

---

TERMS

express trust† A trust created by a direct or positive declaration of trust.

resulting trust† A trust created by operation of law in circumstances where one person becomes vested with legal title but is obligated, as a matter of equity, to hold the title for the benefit of another person, even though there is no fraud and no declared intention to hold the property in trust.

constructive trust† A trust, created by operation of law, that is declared against a person who, by fraud, duress, or abuse of confidence, has obtained or holds legal title to property to which he or she has no moral or equitable right.

that, technically, whoever has possession of them can cash them in and get the money. She's told me, rather informally from my perspective, that they will serve as security to the firm against her divorce matter bills. I'm not really sure if this is a fee advance or if she is trying to hide these assets from her husband.

What are the types of trusts that the bonds might be the property for? Who are the beneficiaries?

Noncash Trust Property

A firm may hold noncash monetary assets, such as securities that cannot be deposited into a trust bank account and other valuable personal property such as rare coins and jewelry. These must be kept in a secure location, usually a bank safe deposit box or fireproof safe in the office. Such property is not listed in the firm's books but should always be listed in full in a comprehensive separate document in the accounting records and the client folder with a separate list for each file or trust. Lawyers also hold title to large items that cannot be kept physically within their reach, such as real property, and even intangible assets like patents.

Practical Application 7–2

Blanche: I'm not sure what to do with all of the items of personal property we're keeping in this very acrimonious divorce case. Would you believe that the final item the couple is fighting over is a blender? It's a very nice one, but I don't like having it around. It won't fit in the office safe, and if I leave it in the file room, someone might think it's there for the taking.

What should Blanche do to secure the blender? What records should be kept? How often should the blender and other property be brought to Blanche's attention by her secretary?

Lawyers pass along cash and endorse over checks made payable to the firm without processing the transaction through a bank account, but keeping written records of such transactions with the client file information. These transactions are usually avoided but may be the only practical way to transfer funds promptly to the ultimate recipient. For example, conduct money, which is provided to people who are required to attend examinations for discovery, trials, and other proceedings, often must be supplied *in cash* as a contribution toward traveling expenses. Although the firm must keep a written record of such transactions, this may be simply a note in the folder instead of a transaction in the accounting records.

Money Held in Trust

Most trust property dealt with by nonlawyer staff in American law firms is:

- money, denominated in United States dollars,

- received by the firm in the form of cash (coin and currency) or check (including drafts, money orders, and confirmed wire transfers), and

- deposited into a bank account, as opposed to being held by the firm in its original form.

Except where specifically noted, this is the type of trust money discussed in this chapter.

Possession of trust money creates obligations of the firm to the beneficiary. Trust settlors (the client and/or other parties) often anticipate that the ultimate beneficiary will be a party other than the lawyer's client. In fact, the express purpose of providing trust money may be to effect a transfer of money from the client to others.

The most commonly encountered client-lawyer trust arrangements in law firms, summarized in Figure 7–1, are:

- *Fee advances,* held by the firm until a bill is rendered to the client. Advances may be the full contemplated sum of the final bill or simply a "down payment" on future fees. Some firms ask that a client pay an advance as an indication of the client's commitment to a potentially problematic case or to provide for significant disbursements.

- *Award or settlement funds in favor of the client,* where the client is the prevailing party. These are paid to the firm by the unsuccessful party or its counsel and distributed to the client, usually net of any unpaid bills from the firm.

- *Award or settlement funds contributed by the client,* where the client is the unsuccessful party. The client provides trust funds to the firm for payment to the successful party, usually through its lawyer's trust account.

- *Conveyance monies or other purchase-related proceeds,* which are paid by the purchaser to effect a property or other major purchase.

- *Estate proceeds* of a deceased, bankrupt, or family, held by the firm pending settlement of the estate.

- *Business and personal transaction funds* provided for the lawyer to conduct transactions on behalf of the client. These are common for out-of-town clients.

Type	Usual Contributors	Usual Recipients	Events
Fee Advance	- client/friend/relative - related company/shareholders	- law firm - client (refund)	- end of file - firm renders bill
Award/Settlement **(in favor of client)**	- unsuccessful party or its counsel	- law firm - client	- release executed - award/settlement paid to firm
Award/Settlement **(client unsuccessful)**	- client	- successful party or its counsel	- client ordered to pay award - client pays settlement
Real Property **Transfers**	- purchaser - bank holding new mortgage	- vendor/vendor's lawyer - real estate agent	- completion date
Estate	- holders of assets (banks, liquidators)	- law firm - creditors/beneficiaries	- firm renders bill - approval of court to pay beneficiaries
Lawyer as Business **Agent**	- client - related company/shareholders	- law firm - third parties (invoices)	- specific client instructions - third party renders invoice

Figure 7–1   Client-Lawyer Trusts

Practical Application 7–3

Curt: We received a large fee advance from Peter's Fish Shop and deposited it to the trust account. Now Peter wants us to use it to pay some creditors who will block the sale of the business if their bills aren't paid. My understanding was that the money in trust was for fees, but the late Mr. Plant handled the file before I got it and I can't find a fee or trust agreement. Now what can I do?

What will Curt take into account when considering Peter's instructions? What could have prevented this dilemma?

Trust Bank Accounts

Law firms need banks to secure trust money and ensure that it can be delivered when necessary. Law firms operate two main types of trust bank accounts:

- **Pooled trust accounts** contain the funds of more than one client. Some states' regulations require that these accounts contribute to

---

TERMS

pooled trust account   A bank account designed to hold the funds of more than one client.

Interest on Lawyers' Trust Accounts (**IOLTA**) programs, which financially support legal services to the disadvantaged. In other states, participation in IOLTA programs is optional.

- **Separate trust accounts** contain the funds of only one client. These accounts often bear interest that becomes part of the trust property. They may also be subject to service charges.

The American Bar Association encourages firms to participate in IOLTA programs where the trust money is a relatively small amount or will be held for a short period of time. IOLTA accounts benefit the firm by eliminating the time-consuming responsibility to account for and distribute small amounts of interest to individual clients. Regardless of whether the funds are placed in a pooled IOLTA or separate account, the firm may not receive any benefit of interest received.

Case 7–3

Found: **Lawyer deposited client funds in money market account in lawyer's name and sought to retain interest for personal gain,** telling client that money had been deposited in noninterest account.

Ordered: Six-month suspension, with proof of rehabilitation and passage of ethics portion of bar examination prior to reinstatement.

Firms whose practices consist mostly of real property transactions tend to have a number of pooled trust accounts in banks whose business they would like to obtain. Small, new banks may aggressively pursue lawyers by pledging referral work in exchange for maintaining a pooled account. The lawyer as trustee, however, has a clear and prevailing obligation to ensure that trust monies are secure.

Aside from concerns about bank stability, firms with substantial numbers of trust transactions consider the following when choosing a bank:

- *Hours of operation.* In urban centers, most banks keep hours consistent with regular businesses. In suburban areas, however, many are closed on Mondays to accommodate Saturday openings.

- *Service to the firm.* Larger branches often have difficulty accommodating the special needs of some firms, such as immediate notification of any dishonored checks or other problems with the account. Promptness in issuing statements, access to key bank personnel, and clearing speed are also important.

--- **TERMS** ---

IOLTA Interest on Lawyers' Trust Account; a program run by a state agency for collecting the interest from pooled trust accounts and directing the income toward publicly supported legal services.

separate trust account A trust bank account designed to hold the funds of only one client, usually bearing interest that becomes part of the trust property.

- *Error incidence.* Internal controls and systems vary greatly between banks, and some experience a greater incidence of errors than others. While the firm may not be held strictly responsible for bank errors, they cause embarrassment and inconvenience.

Banks encourage lawyers' pooled trust accounts for a number of reasons, including the exposure within the business community that lawyers often provide. Pooled trust accounts are also an inexpensive source of reserves (minimum percentages of deposits that banks are required to reserve from lending). Because law firms do not themselves receive interest on pooled accounts, they may be somewhat indifferent about whether terms are competitive.

Practical Application 7–4	Ms. Moss: I would like us to start using the First Green Bank (FGB), which is guided by environment-friendly policies, such as being open only during daylight hours to reduce electricity usage. But here in Alaska, the days can be very short in the winter, and we might need access to the bank when it's dark. FGB has a Twenty-first Century account, accessible by bank machine, and we could use electronic banking, but I'm not sure whether the records produced would be sufficient.
	What are some considerations Ms. Moss needs to take into account before using FGB's facilities? If they were used, what additional controls within the firm would be advisable?

Pooled Trust Bank Accounts

Practically all firms operate at least one pooled trust bank account. This is sometimes called the "regular trust account" or the "general trust account," but these terms are discouraged because of the potential confusion with the firm's general operating bank account. To further avoid confusion between trust and general bank transactions, most firms' trust checks are printed in a different color from the general checks and are kept in a separate place, and deposit books are clearly identified on the cover as being for either the trust or general bank account. Firms that operate more than one trust bank account maintain separate records (journals and ledgers) for each bank account as well as separate client ledgers where an individual client's money is on deposit in more than one bank account.

Trust bank accounts should be clearly identified as such in the bank's records. When a firm establishes any trust bank account, it should inform the bank of the nature of the account, by letter in a standard form, as illustrated in Figure 7–2, which ensures that the bank is aware that the funds do not belong to the firm and are not attachable by the firm's creditors. Copies of bank correspondence, banking agreements, and current lists of signatories are kept in permanent files with the accounting records.

FIGURE 7–2
Letter to Bank to
Establish IOLTA
Account

Carpenter & Cook
Attorneys at Law
2400 - 555 North Ocean Street, Fielding, ST 10001

Telephone: 488-1111
Fax: 488-6666

Pat Carpenter
Sandy Cook
Terry Baker
Lee Mason (Associated)

August 20, 1998

State Eastern Bank
600 North Ocean Street
Fielding, ST 10004

Attn: Branch Manager

Dear Sirs:

Re: Lawyer's Pooled Trust Account Number 7410-86

We have established the captioned account in preparation for commencing practice under the name of Carpenter & Cook, Attorneys at Law, commencing September 1, 1998. We write to inform you that the captioned bank account is a lawyers' pooled trust account and is subject to the state legislation governing such accounts, specifically:

1. This account is to be identified in your records and on all checks and statements issued by you as a trust account.

2. Interest on this account is to be remitted according to state law to an Interest on Lawyers' Trust Accounts (IOLTA) program.

3. No service charges are to be charged to the account, as such charges would render the account deficient.

4. Statements must be produced at least monthly regardless of whether there are any transactions on the account during the month and all canceled checks returned with the statement.

5. The firm must be notified immediately of any dishonored checks returned against the account. Similarly, any deposits to the account not made by our staff that may give rise to an obligation of the firm without its knowledge must be identified by telephone to us at the earliest opportunity.

6. Any concerns with respect to the account should be directed to Pat Carpenter or Sandy Cook, partners. Our administrator, Marty Fisher, will be available in the event we are both unavailable.

7. Only Pat Carpenter and Sandy Cook are permitted signatories on the account, and checks, instructions, and transactions (except for deposits) are to be authorized by one of us.

Thank you for your cooperation and attention. We look forward to a mutually rewarding relationship with your institution.

Yours truly,
Carpenter & Cook

P. Carpenter   *S. Cook*
Pat Carpenter, Partner   Sandy Cook, Partner

This letter was sent to the bank explaining about the pooled trust account. M.

Separate Trust Bank Accounts

Separate trust bank accounts are investments in which the interest accrues to the trust instead of being paid to an IOLTA. If the firm anticipates holding large sums of trust money for a substantial period of time, the lawyer may decide to (or must, under certain circumstances) deposit the funds into a separate account. If the account is subject to bank service charges, the client should be notified.

Staff who are asked to survey appropriate banks to obtain a high interest rate and suitably flexible investment instruments should be familiar with the most common investment accounts available through the firm's established banks. Fixed-term investments usually specify that the principal and interest will be deposited into a certain account upon maturity. This account should be either a savings account operated for the same beneficiary or a pooled trust account. Automatic "roll-overs" into another investment period should be avoided unless the client specifically requests it. Investment maturities are diarized by the accounting staff and by the secretary and lawyer responsible for the file so that reinvestment is discussed before the due date to minimize loss of interest or inappropriate reinvestments that may have negative tax consequences for the client. Automated systems often provide due-date reminder programs.

Practical Application 7–5

Jade: Mr. Gold isn't here and his client's term deposit is due today. We are currently negotiating for an early settlement on this file, but the opposing party needs Mr. Gold's undertaking before they will agree to any settlement. Ms. Silver thinks that the funds should not be reinvested for another thirty days, but she is not the lawyer responsible for this file, and no lawyers senior to Ms. Silver will be available before a reinvestment decision will have to be made.

What should Jade do about the reinvestment? What controls need to be in place in order for Ms. Silver to make the reinvestment decisions?

Separate accounts are set up using either a letter to the bank or a form acceptable to the bank. Often the bank will require that its own internal forms be completed, especially if the signatories are not the same as those for the pooled account. Firms that routinely set up certain types of separate accounts, such as daily interest accounts, for which special terms are not negotiated may have a blanket agreement with the bank that accelerates the process. If the account is not of a conventional type or the terms have been specially negotiated, however, a letter has the advantage of confirming all the terms with the bank.

In some situations, there may be a question about whether monies that are to go immediately into a separate account should first be placed in the pooled account. If the funds are cash, a lawyer's trust check, certified check, or money order, they may be placed into the pooled account first, although there may be no particular reason for doing this. Sometimes trust money must earn interest from the date it is received into trust, even if it is uncertain that a check will clear the drawee bank. If the check were deposited directly into the pooled account, transferred to a separate account, and subsequently dishonored, the bank would charge the returned check to the *pooled account.* This would cause the pooled bank account to become deficient at a minimum, and because funds in separate accounts are often large, the pooled account could become overdrawn. For this reason, many firms place all separate trust monies directly into the separate account.

When trust monies are withdrawn from a separate account for which canceled checks are not received, they should always be transferred into the pooled trust account, and a check should be issued from the pooled account to the final recipient. This ensures that the firm always has access to the check endorsement in the event of a dispute over receipt of the funds and that the firm's normal procedural controls are not bypassed. Transfer instructions to the bank are commonly made by letter of authorization or another form acceptable to the bank, and the firm's copies of these letters and forms serve as the source document for recording the transfer. When a separate account is closed, the passbooks or statements must be kept for the minimum five-year period.

Internal Trust Records

Aside from records it receives from its banks, a firm must retain its own trust records, including letters, instructions, and communications with the client and other settlors and beneficiaries.

The firm's internal trust accounting records show all of the financial activities related to receiving and disbursing trust monies. Other supporting information in the client folders is copied to accounting staff when giving them instructions.

Trust Bank Account Ledgers

Trust bank account ledgers are running registers of deposits, checks, and adjustments on an individual bank account. If the firm operates more than one trust bank account, each account has a ledger. Debits and credits in trust bank ledgers are consistent with other bank ledgers: deposits are debits and checks are credits.

TERMS
---

trust bank account ledgers   A ledger for an individual bank account.

In manual systems, the ledger is often combined with the journals in a synoptic, as illustrated in Figure 7–3. Each individual transaction is recorded on a separate line in the synoptic, with the running balance updated after each entry.

In pegboard and other manual systems, the trust receipt and trust check journals are on separate pages, and only the totals of the journals are posted in the ledger.

Accounting software usually emulates this presentation. Firms often keep the trust synoptic on a computerized spreadsheet, which has the advantage of eliminating time and errors inherent in manual computation

---

Carpenter & Cook

POOLED TRUST BANK ACCOUNT SYNOPTIC

Bank Account: *State Eastern*   Month: *November 1998*

Date	Description	File #	Ref	✓	Receipts DR	Checks CR	Balance
11/01	Balance Forward						33,100.05
11/09	Teal, W. (for Disb)	2162.6		✓	250.00		33,350.05
11/12	Rev New Panorama	2417.4	188	✓		(100.00)	
11/12	Corr New Panorama	2417.4	188	✓		1,000.00	32,450.05
11/12	TT - Peel, D.	2302.8	225	✓		1,346.77	
"	" - Sunrise/Sunset	1861.4	"	✓		500.00	
"	" - Teal, W.	2162.6	"	✓		76.00	30,527.28
11/20	M. Hall/Fee Advance	2377.0		✓	1,000.00		31,527.28

The pooled trust bank synoptic is quite simple, compared to the general account. I had to reverse an error in the subsequent month. M.

FIGURE 7–3 Pooled Trust Bank Account Synoptic

and is not affected by the restrictions in some accounting programs (for example, where the accounting program cannot be accessed because the previous month has not been closed).

General Ledger Treatment

Most firms with manual and nonintegrated automated accounting systems have no trust amounts in the general ledger. Presenting the trust bank and liability balances interferes with the interpretation of the firm's balance sheet from a business perspective because trust transactions are not economic transactions; they do not affect the economic position of the firm in any way unless the trust is breached.

Trust obligations become genuine liabilities if the firm cannot or does not deliver trust property as required under a trustee's duty. If the firm's actions or omissions compromise the value of property with which it has been entrusted, the firm is responsible for restoring it. While there may be practical limits on the firm's liability if it has not acted imprudently, recording a liability arising from a breach is justifiable because the firm's economic activity is, in part, receiving payment to act as a professional fiduciary.

While a lawyer's position as a trustee clearly creates an obligation, trust money cannot be considered assets of the firm. In financial accounting, assets of the firm must:

- be under the firm's control,

- be expected to provide the firm with future *economic* benefits, and

- arise from a previous *economic* transaction.

Strictly speaking, not even the first criterion applies to trust money because the control the firm exercises over the money is in its role of trustee, not as an economic entity, and an event beyond the firm's direct control will oblige it to handle the funds according to the trust arrangements.

The latter two criteria may appear to apply to trust money when a firm anticipates making a trust transfer to pay itself for a client's bill. However, this transaction extinguishes the client's liability to the firm, and the money is not a true asset of the firm until it is earned and deposited to the firm's general account.

Despite the reasons for excluding trust money and obligations from the firm's financial records, accountants sometimes add the trust "assets" and "liabilities" to the balance sheet at year end. The specifications of many integrated automated systems dictate that the trust bank be shown in the current assets section and the trust liabilities in the current liabilities section or as a contra account immediately following the asset.

The only other logical presentations are to show both in a totally separate section of the balance sheet (possibly between assets and liabilities) or under current liabilities, with the funds on deposit offsetting the obligation.

Trust money transactions never appear in revenue or expense accounts, only as assets and corresponding liabilities. Even when the trust transactions are kept completely separate from the firm's financial information and do not appear in the firm's general ledger, debits and credits are treated consistently with regular financial information. Debits increase assets and decrease liabilities, while credits decrease assets and increase liabilities.

Practical Application 7–6

Grant: I don't care what the accountants say—monies under the firm's control are assets, and our obligations to pay those monies are liabilities. It's no different than with a property development company. They may have pending contracts for the sale of property, but until the sale is complete, the property is listed as an asset. Law firms are no different.

Discuss the points that Grant has raised. Are law firms really different? Why or why not?

Carpenter & Squire

CLIENT TRUST LEDGER CARD

Lawyer: _S.C._   Name: _Bishop, Norman_   File: _2015.6_

Opened: _Apr. 17, 1998_ Re: _Dutch Treat Dating Service_ Page No.: _1_

Date	Description	Ref.	DR	CR	Balance
04/17/98	Fee/Disb Advance: N. Bishop	TS0498		500.00	500.00
08/31/98	Transfer to Carpenter & Cook	Memo			
12/06/98	Settlement Proceeds; Brewer & Co.	TS1298		12,500.00	13,000.00
12/12/98	To Carpenter & Cook General	T 276	3,066.13		9,933.87
12/12/98	N. Bishop, Net Proceeds	T277	9,933.87		0.00
12/31/98	FILE CLOSED				

Our trust activity is usually quite limited on all but estate files, so we use a small ledger card. This file started at Pat's old firm and was transferred here. M.

FIGURE 7–4 Manual Trust Ledger

Client Trust Ledgers

The **client trust ledger** is a chronological record of all trust transactions for a particular trust. If a client has trust transactions for more than one file (matter), a separate ledger is kept for each. Figure 7–4 illustrates a client trust ledger card in a manual system.

Transactions are posted to the client trust ledger as they occur, using trust check and receipt journals or the bank synoptic. On the client ledger, receipts are credits and checks are debits. After each transaction, the client ledger running balance is updated. A client's file must never be closed or the folders permanently removed from the office if a trust balance exists.

A client trust statement may be required by a lawyer or secretary or at the request of the client or beneficiary. Many firms automatically produce such statements at the conclusion of a client's file. The statement is basically another version of the trust ledger, reproduced in a more readable format, as illustrated in Figure 7–5.

Trust Journal Entries

A **trust journal entry** is used to record transfers from one client trust ledger to another in the same bank account, without any transactions being processed through the bank account. These entries are authorized in writing by the lawyer, specifying the purpose of the transfer. Because they are relatively rare in all but real property matters, instructions to make them are usually given by individual memo. Firms that routinely assign several file (matter) numbers to the same client, where other firms would combine them, also use this type of entry.

The entries are typically between different files for the same client or files for other family members, or between a corporate client and its principals or a related corporation. They facilitate:

- closing one file while another remains active, with the funds as an advance;

- transferring advanced funds from an open file with no outstanding bills to another file with outstanding bills, to make a subsequent trust transfer; and

- providing funds more immediately required on another file, such as the sale of one property and purchase of another by the same client.

TERMS

client trust ledger A subsidiary ledger listing all trust transactions for a client's funds in a bank account.

trust journal entry A reassignment of trust property between two or more clients without a bank transaction.

FIGURE 7–5
Statement of Trust
Sent to Client

Carpenter & Cook
Attorneys at Law
2400 - 555 North Ocean Street, Fielding, ST 10001

Telephone: 488-1111
Fax: 488-6666

Pat Carpenter
Sandy Cook
Terry Baker
Lee Mason (Associated)

December 12, 1998

Mr. Norman Bishop
P.O. Box 29
State Eastern Bank Building
600 North Ocean Street
Fielding, ST 10004

Dear Mr. Bishop:

Re: Dutch Treat Dating Service (Libel)
      Our File Number 2015.6 - Final Bill

I am pleased to enclose our trust check in the amount of $9,933.87, representing the net proceeds of the settlement in the referenced action. I also enclose our account which, as per our fee agreement, has been paid from the settlement proceeds. Our trust statement is as follows:

4/17/98	From client: Fee advance	500.00	
12/6/98	From defendant: Settlement	12,500.00	
12/12/98	To Carpenter & Cook: Account		3,066.13
12/12/98	To client: Net proceeds		9,933.87
		$13,000.00	$13,000.00

It has been a pleasure to assist you in this matter. Should you require legal services in the future, we would appreciate your consideration.

Yours truly,

S. Cook

Encl.

P.S. Compliments of the season, Norm!

We send a statement like this to contingency file clients when we send them their checks. M.

The posting of these entries does not affect the pooled trust account re-cords, since no money is being received into or distributed by the firm. The only ledger entries are to the client ledgers, as illustrated in Figure 7–6. In practice, many firms prefer that such transfers within the pooled account be made by issuing a check from the trust account and redepositing it. While apparently a redundant activity, this procedure provides a clearer audit trail and secures the required approval documentation. An entry not affecting the bank account, however, is necessary where the withdrawal of funds from an investment would cause a loss of interest.

FIGURE 7–6

Trust Journal Entry Recording Process

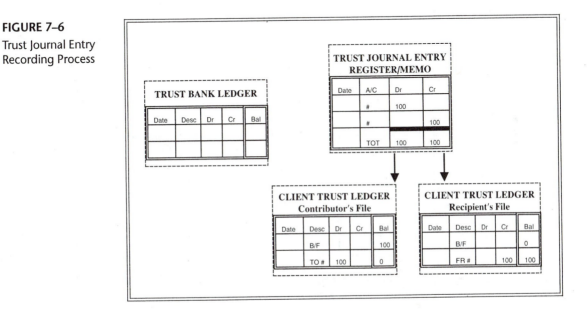

Because there are no external documents supporting the transfer, written instructions for the entry should include:

- *Full file identification* of the contributing and recipient files: client names, numbers, and matter descriptions.

- *The bank account* wherein the transfer is made.

- *The effective date of the transfer.* This is the date that the entry is *verified and approved.* Back-dating or postdating may cause date-sensitive re-ports in automated systems to show a debit balance at a prior date.

- *Purpose of the transfer.*

- *A description* that will appear in each ledger referencing the other ledger. In automated systems it will appear in both.

- *Amount of the transfer.* In many cases, it is simply the balance that should be transferred, but if only "balance" is specified, there is no assurance that anyone knowledgeable about either file has confirmed that the balance appears to be correct. Some firms simply request an estimate of the balance and inform the lawyer if it is not close to the actual balance.

- *Approval of a lawyer.*

Figure 7–7 illustrates a trust journal entry authorization form that would be used in a real property practice that creates a file for both purchases and sales for the same client. Chapter 8 further discusses transfers of funds in real property transactions.

FIGURE 7–7

Trust Journal Entry Form

TRUST JOURNAL ENTRIES							
Date: _Dec. 20, 1998_ Approved: _S.C._							

Amount	Contributor File			Recipient File		
500.00	2417.4	P	United Investment	2409.1	P	United Investment
456.03	2302.8	P	Peel, Don	1844.0	P	Century Textiles

This form is good if there are a number of trust journal entries to make, such as for real estate sale to purchase files that we get a lot of in the spring and summer. M.

Trust Adjustments

There are three types of accounting adjustments (as opposed to error corrections) made on trust accounts:

- *Foreign exchange transactions* record differences between the amount presented on the ledger in the foreign currency and the United States dollar amount on conversion.

- *Interest payments* on separate accounts and investments are recorded when the interest has been received into the firm's control. Normally, there is a separate journal for interest payments, and if the firm has several savings accounts receiving monthly interest, they are all updated at once.

- *Service charges* are often levied on separate savings accounts. These should be recorded separately from the interest payments, not netted against them. Occasionally, service charges are higher than the interest payments, especially during times when interest rates are generally low. These cases should be reported to the lawyers responsible, who will consider alternate placement of the funds. The client's welfare may be better served by returning the money to the pooled account.

Interest payment and service charge amounts often are not available before the monthly records have to be closed. When separate accounts are reconciled, interest and legitimate service charges may be outstanding.

Trust Accounting Controls

Research into rules, opinions, and case law findings provide a starting place for designing and maintaining trust accounting controls but clearly reflect minimum standards that do not address the peculiarities of any particular system or firm. Well-managed firms ensure that all aspects of trust accounting, including training and reference materials, task separation, paper flow, recording and reporting systems, and filing routines, contribute to a strong system with reliable internal controls.

Because trust monies are subject to the client-lawyer relationship, instructions to the accounting staff for handling trust funds are authorized by a lawyer, either directly to the secretary or to accounting staff via the secretary. Lawyers' instructions must always be followed exactly, and clarification should be sought if there are any questions. A strict policy of obtaining signatures approving all trust transactions reduces misunderstandings and mistakes so that appropriate documentation to support trust transactions is readily available when questions arise.

Case 7–4	Found: Lawyer failed to reconcile trust account, had shortage in trust account, failed to comply with promise to use a new trust account, commingled cost deposits, presented overdraft checks for payment, and **allowed non-lawyer to manage trust and general accounts without adequate supervision.**
	Ordered: Three-year suspension.

Trust Bank Account Access

The operation of trust bank accounts is subject first to regulations governing professional conduct and then to the requirements of a particular bank and the firm's desired banking arrangements. Certain instructions must be given to the bank by a lawyer, who must in turn be authorized by the firm to effect the transaction with the bank.

Controlling access to the trust bank accounts is very important in law firms. Clearly, access to checks is restricted, but even access to deposit books should be supervised to prevent improper and erroneous deposits.

Appropriate combinations of trust check signatories should be considered when designing trust accounting controls so that while access levels preserve the trustee's authority, they do not paralyze the firm if a check or authorization is needed immediately. Firms with few lawyers may find it awkward to require more than one signature on trust checks, and the reasons behind such a requirement should be carefully considered. If the partners want access to be highly restricted, they might consider approving the signature of either one partner alone or two staff lawyers together. Most important of all considerations is that *the combination of signatories should preclude the necessity for any lawyer to ever sign a blank trust check.* Lawyers' signatures are required for very good reasons, which are defeated if blank checks are signed.

Practical Application 7–7

Newton: I'm afraid I find this situation terribly frustrating! I need to get some funds transferred into our pooled account to cover a check that we issued last week in error. The check really isn't wrong, except that it should not have been dated until tomorrow. There are no signatories on the separate account here today, and by tomorrow, our pooled account may be overdrawn. I'm a senior associate, and I should be able to make these transfers. The partners are always in court when these things need to be signed. I know that our administrator has the authority to make the transfer over the phone, but he won't do it without a partner's signature. Why are people trying to make things difficult for me?

What needs to happen in this firm? Write a brief memo to the appropriate person(s) about advisable changes in the authorized signatories.

Other types of access that require control include:

- *On-line access to transactions via modem.* Many major banks now allow their customers access to account information and transactions through use of a password. While the firm may want staff to be able to *view* trust account information, it typically cannot simultaneously restrict the ability to *execute* transactions.

- *Authorizing transfers between pooled and separate accounts.* Some firms establish procedures with their banks to allow transfers between pooled and separate accounts by telephone, later confirmed in writing. This is intended to let the bank prepare the documentation for proper signature and set up the necessary accounts, but it invariably leads to errors and usually saves little time or interest. A sound internal procedure, with everyone understanding the need for promptness, produces better results.

Many larger firms operate several pooled accounts for different purposes and find it easier to manage a large number of trust contributions if they are segregated by purpose when deposited. Trust reports for particular banks can then be reviewed, keeping in mind the purpose of the funds. For example, all client advances for fees are placed in an account that is reviewed weekly by the trust accounting supervisor to see if there are trust transfers to be made. The account might also require the signatures of one lawyer plus the accounting supervisor, while conveyance monies are placed in a bank account that is reviewed daily and requires only one partner's signature.

Trust Errors

The best cure for trust errors is prevention, which is why such great attention is paid to trust procedures and controls. However, despite everyone's best efforts, errors occur, and it is always best to deal with them in a direct manner focused on resolving the current problem and preventing its recurrence. Attempts to hide errors are not only unsuccessful in most cases, but compromise the integrity of the firm if discovered by the client, accountant, bar, or other authority. Many problems can be rectified quickly when the trustee lawyer is made fully aware of the circumstances. Notes and correspondence related to the occurrence and correction of trust errors are kept with the reconciliation for the month(s) affected or in a separate folder.

Most trust transactions are quite simple: deposits to the trust bank accounts and checks distributing funds to the appropriate parties. Yet it is in processing simple transactions that most errors occur and where recording errors are most likely to cause troublesome substantive errors. Errors in processing routine transactions tend to arise from inattention and lack of clarity about responsibilities within the office. Problems with nonroutine transactions usually arise from a weak grasp of trust concepts and banking procedures rather than from inadequate internal processes.

Most recording errors are discovered soon after they occur while the month's records are still open and can be corrected. Types of recording errors that must be corrected are:

- incorrect dates, amounts, names, and reference numbers (check numbers especially)

- entries to the wrong client ledger

- entries to the wrong bank account ledger

- entries that were omitted

- entries that should not have been recorded (either duplicate entries or entries that should have been canceled)

The only trust recording error that is usually not corrected is a simple and obvious spelling error. Figure 7–8 illustrates a trust entry correction.

FIGURE 7–8

Trust Ledger: Error Correction

Carpenter & Cook

CLIENT TRUST LEDGER CARD

Lawyer: _S.C._   Name: _United Investment Corp_   File: _2417.4_

Opened: _Oct. 17, 1998_ Re: _Public Company Investments_ Page No.: _1_

Date	Description	Ref.	DR	CR	Balance
10/17/98	I. Cantor - Deposit	TS1098		5,000.00	5,000.00
10/24/98	New Panorama Development	188	100.00		4,900.00
10/31/98	Carpenter & Cook; bill # 86	192	467.23		4,432.77
11/12/98	Rev New Panorama 10/24/98	188		100.00	4,532.77
11/12/98	Correct New Panorama	188	1,000.00		3,532.77

Here is an example of how to correct errors; reverse the original (wrong) entry completely, and then make the correct entry. M.

Some automated systems will not allow an entry that will create a debit balance in a client trust ledger, which may be necessary when reversing a deposit and entering it correctly *if* the funds have been disbursed before the correcting entries are made. In this case, the correction must be posted before the reversal.

Substantive errors that result in deficiencies or misallocations are the most serious trust errors and must be rectified immediately. A firm must maintain sufficient resources to cover trust obligations, and if an account becomes deficient, the firm must eliminate any shortage in *either* total trust resources or in a particular trust bank account. Lawyers are aware that the firm's operating funds are not to be deposited or withdrawn from trust bank accounts, as this constitutes commingling and/or misappropriation.

Case 7–5

Found: **Lawyers used clients' funds in trust account to pay operating expenses,** causing clients' checks to be returned for nonsufficient funds. All (three) lawyers culpable if each lawyer individually continues practice of commingling; culpability not mitigated by "poor accounting procedures."

Ordered: All disbarred.

A client's trust ledger must never be allowed to fall into a debit balance. If it does, the firm must eliminate the deficiency immediately, because a failure to do so would mean that there are insufficient funds on deposit to cover the firm's obligations in respect of other clients' matters.

Wherever possible, the firm issues its own checks to correct its own errors. To make subsequent reconciliations easier, deposits to correct errors are made as separate bank transactions (deposit slips), and not included with other trust deposits.

The most common substantive trust errors are:

- *Bank errors* including erroneous service charges, posting deposits to the wrong bank account (usually the firm's general account), incorrect amounts, omissions, and duplications. Bank errors should be corrected by the bank so that they clear the bank side of the trust reconciliation. A letter describing the error, copies of pertinent documents (checks or deposit slips recorded incorrectly by the bank), and a copy of the related bank statement should be delivered to the bank at the earliest opportunity after the error is identified. These letters are signed by required signatories of the subject bank account to avoid delays in correction.

- *Deposits made to the trust account that belong in the general account,* as when a client pays a bill already rendered. This is corrected by immediately issuing a check for the amount and depositing it into the general account, as with a trust transfer. Where the deposit is a check that may not clear, the check must be allowed time to clear before the money is transferred into the general account to prevent a trust account deficiency.

- *Deposits made to the general account that belong in the trust account.* This is more serious than the opposite error because it creates a trust shortage, and the funds must be transferred from the general account to the proper trust account without delay. However, if the check is not honored and the firm's legitimate general funds are insufficient to cover the amount, the general account would become overdrawn. The funds would be transferred back into the general account because the firm no longer needs to safeguard funds it never really received.

- *Transactions that place the client's trust ledger balance into a debit balance,* or when the deposit has not yet been made but a check against it has been drawn. Usually making a deposit and documenting the occurrence are the only steps necessary. The lawyer reports the deficiency if required by law or the trust agreement.

- *Deposits or withdrawals of funds using the wrong trust bank account* in firms that operate several trust bank accounts. These errors do not cause a shortage of *total money* to *total obligations,* but must be rectified immediately and reported if necessary.

All three levels of internal control are important in performing basic trust transactions because of the acute need to minimize error incidence *and* to locate and correct errors at the earliest possible moment. A critical primary control for trust transactions is effective communication between lawyer and secretary and accounting staff have little control over this.

Another essential control, the plausibility assessment, relies on the conscientiousness and experience of everyone involved in trust transactions. All proposed transactions should make sense to informed people who authorize and handle them.

Foreign Currency Transactions

Firms may receive funds denominated in a foreign currency that are to either be held in that currency or converted to American funds. Where the funds are to be held in a trust bank account, as opposed to safekeeping in their original form, there are very real risks to both the client and the firm of exchange rate fluctuations. Trust accounts denominated in foreign currencies may be subject to significant loss of value. If the funds are intended to cover a client's obligation to a third party, the client's ability to meet the obligation could be compromised. If the firm has undertakings to third parties with respect to the trust funds, the firm's ability to meet its undertakings could be compromised. Although state regulations may be silent on foreign currency transactions, firms must use judgment to prevent deficiencies arising *even though the funds have not been distributed.*

Practical Application 7–8

Jasmine: We have an unusual client matter where we hold trust money only in lire and sterling, because our client's British subsidiary is involved in purchasing an Italian company. The exchange rates are always fluctuating, and the firm tries to time the transactions to get the best rates. Mr. Cross, the partner responsible for the file, thinks that we should adjust the trust ledgers every month, converting all funds to American dollars, because that is the principal currency of the client conglomerate. His partner Ms. Moody thinks that we should not make any adjustment but is concerned because the client has pledged a "down payment" in lire on the purchase that, in the event the sale is not completed, will represent liquidated damages against our client. At various times, the lire balance is insufficient to cover the pledge. Because I'm the trust supervisor, Mr. Cross and Ms. Moody think I should know what to do. No one in the firm wants us to have trouble with this client because they are very influential in our local community.

How should Jasmine go about getting adequate instructions on handling these funds? What advice can she give the partners about the funds? What should she provide as simple information?

Even if a check drawn on a foreign bank is denominated in United States dollars, the clearing process will often result in an amount not equal to the figure amount if the check is not drawn on *an account denominated in United States dollars.* Checks drawn on foreign banks take a long time to clear so extra consideration should be given to the holding period before the funds are distributed by the firm.

Unfamiliarity of foreign checks (language, alphabet, stability of the drawee) may cause banks to refuse to credit the trust account until the check has been accepted by the drawee. The bank will send the check "on collection" and credit the trust account when it receives the assured United States dollar amount. Because it usually takes at least two weeks for collection items to be *settled* (credited to the firm's trust account), the responsible lawyer always approves collection of trust receipt items before they are surrendered to the bank. Collection items are easily forgotten so the secretary should diarize the expected settlement date. In most cases, it is not appropriate to make an accounting entry until the funds are settled.

Separate foreign currency trust accounts may be in the form of a pooled trust account but contain the funds of only one client. This is common where a firm maintains a trust checking account denominated in foreign currency to effect business transactions for foreign clients. Trust accounts denominated in foreign currency may not have the same deposit insurance as those denominated in United States dollars, so the bank should be consulted if the lawyer considers deposit insurance an important issue.

Unclaimed Trust Funds

Unclaimed trust funds are those held for clients the firm has been unable to locate for two years. Often, the file work has been concluded and the client is no longer in regular contact with the firm. Until the funds are disbursed properly to the correct party, the firm still has responsibility for them.

Case 7–6	Found: **Lawyer failed for three years, despite repeated inquiries from beneficiaries' counsel, to remit proceeds of sale of residence of deceased; also failed to cooperate with censor [sic] committee investigation to determine if funds were improperly handled.**
	Ordered: Suspended for six months or until audit completed. Further disciplinary action considered when results of audit known.

Firms with weak internal controls often have records of unclaimed trust funds only as outstanding trust checks on the bank reconciliation. If the check was for the final distribution of trust funds, the balance shown in the client trust ledger will be zero, and the lawyer responsible for the file may be unaware that the firm still has charge of the funds. Firms with strong internal controls often set a period of forty-five to sixty days from the check date for investigation of outstanding trust account checks.

Guy: We interview our clients carefully to make sure they understand everything that will happen to the monies we hold in trust for them, but we can't control the other beneficiaries! Six months ago we had a real estate closing, where the vendor more or less refused to negotiate [cash] our trust check in the mistaken belief that the sale would be void if she held on to the check! Our trust reconciliation has shown a check for over $50,000 outstanding for six months! The partners are very concerned. The vendor's behavior is beyond the firm's influence, but we now have a stale-dated check, and we may still be responsible for the custody of the funds!

What options are available in various states for handling the funds? What are the firm's responsibilities? How could this situation have been avoided?

Trust Receipts

Many procedures for handling trust receipts are similar to those for handling general receipts (discussed in Chapter 6). There are some special considerations, however.

Most trust funds arriving in the office are anticipated by the lawyer and/or secretary, who provide instructions for depositing them and give the contributor a **trust receipt** if the funds are cash. Usually no receipt is issued to other lawyers who forward funds to the firm.

Trust money should be deposited promptly and never removed from the office by staff, except to be deposited. If money is received after banking hours, it is placed in the office vault or other designated location in the office until the next banking day.

All banks should be instructed to inform the firm immediately if a check deposited to a trust account is dishonored. Because lawyers are obliged to cover deficiencies in trust accounts, firms have holding policies whereby funds received in the form of an uncertified check are not disbursed until the check has had time to clear. Some firms request certified trust checks if they are for large amounts that must be paid out immediately, especially if the contributing firm is not a familiar one.

TERMS
---

trust receipt   Funds given to the firm for safekeeping.

Cash trust receipts, like general cash receipts, must be handled responsibly and preferably under a lawyer's supervision. Some firms allow the practice of depositing funds into the trust account when it is uncertain whether they are trust or general funds. This is commingling and is not appropriate. The account the funds belong in is determined *before* the deposit is made.

Case 7–7	Found: **Lawyer sought to defeat judgment creditors of firm using trust account for firm's operating expenses.**
	Ordered: Disbarment.

Practical Application 7–10	Belle: We have a very specialized field of practice: collection of overdue family maintenance payments in circumstances where no government agency can help. Our fee agreements with clients invariably state that we can take any funds received and apply them to our outstanding bills. The accounting staff look at the outstanding accounts for a client and deposit the money to our general account if there are outstanding bills. If there are no outstanding bills, we deposit the money to out trust account. But often the payments are mixed—part is to go to pay bills and part to the client. We put these payments into trust first, and then transfer the payment for outstanding bills to our general account. But sometimes we get maintenance payments for disabled dependents where part of the money goes to a public trustee. Should we take our payments first, or pay the trustee first?

What questions does Belle need answered before she can determine where to deposit the funds? Whom should she ask? At what point?

Documenting Receipts

Ideally, the secretary who handles the client's lawyer's mail is responsible for documenting trust receipts because the secretary is familiar with the file, client, and purpose of the funds and has closer access to the lawyer if problems or questions arise.

All checks deposited by the firm are proofed to ensure that there will not be a problem negotiating them (see Chapter 1). The payee, which may include the firm "in Trust"; drawee bank (especially for large amounts); and any previous endorsements should be examined especially carefully for trust receipts.

**Practical
Application
7-11**

Dan: We got this check from a client for a fee advance, but I'm a little nervous about it. It was issued by another law firm to someone we don't even know and has been endorsed by that person and a few others before it came to us. One of the endorsements says "Wishy Washy." Is this a weird joke, or is it someone's name? I don't want to insult anyone, but what can I do to make sure that we will not eventually be held responsible for a fraud or something?

What can and should Dan determine about the check? What are various rules about negotiable instruments and being a "holder in due course"?

Any problems that become evident in the proofing process are immediately brought to the responsible lawyer's attention. If that lawyer is not available and the funds must be disbursed without delay, another lawyer or direct supervisor is consulted before the check is deposited.

An in-house form similar to the general receipts form in Figure 6–2 (illustrated in Figure 7–9) or a carbon copy or photocopy of the receipt issued to the contributor accompanies the funds when they are forwarded to the accounting staff, who double-check all documentation and re-proof the check when preparing the deposit. Data needed to complete the trust accounting records are:

- *Full identification of the file* to which the funds are to be credited: name, matter description, and file number. This is especially important where a client may have more than one file.

- *The bank account* the funds are to be deposited to if the firm operates more than one trust bank account.

- *Date* the funds were received into a lawyer's trusteeship. Whenever possible, they should be deposited on the same day.

- *Form of the funds:* cash, check, lawyer's trust check, money order.

- *Nature or purpose of the funds:* fee advance, settlement, judgment, sale proceeds.

- *Identity of the contributor,* often the client or a relative or friend, a related corporation, another law firm, an insurance company, a bank, or an unsuccessful opposing party.

- *Amount* of the funds. Special attention must be paid to foreign currency amounts. In the case of cash, the contributor may not have the correct amount to be deposited and change will be taken from petty cash. Only the *correct* amount of the funds is deposited.

- *Individual who has prepared the form,* usually the secretary who has also proofed the check.

- *Holding period* before the funds can be disbursed. If the drawee bank is local, this is usually not more than eight banking days. For out-of-town and foreign banks, the firm's policy may be to hold the funds for up to one month.

- *Special instructions* for handling the funds: investment, transfers for the firm's outstanding bills, payment of third-party disbursements.

   A copy of the trust receipt form and/or check is made and kept by the secretary before forwarding the funds for deposit.

FIGURE 7–9

Trust Receipt Form

Carpenter & Cook
TRUST RECEIPT

Prepared by __L.S.__

File	2377.0	Hall, Miles
Date	11/20/98	Lily; Peter
Amount	1,000.00	Form Check
Bank	State Eastern – Pooled	
Purpose	Fee Advance	
Instructions	do not transfer until final bill	

Deposited by	L.S.
Receipt entered by	M.F.

M. HALL 100

17833 Eastern Way
Suadown, ST 10010

Nov. 19 19 98

PAY TO THE
ORDER OF __Carpenter & Cook - in Trust__ $ 1,000.00

------------------ one thousand ------------------------------00 /100 DOLLARS

RE __Legal Advice__

The Bank of the East
149 - 340 John Street
Fielding, ST 10101

M. Hall

000100   29873   10 467 184

This is the trust receipt form that goes with Mr. Hall's check that I showed you earlier. Sandy wants to hold this amount against the final bill, so the funds should not be transferred without specific instructions. M.

Banking Procedures

The accounting staff responsible for completing the bank deposit slip use the check and the receipt form as source documents. Although some firms balk at writing the client's name on the bank deposit slip, some identification of the file to be credited, such as the number, must be clear on the bank's copy of the deposit slip. Most bank deposit books/slips permit duplicates to be made at the same time as the original. If the bank's forms do not allow for duplicate copies, one is made by photocopying the original slip, marking it "COPY," and presenting it with the original to be validated by the bank. The bank-validated copies are checked for clarity before leaving the bank.

All checks should be photocopied before they are deposited into trust accounts, and a photocopy filed with the receipt form in the accounting records. If a problem arises and the check is unavailable, the firm must have access to the check information.

If the firm does not have an endorsement stamp for each trust account, the accounting staff write the bank account number on the back of the check so that the bank can complete the endorsement by stamping the back with a "PAYEE" stamp. Endorsements are particularly important on checks from insurance companies and certain government agencies. Unclear endorsements may cause the check to be returned by the drawee, requesting a *guaranteed endorsement* from the cashing bank.

Validated copies of deposit slips are kept permanently in the deposit book or removed and filed chronologically or with the bank statement when received. As deposit books are removed from the office to be taken to the bank, some firms separate deposit slips from the book immediately after the deposit is made to minimize loss of records if the books are mislaid.

Recording Trust Receipts

Trust receipts are entered to the trust receipts journal using the supporting documentation. Usually the journal is for trust receipts only, but sometimes, especially in pegboard systems, combination journals are used.

Trust receipts are not entered into the journal until the validated copy of the deposit slip is returned to the office. The validated copy confirms that the deposit has been made by the firm and accepted by the bank and that the funds were not misplaced or misappropriated in transit. In some cases, urgency requires that the receipt be posted before the copy is returned so that a check can be issued and signed. The signing lawyer must be told that the receipt has not been returned, and the check must *not* leave the office until the deposit has been verified.

The trust receipt form and/or check photocopy and/or the validated deposit slip are used to make the entry to the trust receipts journal. A unique reference number is assigned to each deposit to help trace the entry if necessary. If the firm makes only one trust deposit per bank account per day, however, the date is a sufficient reference. The client ledger entries are posted from the journal, often with the added description of the form of the funds received (cash or check) and the purpose (fee advance, settlement proceeds). This will be simultaneous in pegboard systems and many automated systems. Figure 7–10 illustrates typical trust receipt procedures.

FIGURE 7–10

Trust Receipt Recording Process

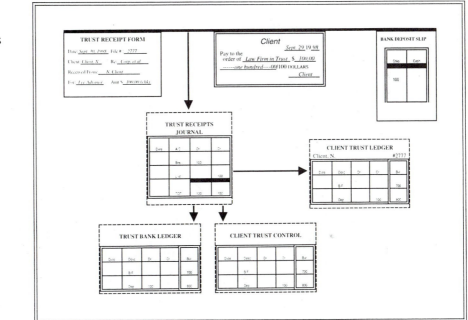

Dishonored Checks

Most people are familiar with checks being dishonored for the reason of nonsufficient funds (NSF), but many do not realize that there are other reasons why drawees do not accept checks for payment, some of which are not the fault of the drawer. From a conduct perspective, therefore, some caution is warranted when approaching contributors about dishonored checks.

When checks deposited to the trust bank account are returned unpaid by the drawee, the firm must be notified immediately by the bank. An entry recording the returned item (dishonored check) is made in the trust journals as well as in the client trust ledger. These entries may be made as "negative" entries in the trust receipts journal, but certain systems require that they be made by separate journal entry or through the trust check journal.

Returned items must always immediately be brought to the lawyer's attention. If the funds have been disbursed, there may be a trust shortage, which must be eliminated and if necessary reported.

Practical Application 7–12

Rowan: We have a real problem with this dishonored check. The client did not complete the body amount, but I know it should be for $1000. The drawee bank has returned it because they read the figure as being $10.00. We knew the client was good for the check and paid out of trust for it. I've been told to call the client like I'm "just" the trust clerk and can we have another check, please? In the meantime, I have to keep track of deposits to trust to make up the "deficiency," and the payments back to general when the correct amount is received, and . . . I don't think I like this.

What should Rowan do before calling the client?

Trust Checks

Much importance is placed on the custody and policy surrounding trust checks because they are widely accepted as being "as good as cash," and in some ways issuing trust checks is similar to issuing disbursement checks (discussed in Chapter 4). It is especially important that access to supplies of blank trust checks be confined to those whose job it is to issue them. Special care must be taken when issuing trust checks for funds that may not have cleared the drawee bank, as the firm is responsible if it disburses funds that have not yet cleared and there are subsequent trust bank deficiencies.

Many firms prefer that whenever possible, client file disbursements be paid from the general account, and not from the trust account, because:

- Trust checks require greater attention than general checks. An uncleared general check poses fewer problems than does an uncleared trust check. More trust checks mean more potential problems. Many firms require two signatures for a trust check but only one for a general check.

- The firm wishes to avoid the added complexity of having two filing systems, one for supporting documents for client file disbursements paid from the general account and one for those paid from the trust account.

- In automated systems especially, it may be easier to prepare an accurate application for court-awarded costs if all disbursements are recorded in one place.

Firms in highly competitive areas of practice such as residential real property may prefer to pay all direct disbursements from trust and absorb all incidental disbursements in the quoted fee. Conveyancing firms also tend to have highly standardized trust accounting procedures and controls that alleviate most of the foregoing concerns.

Practical Application 7–13

Candy: I'm not sure about the way we do our conveyance billings. I came across a copy of a bill from another firm that showed only photocopies and faxes for disbursements, and quite a low fee. It's simply not possible that they absorb all of the filing and other disbursements into their fees—they'd lose money every month! What is going on?

Rich: I think I know the firm you're talking about. To appear "competitive" they quote a low fee and say that disbursements will not exceed ten percent of the fee. But you and I both know that the filing and other large direct disbursements are bigger than that fee. Don't the clients see that the file disbursements are being paid from trust? They must see that on the Statement of Adjustments.

Candy: Do they? These are mostly residential conveyances that clients are involved with perhaps once in five years. They don't know the difference. Is the other law firm treating them properly? Should our firm do the same thing and get more clients?

Candy and Rich are concerned about the clients' understanding of the payment of disbursements. What documents would serve to inform clients of what they are really paying "to the firm" and what is absorbed into the Statement of Adjustments?

Check Requests

Most trust checks are requested by the lawyer, often through the secretary, from the accounting staff using a form similar to the one illustrated in Figure 7–11 that specifies:

- *date of the request* (when it was forwarded to the accounting staff);

- *date and time the check is to be available* (often the same day, or as soon as possible);

- *where the check is to be forwarded* (sometimes the accounting staff will forward it, but usually the secretary will include it with other correspondence);

- *full identification of the file* to which the check is charged (name, matter description, and file number);

- *the bank account* on which the check is to be drawn (in some cases this will be obvious, as the file shows funds in only one bank, but this should still be double-checked);

- *full and correct payee name*(s) (often the client, another law firm, a bank, a successful opposing party, or the law firm itself for payment of a bill already rendered to the client);

- *nature of the payment* (trust transfer, settlement, judgment, fee award, sale proceeds, file disbursement, refund of fee advance);

- *amount of the check* (before issuing the check, the client ledger must be consulted to ensure that adequate funds are on deposit, which is another reason for not recording trust receipts until the deposit has been made);

- *approval* from the appropriate person, usually the lawyer; and

- *specific instructions* (sometimes payments must be made by money order or bank draft in a foreign currency; the payee is usually the bank issuing the money order).

Other information such as check number and check date is completed by the accounting staff after the check has been issued.

FIGURE 7–11

Trust Check Request Form

Carpenter & Cook

TRUST CHECK REQUEST

Request date _Oct. 21, 1998_

Approved by _S. Cook_

Date required _Oct. 25, 1998_

at: _____

Forward to _C.W._

Client _2417.4_

United Investment Corp.

Public Company Investments

Amount _$1,000.00_   Bank _State Eastern - Pooled_

Payee   _New Panorama Development_

Purpose   _purchase warrants: 1,000 @ $1.00_

Other instructions _____

Check number	T - 188
Check date	Oct. 24, 1998
Check prepared by	M.F.
Check entered by	M.F.

Trust check requests are always approved by a lawyer before anyone issues the check. If I'm not here, Kim usually issues them. M.

Issuing Trust Checks

Trust checks are issued in numerical order on checks marked "Trust" or "Trust Account." If for some reason the checks are not numbered already, such as a counter check, one is assigned and written on the face of the check and all supporting documents even if it is subsequently voided and a new check is issued.

Because they are usually for large amounts and are drawn against money that does not belong to the firm, trust checks should be prepared with extra care. Chapter 1 introduces the preparation of checks, and the following items are of additional concern for trust checks:

- *The payee* must be specific, not "cash" or "bearer." Particular care is needed here because when two or more payees are stated as "and" instead of "or," the endorsements of *all* payees will be required to negotiate the check.

- *The reference line* should be completed with care. While it is practical to disclose some explicit reference on the face of a check when forwarding funds to another law firm, some payees may not want others, even their bankers, to know the nature of the payment. The file number is usually sufficient.

- The signature by a lawyer. Some firms require the accounting staff person responsible for trust accounting to sign the check before it is presented to a lawyer for signature. This procedure is intended to assure lawyers that the other signatory has verified that adequate funds are on deposit.

Technically, a trust check is "issued" when it leaves the firm's custody. The lawyer and secretary ensure that the check is forwarded to the correct place by suitable means. Many checks are forwarded by regular mail, but large checks are often delivered by courier, registered mail, special delivery, or other expedited method, some of which provide verification of receipt. Such verification may not be necessary to show proper diligence in the event of a dispute over delivery, but it is a cost-effective way of reducing misunderstandings and friction with clients.

Case 7–8

Found: **Lawyer was not negligent in sending large cashier's check to client by ordinary first-class mail.** Check was not received by client who refused to post bond in order to receive replacement check.

Ordered: No award to client for lost interest.

Particular attention is needed when giving a client a full or partial refund of a fee advance. The responsible lawyer must be satisfied that there are no legitimate outstanding amounts to be paid to the firm from the advance. The refund of an advance, however, does not necessarily end the firm's responsibility to the client.

Case 7–9

Found: **Lawyer attempted to limit malpractice liability to clients by placing restrictive endorsement on trust check refunding fee advance.**

Ordered: Indefinite suspension, reinstatement after two years subject to review.

Recording Trust Checks

The check stub and/or trust check request form are used as source documents in preparing the trust check journal. Pegboard systems create the trust check journal and post to the client ledger at the same time the check is written. Advanced automated systems may print the actual check on a special form and enter the check simultaneously. As an additional control, such systems either will not print a check or will require an override code to print one if adequate funds are not recorded as being on deposit. A typical trust check procedure is illustrated in Figure 7–12.

FIGURE 7–12

Trust Check
Recording Process

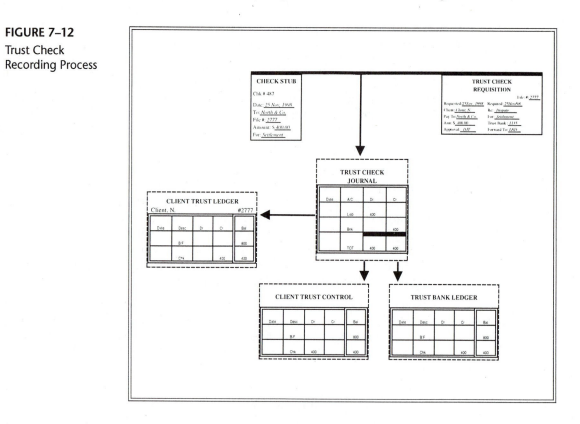

Trust checks should be recorded as soon as they are written, and always before they leave the firm's hands.

<table>
<tr><td>

Practical Application 7–14

</td><td>

Virginia: I'm really steamed and I don't know whom to blame! My secretary requested a trust check for a third party—that was fine. Then Dirk asked for the same check, and Willy the trust clerk issued it. The first check (the one I'd signed the authorization for) was issued by Joy, the trust supervisor. Problem is, she gives all of her posting to Willy, who didn't look in his in-tray to see that the check had been issued, and now it's been issued twice. As the lawyer responsible for the file, what do I do? What is the management committee going to do about this type of thing?

What has happened that shouldn't have? How should it be fixed and who should be responsible for seeing that it is fixed?

</td></tr>
</table>

Procedures for voiding checks and recording void checks are explained in Chapter 1.

<table>
<tr><td>

Practical Application 7–15

</td><td>

Tip: We issued this trust check over a year ago, and I would like to clean up the reconciliation and record it as void. Ms. Hail says not to worry—the client will cash it eventually, but I know that our bank won't accept it. The check is for about $3,000, and the bank verifies dates on all checks over $1,000.

What can Tip, as the accounting supervisor, do to convince Ms. Hail that the matter requires investigation?

</td></tr>
</table>

Trust Transfers

Trust transfers are basically a simple way for the firm to pay its bills from funds held in trust on a file, instead of issuing the bill to the client and receiving payment from the client. All trust transfers, however, must conform to the fee agreement or be specifically authorized by the client.

<table>
<tr><td>

Case 7–10

</td><td>

Found: Lawyer billed expenses of law clerks, secretarial assistance, **a sumptuous meal and other exorbitant charges to client trust account in absence of agreement with respect to the expenses.**

Ordered: Public censure.

</td></tr>
</table>

Trust transfers for several files may be included in one trust check, but the component amounts must be separately attributable to the individual files, and the total not a mere lump-sum estimate.

———————————————————— **TERMS** ————————————————————

trust transfers   Amounts transferred by the firm from a trust account to the firm's general account to pay a client's bill.

A trust transfer request form is completed by the secretary and bears the lawyer's approval. Requests are made using:

- The same form used for a trust check, with a special space for denoting a trust transfer, or submitted together with a general receipt form.

- A written memorandum dealing with one or more files.

- A form or memorandum produced by accounting staff and then approved by the lawyer.

- A special trust transfer form that is used as both a trust transfer request and general receipt form for recording, as illustrated in Figure 7–13. These will require either a special binder or a duplicate copy filed with both trust check and general receipt records.

FIGURE 7–13
Trust Transfer Form

Carpenter & Cook

TRUST TRANSFERS

Bank Account _State Eastern - Pooled_   Total _1,922.77_

Check Date _Nov. 12, 1998_   Check Number _T-225_

File No.	File Name	Total	P	Bill	Lwyr	Fees	Disb.	Tax
2302.8	Peel, Don	1,346.77	P	145	TB	1,100.00	213.77	33.00
1861.4	Sunrise/Sunset	500.00	P	123	TB	485.44		14.56
2162.6	Teal, W.	76.00	P	121	PC	0.00	76.00	76.00
TOTALS		1,922.77			TB	1,584.44	289.77	123.56

Date Prepared _Nov. 10, 1998_   By _D.M._   Approved _P.C._

When there are a number of trust transfers, I do them on one check with this form as documentation. Always make sure that you know you are supposed to make the transfer (usually it says at the bottom of the bill). M.

In some firms, the secretaries and/or accounting staff monitor trust and accounts receivable balances and complete the authorization forms for the lawyer's approval to transfer funds from the trust account to the firm's general account. Also, a copy of the *signed* bill to the client showing the trust transfer may be used as authorization.

Trust Reports

The monthly trust reconciliation is reviewed by a partner to confirm that the reconciliations are being prepared as and when required. In any firm of appreciable size, however, this does not help individual lawyers identify files that should be reviewed. Small trust amounts often cause large problems, and lawyers may not be aware that potentially troublesome amounts remain in the firm's custody.

Types of useful trust reports include:

- *Trust balance listings by last trust transaction date.* These reports help to identify dormant files. Like client folders for closed files, they create more problems as they get older.

- *Trust balances under a threshold amount.* Balances of less than $100, especially if they are relatively old, should be reviewed.

- *Trust and accounts receivable balances by client.* Often trust transfers can be made from fee advances on deposit.

- *Trust and WIP balances by file.* Billing WIP and making a trust transfer can clear the ledgers in preparation for closing the file.

- *Schedules of separate accounts,* due dates of term deposits, and the status of all trust investments. These remind lawyers that there are substantial sums still under their control.

- *Periodic listing of any items in safekeeping.* Lawyers may need to be reminded that property items are still with the firm. Many are personal items that should be returned to clients.

At least monthly, all lawyers receive a list of trust balances remaining in their files. Dealing with small, old trust balances can be wearisome, but these balances should be addressed while the lawyer's memory is fresh and the client can be located easily.

Practical Application 7–16

Ms. Snow: This client refuses to return my calls, and I know that he is in town most of the time. His secretary is screening his calls and lets on that he is "unavailable." I send letters that are never answered. The silly thing is, all I want to do is have him execute this release so that we can give him a few hundred dollars that has been sitting in trust for three years because Ms. Carver did not have the time to clean up her files before she became so ill. It's just a formality, but I can't release the funds until he's signed. There are no legal issues—I just need a signature.

How does this outstanding amount affect the accounting efficiency of the firm? What are some options in your state for dealing with these funds?

Trust Account Reconciliations

A reconciliation of each and every trust bank account is prepared as of the last banking day or calendar day of each month, bearing the date it was prepared and the signature of at least one partner to confirm that the reconciliation has been reviewed.

Ideally, the bank's records should mirror the firm's trust records and, with the exception of uncleared checks, balance to the firm's ledgers. The four items to reconcile to one total *for each bank account* are:

- *the bank's records* (statements);

- *total client trust ledger balances* for the bank account;

- *the trust bank general ledger account* or other supplementary ledger (or synoptic) where the trust assets do not appear in the general ledger; and

- *the general ledger liability (control) account* corresponding to the bank asset, if one exists.

In most automated systems, the input protocols make it theoretically impossible for the last three not to show the same total if only one pooled trust account is operated. If any client trust ledgers are incorrect, however, the *correct* balance is stated on the reconciliation.

Reconciling (outstanding) items should show only as adjustments to the bank's reported balance. Many firms' systems do not allow additional entries after the month-end closing, and the bank statements may not be received before the date the month must be closed to avoid backlogs. Any required adjusting entries are made at the earliest possible opportunity in the following month, with a reference to the date the actual transaction occurred. Automated systems may provide useful reports such as outstanding check lists and deposit summaries, which help in reconciling very active bank accounts.

In pooled accounts, the most common reconciling items are outstanding checks, erroneous bank charges and other bank errors, and outstanding deposits. The last of these should always appear in the bank's records on the first banking day of the following month. Auditors are very aware that "outstanding deposits" are often recorded to hide actual deficiencies in the trust bank account detected by the firm during the reconciliation process after an inappropriate distribution has been made. Outstanding checks older than two months should be investigated.

All reconciling items appear where the item will ultimately be cleared. Outstanding checks will eventually show on the bank's records and are listed there. Similarly, any bank errors to be corrected show with the bank adjustments. Recording errors or omissions appear in the firm's ledger adjustments, as illustrated in Figure 7–14. One-step reconciliations, which list all outstanding items in one section, are not used because they do not show how items will clear.

FIGURE 7–14
Trust Bank
Account
Reconciliation

Trust Reconciliation at October 31, 1998

POOLED ACCOUNT — State Eastern Account # 7410 - 86

Balance per bank	$41,036.17	

Outstanding checks

187	1,106.84	
189	74.22	
190	7,680.56	
		(8,861.62)

Bank service charge October 31, 1998
(to be reversed by State Eastern)   25.50

Adjusted Bank Balance   32,200.05

Balance per bank synoptic   33,100.05

Posting error # 188   (900.00)

Adjusted Ledger Balance   32,200.05

Client Trust Balances

1512.3	1,000.00
1513.1	1,000.00
1514.9	1,000.00
1717.8	22,864.48
1861.4	500.00
2015.6	500.00
2302.8	1,802.80
2417.4	3,532.77

Total Client Trust   32,200.05

Approved: _Pat Carpenter_   Date: _Nov. 6, 1998_

I reconcile the trust bank account as soon as possible after getting the bank statement. Pat likes to approve them, but Sandy can also do it. M.

External Trust Reports and Reviews

Most states have some form of reporting requirement for lawyers' trust accounts. Sometimes all that is required is a periodic declaration that accounts are properly reviewed and maintained. Some jurisdictions have much more stringent requirements than others.

Case 7–11   Found: **Lawyer maintained inadequate client trust account records, was out of trust (deficient in trust account), and failed to disclose that fact in trust accounting compliance certificate, falsely representing to professional conduct committee that trust fund shortages had been corrected;** failed to inform committee of certain arrest; and falsely represented to committee that property sale proceeds would meet obligations to client.

Ordered: Disbarment.

Preparation of trust reports is generally assigned to a senior member of the accounting staff, who presents them to a partner for approval.

Although audits or reviews by an external accountant are not required in all jurisdictions, an examination or spot-check of the trust accounting records is performed by the accountant, usually when the year-end financial statements are being prepared. These reviews serve several critical functions:

- Assuring the partners that the firm's accounting staff are performing record-keeping duties competently and honestly.

- Reminding everyone involved in the trust accounting function that the records will be reviewed and errors will be investigated, especially those errors that were concealed by staff responsible for them and not properly revealed to the partners.

- Identifying inefficiencies and proposing recommendations for improvements to the system.

Under no circumstances should the firm's employees be permitted or requested to conceal information during any legitimate review.

Case 7–12   Found: Lawyer failed to diligently pursue legal matters entrusted to his care, **misappropriated client trust funds, failed to keep adequate client trust account records, and experienced $140,000 shortage in client trust account.**

Ordered: Disbarment.

Laundering

Laundering is the crime of processing illegally obtained funds through a legitimate vehicle for the purpose of concealing its source.

--------------------------------- TERMS ---------------------------------

laundering   The unlawful concealment of the source of illegally obtained funds to give an appearance of legitmacy.

Any lawyer that knowingly participates in this activity through a trust account, or in any other way, participates in laundering. In some cases, lawyers are deemed to be wilfully ignorant of laundering. They are presented with a suspect transaction, for example, but ask no questions about it.

The Internal Revenue Service (IRS) requires that lawyers who receive more than $10,000 in cash report the transaction on IRS Form 8300 illustrated in Appendix B.

Comprehensive Exercises

1. Design a checklist for the complete trust accounting procedures for a firm with two pooled trust accounts. The list should have at least fifty items.

2. Design a checklist for the complete trust accounting procedures for a firm's separate trust accounts. The list should have at least thirty items.

3. Draft a manual of procedures for the firm of Carpenter & Cook for the pooled and separate trust accounts. Do not restate the reconciliation process in detail. Address in particular the approvals and bank signatories. Describe how your system addresses the requirements of the ABA Model Rules (Rule 1.15 in particular).

4. In the following example, explain what steps the firm should have taken to avoid the problem.

    A check for 100,000 British pounds (£) drawn on a British bank, is converted to American funds ($) at the time of deposit at a rate of £ 1.00 = $1.80, and the trust account is credited with $180,000. The check is subsequently dishonored when the rate is £ 1.00 = $1.85, and the trust account is charged $185,000. A deficiency of $5,000 has occurred even though the firm has done nothing but deposit the check. Banks have no obligation to charge back only the amount originally deposited when an exchange rate changes between the time of deposit and the receipt of the dishonored check.

5. Describe some concerns that trust transfers aggravate in a large firm where many people do trust accounting.

CHAPTER 8

ACCOUNTING IN CLIENT DOCUMENTS

As part of performing legal services for clients, firms are often required to prepare documents using the client's accounting information. Lawyers also use the accounting information of opposing and other parties for such purposes as analyzing the **quantum** (dollar value) of a client's litigation claim.

Although many calculations and presentations are specified in statutes and regulations, basic accounting information is the foundation for many of these documents. This chapter provides a brief overview of the types of transactions and terminology encountered in client accounting documents.

Case 8–1   Found: **Lawyer incorrectly prepared real estate closing statements, resulting in overpayments from trust account.**

Ordered: (for this and other issues) Three-year suspension.

Time Value of Money

People in industrialized societies understand the basic concept of **interest**, which is essentially payment to one party (the lender) by another party (the borrower) as consideration for forfeiting current use of the money lent (**principal**). People must be paid to forego the benefits of spending money (deferral of consumption) until a later date. **Interest rates** are expressed as annual percentages of the principal amount and are adjusted for part-years as either one-twelfth (for monthly periods) or as a fraction of 365 for more precise calculations.

The **nominal interest rate** is the stated rate of interest for a loan such as a mortgage, an unpaid credit card balance, or a government bond. Nominal interest rates, determined either by statute or regulation or agreed on by the parties, have three components:

TERMS
---

quantum The amount of monetary compensation sought or awarded.

interest Amount charged by a lender to a borrower for the use of money.

principal Initial or capital sum.

interest rate The percentage of the principal to be charged as interest, usually expressed on an annual basis.

nominal interest rate Stated rate of interest for a lending arrangement. The nominal rate may or may not reflect the effective rate of borrowing.

- **Real interest** is the cost of deferred consumption the borrower must pay the lender. Many financial analysts believe that in the past century, it has been fairly consistent at around three percent.

- **Anticipated inflation** causes an increase in the nominal rate when lenders anticipate that money will lose purchasing power over time and/or the money supply will be restricted. Negative inflation (deflation) causes a reduction in the nominal interest rate. Inflation reflects general economic trends in an economy and affects concurrent lending transactions within an economy more or less equally without regard to the individual borrowers involved.

- **Risk premium** is additional interest charged by lenders to compensate for the risk that a particular borrower may not be able or willing to pay back the loan. Risk premiums are a reflection of a specific borrower's creditworthiness, not general economic trends.

Calculations of interest amounts also depend on other **lending terms** in the agreement, including the method of interest calculation and the amounts and frequency of repayments. There are two basic methods of interest calculation:

- **Simple interest** is a fixed percentage of the principal that will be paid, usually in a lump sum when the principal is completely repaid. Simple interest is not common in business arrangements except for short time periods, low nominal interest rates, or very small amounts. It is more common in lending arrangements between family members and friends. Figure 8–1 illustrates a simple-interest lending arrangement.

- **Compound interest** recognizes "interest on the interest," which is important to the lender when nominal interest rates are high, the time period is longer than one year, or the principal amount is large.

TERMS
---

real interest Basic cost of deferral of consumption.

anticipated inflation The expected rate of decrease in the value of money in the figure, usually expressed as an annual percentage.

risk premium Additional compensation required for a lender to advance funds to a particular borrower.

lending terms Conditions of the lending arrangement, including interest rate, basis of interest calculation, timing, and amount of payments.

simple interest Interest calculated as: principal × annual rate, × years (or fractions of years)

compound interest Interest calculated on the assumption that unpaid interest becomes part of the principal for the next compounding period.

FIGURE 8–1

Simple Interest
Calculation

Computer Loan Schedule

TERMS:

Principal Amount $10,000.00
Nominal Interest Rate: 9%
Basis of Calculation: **Simple Interest**
Lending Period: September 10, 1998 to December 31, 1998 (112 days)

$10,000.00 × 9% × 112/365 = $276.16 **total interest**

Total due December 31, 1998 = $10,276.16

This is a calculation of loan interest I prepared for Pat and Sandy when they thought they would borrow the $10,000 for the computers from Pat's parents and pay it back on December 31, 1998. M.

With compound interest, the nominal interest rate is not the same as the **effective interest rate**, true annual interest rate paid by the borrower. Figure 8–2 illustrates a compound interest calculation.

The amount and frequency of payments are important factors in calculating the total interest to be paid. Some lending arrangements require only that **accrued interest** be paid each month, quarter, half-year, or year (as with bonds), and the principal is repaid all at once at the end of the lending period. Others allow flexibility for the borrower to repay interest and principal as cash flow permits, providing that all payments are credited first to interest and then to principal. Revolving arrangements such as credit cards and lines of credit allow borrowers to draw on credit and repay as they choose, provided they do not exceed a certain credit limit. Often the interest rate is subject to fluctuations reflected in the **prime rate**.

There are four variables in a loan payment calculation:

- the *principal,* or original amount;
- the nominal *interest rate per period* (if the compounding frequency is monthly, the annual rate is divided by twelve);
- the *number of payments* or interest periods if payments are not made each period; and
- the *amount of each payment*.

Any three of the four are sufficient to calculate the other variable.

TERMS

effective interest rate The true interest rate in a compound interest calculation.

accrued interest Interest incurred but not yet paid at the effective date of the accrual.

prime rate The rate charged by major financial institutions to their most creditworthy borrowers; the "risk-free" rate.

FIGURE 8–2

Compound Interest Calculation

Computer Loan Schedule

TERMS:

Principal Amount: $10,000.00
Nominal Interest Rate: 9%
Basis of Calculation: **Interest Compounded Monthly**
Lending Period: September 10, 1998 to December 31, 1998 (112 days)

Period	Principal	Rate for Period	Interest
Sept. 10–30	10,000.00	*.53%	52.50
Oct. 1–31	10,052.50	.75%	75.39
Nov. 1–30	10,127.89	.75%	75.96
Dec. 1–31	10,203.85	.75%	76.53
Total Interest			280.38

* .75% × 21/30

Total payable December 31, 1998 = 10,280.38

Effective Interest Rate: $\dfrac{280.38 \times 365/112}{10,000.00} = 9.14\%$

This is the same loan terms, except with compound interest. M.

The most common arrangement for the purchase of capital (durable) property is the **term loan,** in which the amount, frequency, and number of periodic payments as well as the interest rate are all agreed on in advance and may not be changed except by mutual agreement. Figure 8–3 illustrates a term loan arrangement corresponding to the loans depicted in Figures 8–1 and 8–2.

Bonds issued by governments, utilities, and corporations are loans involving one borrower and many lenders. They are often secured, but **debentures** (unsecured bonds) are common in some industries.

TERMS

term loan A loan for a definite period, often specifying the frequency and amount of payments.

bonds A written promise, secured by specific property, to pay a specified amount on a certain date, with or without interest payments before the due date.

debentures Unsecured bonds.

FIGURE 8–3

Term Loan
Calculation

Bank Loan Schedule

TERMS:

Principal Amount: $10,000.00
Nominal Interest Rate: 9%
Basis of Calculation: **Interest Compounded Monthly**
Lending Period: September 10, 1998 to December 31, 1998
Payments: 4 equal installments of $2,541.41 to be paid at the end of each month

Period	Amount owing	Days owing	Interest paid	Principal paid
Sept. 10–30	10,000.00	21/365	51.78	2,489.63
Oct. 1–31	7,510.37	31/365	57.41	2,484.00
Nov. 1–30	5,026.37	30/365	37.18	2,504.23
Dec. 1–31	2,522.14	31/365	19.27	2,522.14
		Totals	165.64	10,000.00

This was the initial term loan schedule proposed by the bank. M.

Aside from express lending arrangements, the time value of money is calculated for such amounts as court-ordered or equitable interest, the **present value** of long-term damages such as lost wages, and the funding of **annuities** in structured settlements. If the amounts and frequency of the payments are constant, financial calculators or books of tables are used to determine the values. Complex calculations are best done on an electronic spreadsheet.

Present Value

In calculating the payments for term loans, the principal is known at the beginning of the agreement. In situations where a value must be determined that *replaces* a flow of income (or payments), only the nominal

───────────────── TERMS ─────────────────

present value   The dollar value of some amount(s) to be received in the future, as though the amounts were received today.

annuity   A series of equal periodic payments. In an ordinary annuity, payments are received at the end of the period; in an annuity due, the payments are received at the beginning of the period.

interest rate and frequency and amount of payments are known. The "principal" in this type of calculation is called the *present value*. Figure 8–4 illustrates a present value calculation.

Another type of present value calculation involves not a series of payments, but a lump sum to be received at some point in the future after a number of compounding periods have elapsed, such as an agreement to pay for a franchise in five years even though it is used from the present day. Alternatively, the same type of calculation of the **future value** of an amount agreed on today can be calculated.

Sometimes a present value calculation combines both a series of payments and a lump sum payment, such as an equipment lease with a purchase option at the end of the lease term. A calculation found more frequently in finance than in law firms is one that determines not dollar values but the **imputed interest rate,** the nominal rate that is implicit if all other variables are known. This calculation is often used to compare leasing a piece of equipment through a leasing company to paying a known interest rate to a bank.

FIGURE 8–4

Present Value Calculation: Series of Payments

Daisy L. Carpenter
Present Value of Future Care Costs
to Age 90 (15 years)
From January 1, 1999

Interest Rate: 9% p.a.

Homemaker: $12,000/year ($12,000 X 8.06069*)	$96,728.28
Special Bed Needed in Ten Years ($3,000 X .42241*)	1,267.23
Special Therapy Required after Age 80: $6,000/year [$6,000 × (8.06069 - 3.88965)*]	25,026.24
Present Value	**$123,021.75**

* used present value tables

For Ms. Carpenter's personal injury claim, Chris and I calculated her future care costs and determined the present value of the claim. M.

TERMS
---

future value The nominal value to which a series of payments will grow at a given interest rate.

imputed interest rate The rate of interest implicit in a calculation if all other variables are known.

**Practical
Application
8–1**

Bob: These present value calculations are quite complicated, especially when the cash flows are not consistent. Can't we just average them over the whole time period?

Answer Bob's question. Use an illustration of very uneven flows to compare the calculation methods.

Annuities

Annuity calculations are used to determine the amount of money required at present to secure a series of payments for a number of periods into the future.

Annuity calculations correspond to present value calculations, except in cases where the payments are assumed to happen at the beginning of each time period (an annuity due). The present value of an annuity represents the amount of principal required to fund a series of payments, as illustrated in Figure 8–5.

FIGURE 8–5

Annuity

Peter Hall
Annuity to Age 18
Funding and Payment Schedule

Interest Rate: 9% p.a.
Annual Payment: $15,000
Years to Age 18: 5
Payment Date: December 31, 1999 to 2003
Funding Date: January 1, 1999
Principal: 15,000 × 3.88965 = $58,344.75

Year	Balance at January 1	Interest earned for Year	Payment made December 31
1999	58,344.75	5,251.03	15,000.00
2000	48,595.78	4,373.62	15,000.00
2001	37,969.40	3,417.25	15,000.00
2002	26,386.65	2,374.80	15,000.00
2003	13,761.45	1,238.55	15,000.00

Chris and I calculated the amount Miles Hall needs for funding his son's annuity to age 18, which was part of the custody and support agreement. M.

Business Accounting

Transactions such as loans are not peculiar to businesses. Many individuals and nonbusiness organizations deal with them routinely. Some types of transactions apply only to businesses, and some only to certain types of businesses. In fields of practice such as incorporations and **securities,** business structure is of primary importance in ensuring that the organization functions as its owners intend.

Capital Structure and Securities

There are three types of profit-seeking businesses, and to outsiders, their daily operations may appear to be similar. Their true differences lie in their capital structures and the relationship of management to ownership. *Proprietorships* have one owner, who owns all of the equity in the business and has the authority to make all business decisions. There is no stock or retained earnings, only "owner's capital." The owner is personally liable for the obligations of the business.

Partnerships are owned by two or more natural or corporate persons, with capital accounts showing their respective equity portions. Both decision-making authority and percentages of ownership interest are subject to a partnership agreement that, if not explicit in an oral or written agreement, is at least implicit in common law and is generally subject to statutory rights. Partners have obligations to each other in the form of **mutual agency,** the capacity of any partner to commit the partnership to a contractual liability, coupled with the obligation of each partner to act in the partnership's best interests.

Case 8–2

Found: **It is a (law practice) partner's duty to see to the completion of the partnership's contractual, professional obligations and, in performance thereof, the fiduciary character of their relationship as partner continues.**

Ordered: No compensation for departing partner's work in administering files through dissolution of the partnership.

In **general partnerships,** all partners are jointly and severally responsible for the obligations of the business to the extent of their assets

---

TERMS

securities† Certificates that represent a right to share in the profits of a company or in the distribution of its assets, or in a debt owed by a company or by the government.

mutual agency The responsibilities and duties owed between partners.

general partnership A normal partnership.

held outside of the business, and all partners are empowered to commit the resources of the partnership. In **limited partnerships,** only general partners are responsible for partnership liabilities that cannot be met with the partnership assets. Limited partners usually have little control over the operation and cannot be held liable for business obligations except to the extent of the contribution of their assets. Notwithstanding the restrictions on their liability and control, limited partners are entitled to full disclosure of the material details of the enterprise.

Case 8–3   Found: **Failure to provide limited partner (of client) with instrument describing the parties' rights is breach of fiduciary duty.**

Ordered: (for this and other issues) Three-year suspension.

Joint ventures between companies are like limited partnerships with no general partner, except that they are usually only formed for a specific project and/or definite period of time.

Corporations (companies) may have one or more owners who own **common stock** and hold voting power in relation to their common stock ownership. Voting power is not necessarily the authority to make day-to-day business decisions. It is the authority to vote for members of the Board of Directors, who in turn appoint the corporate officers who manage the business. In large **widely held corporations,** most stockholders have limited influence in daily business operations. Corporations have many advantages over proprietorships and partnerships, including limitation of the business liabilities of the owners. In corporations, owners

---

──────────────── TERMS ────────────────

limited partnership A limited partnership with (usually) one general partner who is responsible for the management of the enterprise and whose liability is not limited to its investment in the partnership. Limited partners usually do not become involved in management of the enterprise, and their liability is limited to the amount of their investments.

joint venture† Sometimes referred to as a joint adventure; the relationship created when two or more persons combine jointly in a business enterprise with the understanding that they will share in the profits or losses and that each will have a voice in its management.

corporation† An artificial person, existing only in the eyes of the law, to whom a state or the federal government has granted a charter to become a legal entity, separate from its shareholders, with a name of its own, under which its shareholders can act and contract and sue and be sued.

common stock† Ordinary capital stock in a corporation, the market value of which is based upon the worth of the corporation.

widely held corporation A corporation with no clear majority or influential stockholders.

are not obliged to meet corporate liabilities from their own resources. The most they can lose is what they have invested.

Investments in a corporation's stock are made to achieve two types of returns:

- **Capital gains** are increases in the value of the stock price, which may be the result of a merger or acquisition of the company. Short-term investors and those who have a certain tax status prefer these returns.

- **Dividends** are periodic payments to stockholders on the basis of earnings. Long-term investors and those with a certain tax status prefer these returns.

Private corporations are usually small and closely held, with less than fifty stockholders. Stockholder agreements often specify restrictive terms of transfer, and transfers of stock between existing stockholders are usually less restricted than transfers to new stockholders.

Public corporations offer common stock for sale to the investing public through a **primary offering** of common stock, which increases the capital available to the corporation. An **initial primary offering** is made when a company "goes public."

After the stock has been sold in a primary offering, it can be traded on one or more stock exchanges (the secondary or **stock market**). Holders of prepublic (seed) stock believe that going public will increase the value of their stock and the status of the corporation. Public companies, however, are subject to many regulations and filing requirements that private companies are not. The Securities and Exchange Commission (SEC) monitors and regulates corporate public financing activities.

There are many combinations of classes of stock and other securities. Corporations may have numerous classes of common stock that confer different terms and benefits on owners. Different classes may be

---

TERMS

capital gain† Financial gain resulting from the sale or exchange of capital assets.

dividend† A payment made by a corporation to its stockholders, either in cash (a cash dividend), in stock (a stock dividend), or out of surplus earnings.

private corporation† A close corporation or other privately held corporation, as distinguished from a corporation whose stock is traded on a stock exchange.

public corporation† A corporation whose stock is traded on a stock exchange, as opposed to a closely held corporation.

primary offering The first presentation of a stock issue to the public.

initial primary offering The first primary offering of a public corporation.

stock market† A market where securities are bought and sold.

used to provide **warrants** (opportunities to purchase additional stock at a future date at a specified price) to stockholders. There is also **preferred stock**, which in some ways is like a bond and in others like common stock.

The stock structure of a corporation is defined in its articles of incorporation, a document forming the corporation that is filed with the appropriate state agency. The articles define the maximum number of shares (units) of each type of stock that may be issued by the company.

Practical
Application
8–2

Jan: I think corporations are better than proprietorships and partnerships. These days you have to make sure you can't be sued personally for damages arising from business transactions.

Tad: But on the other hand, corporations are more work to administer, and it costs a lot to incorporate if you just have a small business. If you're worried about being sued, just buy business insurance.

Discuss Jan's and Tad's opinions. Research the relative costs in your jurisdiction.

Standard Financial Statements

The balance sheet and income statement introduced in Chapter 1 are the most widely used financial statements and are often produced monthly in a law office on an informal basis by internal accounting staff. Formal financial statements also include two other statements:

- The **statement of cash flows** is usually produced only when formal financial statements are issued. It illustrates businesses' sources and uses of cash during the year. Figure 8–6 illustrates such a statement.

- The **statement of retained earnings** (or proprietor's or partners' capital) shows the beginning balance, changes resulting from the year's operations, and the ending balance of the capital accounts arising from earnings. In corporations, dividend allotments are also included. Figure 8–7 illustrates partners' capital.

TERMS

warrant† A certificate issued by a corporation evidencing the right of its holder to receive a specified number of shares of stock in the corporation; i.e., a stock warrant or share warrant.

preferred stock† Corporate stock that is entitled to a priority over other classes of stock, usually common stock, in distribution of the profits of the corporation (i.e., dividends) and in distribution of the assets of the corporation in the event of dissolution or liquidation.

statement of cash flows A financial statement showing the flow of cash within a business.

statement of retained earnings A financial statement showing the activity of capital and retained earnings during a period.

FIGURE 8–6

Statement of Cash Flows

Carpenter & Cook

STATEMENT OF CASH FLOWS
Four Months to December 31, 1998

Opening Cash Balance		0
Cash Flow from Operations		(14,054)
Cash Flow from Financing		
P Carpenter (net)	17,000	
S Cook (net)	17,000	
		34,000
Cash Flow from Investing		
Computer Purchase		(10,100)
Cash at End of Period		
Petty Cash	100	
Operating Account	9,746	
		9,846

This is the statement fo cash flows I prepared from the cash basis financial statements. M.

FIGURE 8–7

Statement of Partner's Capital

Carpenter & Cook

STATEMENT OF PARTNERS' CAPITAL
December 31, 1998

	P Carpenter	S Cook	Total
Opening Capital (September 1, 1998)	0	0	0
Contributions	29,000	29,000	58,000
Income (Loss) from Period	(7,027)	(7,027)	(14,054)
Drawings for Period	(12,000)	(12,000)	(24,000)
Ending Capital	9,973	9,973	19,946

This is the statement of partners' capital I prepared form the cash basis financial statements. M.

At least once per year corporations produce formal financial statements for income tax purposes. Public corporations and larger private corporations also produce an annual report for their stockholders, creditors, and potential investors, presenting the financial statements and other supplementary accounting information as well as a narrative summary of the year's operations and future outlook.

Statements for corporations that have non–arm's-length shareholders are usually prepared by a designated accountant who is familiar with the standards for preparing financial reports for evaluation by external parties who are entitled to rely on the reports to make decisions about their relationship to and risk involving the business.

Case 8–4	Found: **Lawyer delivered a signed financial statement (of client) to bank, false and fraudulent in material respects, with the intent that the bank rely on the financial statement in extending credit.**

Ordered: (for this and other issues) Disbarment.

Real Property

Transfers of real property require accounting for the transaction for both vendor and purchaser. Some items such as the sale price are used in calculations for both parties. Other items such as the agent's commission affect only one party.

A number of **mortgages** are usually involved, especially in residential transfers where both the vendor and the purchaser are involved in other essentially simultaneous transfers. The vendor is purchasing a new residence, and the purchaser is selling a former residence.

Because most transfer dates do not coincide with a mortgage payment date, the interest owing for the partial period must be calculated. Normally, the **mortgagee** financial institution holding the (current) vendor's mortgage provides an interest payout figure effective on the proposed date of the transfer. However, payouts are sometimes a day or two later than expected, and a *per diem* amount is either provided by the mortgagee or calculated by the vendor's lawyer. In calculating *per diem* interest, a mortgage is treated like other loans. The principal is multiplied by the annual interest rate and by the number of days outstanding, and then divided by 365.

TERMS
---

mortgage†   A pledge of real property to secure a debt.

mortgagee†   The person to whom a mortgage is made; the lender.

The other components of transfer calculations depend on the jurisdiction and other factors specific to the property, such as the proration of taxes and provision of insurance coverage. Figure 8–8 illustrates a typical closing worksheet showing the calculations for both the vendor and purchaser.

Personal Income

Lawyers in fields of practice like personal injury, labor, and family law need information about their clients' and others' personal income.

CLOSING WORKSHEET

Whose Entry (B/S)	Item (RESPA Number)	Buyer Debit	Buyer Credit	Seller Debit	Seller Credit
B&S	Sales Price (101/401)	350,000			350,000
B	Earn. Money (201)		52,500		
S	Rltr's Comm. (700/703)			21,000	
B	Mortgate Loan (202)		245,00		
B	Loan Fee (802)	3,675			
B&S	Transfer Tax (1204)	2,625		4,375	
B&S	Fuel (1303)				1,500
B	Survey (1301)	375			
B	Appraisal (803)	250			
B	Credit Report (804)	90			
B	Interest Deposit (901)	855.82			
B	Tax Deposit (1004)	2,100			
B	Title Insur. (1108–10)	1,500			
B&S	Legal Fees (1107)	750		800	
B&S	Recording (1201)	90		30	
B&S	Fire&Haz. Ins. (111/411)	1,272.33			1,272.33
S	Mechanic's Lien (515)			2,250	
S	Termite Inspection (1302)			850	
S	Mortgage Payoff (504)			215,00	
B&S	R.E. Taxes (107/407)	4,579.73			4,579.73
	Totals	$369,662.88	297,500	244,305	357,352.06
	Needed to Close		72,162.88		
	Due to Seller			113,047.06	
	Balances	$369,662.88	369,662.88	357,352.06	357,352.06

Source: Kearns, The Law of Real Property (Lawyers Cooperative Publishing), p. 25

FIGURE 8–8 Real Property Transfer Worksheet.

If the client is the plaintiff (for example, in a tort action to recover loss of future income), it is important to schedule not only the normal income arising from employment as reported in an income tax return, but other monetary and nonmonetary benefits lost by deprivation of employment. For example, a store manager might receive discounts on purchases that do not appear in any official income records. Forfeiture of the use of a company vehicle, reduced professional development opportunities, and a decline in the social contacts consequent upon an elevated socioeconomic status are all real losses, whether or not they are easy to quantify.

Calculation of personal income often starts with a perusal of the client's previous two to five years' income tax returns. Passive income such as interest and dividends is usually not affected by the event related to the damages. Income derived from rental property and copyrights, however, is affected if the client can no longer perform the functions required or must hire someone else to perform them.

Practical Application 8–3	Mary: Our new client, the rock star Red Rocket, was injured in a car accident and can't make appearances for a year. She'll still have income from her recordings, but everyone knows you need to do concerts to keep the fans happy. Should we claim her lost royalties? How might we calculate them?

Answer Mary's questions.

Income calculations include:

- income from an employment or office, including directorships and self-employment
- perquisites of monetary value, such as a company vehicle or annual conferences
- opportunities for marketing a product, or intellectual or intangible property owned by the client
- accumulation of time and employer's contributions toward a pension or retirement plan

Case 8–5	Found: **Lawyer failed to assert claim of wife (client) against husband's military pension.** Ordered: Lawyer negligent.

These amounts are usually determinable but may occur unevenly over the time period in question.

In certain situations, income loss is expanded to include:

- loss of professional status and advancement;

- lost opportunities for travel, sabbatical time, or other educational opportunities inherent in the position; and

- loss of social benefits and status resulting from an inability to contribute to political, community, and volunteer activities.

These amounts are more difficult to determine and usually must be estimated. Law firms hire economic consultants to perform complex calculations for income loss and other damages that require a significant amount of research.

Quantum in Torts

Damages resulting from torts include not only income loss but other personal losses as well. Pain and suffering damages are generally subject to precedent, but others such as loss of childcare or homemaker benefits are determinable and often must be calculated on an individual basis.

There are also direct expenses incurred as a result of injury, including prescriptions and medical treatment, in-home care, and transportation to medical appointments. Lawyers ask clients to record these expenses, as they are often completely recoverable in the action. Figure 8–9 illustrates a form that law firms can provide to clients in a motor vehicle personal injury action.

Practical Application 8–4

Andrew: I got this statement of lost earnings from the plaintiff's counsel in the Twin Mountain case, but something is wrong. The plaintiff will not have to pay income tax on the damages, so I think they should be subtracted from the loss.

Do you agree with Andrew? Why or why not?

Labor Law

Clients who experience loss of income and/or status as a result of a dispute with their employers often seek compensation through administrative channels. Many states' enactments are intended to ensure that an employee can act *pro se* with the assistance of a state board. Some employees' situations, however, indicate that they should be represented by a lawyer, often because a particular government agency is not equipped to recognize and assert all of the client's claims or the claims are conflicting between jurisdictions.

Carpenter & Cook

CLIENT THERAPY REPORT

Please help us to help you!

It is very important that you make a note of all of your therapy and medical appointments and expenses, so that we can help you to recover these costs.

Please also keep a diary in the separate notebook that we have given to you. You should make at least one entry for each day, even if you do not feel that your condition changed that day.

APPOINTMENTS: Please make a note of all of your medical and therapy appointments.

Date	Doctor	Cost	Taxi	Description/Outcome

HOME CARE AND HELPER LIST: Please note your home care and other assistance you require because of your accident or illness.

Date	Helper	Agency	Cost	Service Description

PRESCRIPTION AND OTHER EXPENSES: Please list all of your prescription and other expenses that you have paid because of your accident or illness.

Date	Doctor	Cost	Description

We give these expense forms to our personal injury clients so that they remember to keep track of all of their injury related costs. M.

FIGURE 8–9   Personal Injury Client Expenses Form

Case 8–6

Found: Lawyer failed to take action on client's tort claim and failed to file workers' compensation claim for several months, constituting neglect.

Ordered: (for this and other issues) Disbarment.

In labor law cases, often there is only a loss of income and some type of nonpecuniary damages such as mental anguish. Labor issues in an organized (unionized) work environment are generally undertaken by the union's lawyers.

Family Law

Full disclosure of income is important in family law because the futures of children and other dependents are involved. However, spouses tend to minimize their own incomes and maximize each other's, creating disagreements surrounding equity issues in spousal and child support.

Permanent spousal support (alimony) is becoming less common, although many courts award rehabilitative alimony to a spouse who has foregone career advancement to be the family's primary homemaker and childcare provider. As divorce and remarriage create more step- and half-relationships within families, courts and even well-intentioned parents and their new spouses have trouble establishing and maintaining equitable support agreements.

Practical Application 8–5

Judith: Our latest family law case is very complicated, because every child of the couple has a different relationship to the parents and each other. We are going to have a fight about support payments, I know that, but I'm not sure which children get priority for support. Is it natural children, then step-children? Or are they all treated the same?

Research your state laws on the priorities for support payments.

Attachment and Garnishment

Attachment (postjudgment) and garnishment (prejudgment) orders provide a litigation creditor with access to the financial resources, both assets and income, of the debtor. Creditors naturally prefer to obtain assets in satisfaction of the judgment as quickly as possible, but assets are often either insufficient or cannot be located or properly garnished or attached.

Where the available assets are insufficient to satisfy the order, creditors attach the income of an individual or corporation. If an individual's employment income is attached, the order is served on the employer, who withholds the amount stipulated in the order. Orders attaching employment income are limited to ensure that the employee receives a reasonable subsistence amount. If the debtor is self-employed or a corporation, customers or clients who owe the debtor money are served with the order(s).

Personal Assets

Like personal income, personal assets may be subject to attachment or garnishment in a litigation matter. Examples of personal assets are:

- money in currency or deposited with a financial institution;

- income-generating assets of self-employed people, including some intellectual property;

- ownership equity in some kinds of businesses;

- the equity in real property, owned solely or jointly;

- personal property (chattels) that can readily be sold, such as vehicles, jewelry, coin and stamp collections, works of art, and valuable animals; and

- personal and household effects that are required to maintain a reasonable standard of living (clothes, furniture, and household pets). These are usually not attachable if they are considered basic necessities.

In most professional businesses, including corporations, the portion of the equity owned by an individual that is attachable to satisfy a judgment is restricted to the amount of capital that can be paid out. It is not appropriate for lay or professional outsiders to own any voting equity or other controlling interest in a professional practice.

Case 8–7	Found:	**Lawyer-partner's widow sought to claim goodwill of deceased husband's share of partnership through fee-splitting arrangement with surviving partners.**
	Ordered:	Contract illegal and against public policy and therefore not enforceable.

A creditor may obtain an order requiring that all distributions of capital in a partnership be surrendered, but the creditor cannot take control of the voting interest. Certain types of partnerships and non-professional corporations, where ownership agreements stipulate that transfers of ownership be approved by the other owners, may also be protected from an arm's-length creditor exercising control over the business.

In family law, it is becoming common for assets such as a company pension to be claimed in part by the nonbeneficiary spouse. Likewise, the value of one spouse's education may be claimed when the other actually paid for the education or at least supported the spouse during educational years. Increasingly, estimates of the monetary value of each spouse's contribution to the family unit, whether or not the contribution is recognized outside the family unit, are recognized as being assets.

Practical Application 8–6

Peter: Certain types of assets are only valuable in one person's hands. Another person would not be able to use them. An example is goodwill in a professional practice like law. No one else can use it.

Paul: Not necessarily. A lawyer who purchased the practice might receive some value from the established client base.

Peter: Maybe, but goodwill is very hard to quantify, and when it's transferred, it would be even harder to determine a dollar value.

What good points do Peter and Paul make? What are the weaknesses of their positions?

Asset Inventory

Producing complete asset inventories for the client is important in all fields of practice, even if some assets are not attachable. The lawyer must review all items in the context of the case and precedent law to prepare for the opposing party's assertions about them.

Case 8–8

Found: **Lawyer engaged in pattern of deception and misrepresentation in divorce action concerning client's assets and liabilities, including counsel fees, to obtain a more favorable settlement.**

Ordered: (for this and other issues) Two-year suspension.

Many clients forget to mention resources that they have never considered to be assets or provisions such as disability and other insurance that confer a benefit only under certain circumstances.

Lawyers may find themselves in a difficult position if property they hold in trust related to a client's matter becomes subject to creditors' claims. Although lawyers must act in their clients' best interests, they also must abide by the law, both letter and intent.

Practical Application 8–7

Mr. Bush: I'm a little bit worried about my new bankruptcy client. She gave me a fee advance, which I deposited to the trust account, but I'm not sure whether another creditor can attach our trust account and get the money. It's quite a large sum, intended to cover all of our legal fees.

Should Mr. Bush be worried? Why or why not?

Insolvency

The law of equity provides that a person unable to meet financial obligations may be forgiven debts under certain circumstances and allowed, during the period between petition and discharge, to maintain a reasonable though not extravagant, existence.

Case 8–9

Found: **Lawyer's acknowledged inexperience in bankruptcy and failure to file petition (on behalf of client) for one year, during which client's wages continued to be garnished, constitutes neglect and failure to seek the lawful objectives of the client.**

Ordered: Reprimand.

Creditors' claims, including claims secured by property, must be satisfied to the extent possible while allowing the debtor sufficient resources to start afresh and become self-supporting. Most bankruptcies are voluntary; the debtor files a petition to seek relief from harassment by creditors. Involuntary bankruptcy is commenced by unsecured creditors, acting alone or together, who hold in aggregate a statutory minimum claim. Technically, a petition might be filed in which the assets at liquidated value are sufficient to satisfy the creditors' claims, but this is not usually the case. Most petitioners in bankruptcy have debts far in excess of the most optimistic liquidation value of their assets.

In reviewing the financial situation of debtors, lawyers need complete knowledge of their income and assets and the priorities of creditors' claims. In some cases, a declaration of bankruptcy that seems inevitable can be handled as a reorganization of debts that provides substantial satisfaction of creditors' claims.

Grounds for refusing to grant a discharge from bankruptcy include failure to keep accurate records of transactions. If the law firm keeps these records, they must be accurate and current. The number of forms and schedules required to summarize the records depends on the nature of the debtor's assets and liabilities. Typically, however, the schedules in Form 6 illustrated in Figure 8–10 must be completed.

Official Form No. 6 Schedules of Assets and Liabilities

[Caption as in Form No. 1]

Schedule A.—Statement of All Liabilities of Debtor.

Schedules A-1, A-2 and A-3 must include all the claims against the debtor or the debtor's property as of the date of the filing of the petition by or against the debtor.

Schedule A-1.—Creditors having priority.

(1) Nature of claim	(2) Name of creditor and complete mailing address including zip code	(3) Specify when claim was incurred and the consideration therefor; when claim is subject to setoff, evidenced by a judgment, negotiable instrument, or other writing, or incurred as partner or joint contractor, so indicate; specify name of any partner or joint contractor on any debt	(4) Indicate if claim is contingent, unliquidated, or disputed	(5) Amount of claim
a. Wages, salary, and commissions, including vacation, severance and sick leave pay owing to employees not exceeding $2,000 to each, earned within 90 days before filing of petition or cessation of business (if earlier specify date).				$ . . . .
b. Contributions to employee benefit plans for services rendered within 180 days before filing of petition or cessation of business (if earlier specify date)				$ . . . .
c. Claims of farmers, not exceeding $2,000 for each individual, pursuant to 11 U.S.C. § 507(a)(5)(A).				$ . . . .
d. Claims of United States fishermen, not exceeding $2,000 for each individual, pursuant to 11 U.S.C. § 507(a)(5)(B).				$ . . . .
e. Deposits by individuals, not exceeding $900 for each for purchase, lease, or rental of property or services for personal, family, or household use that were not delivered or provided.				$ . . . .
f. Taxes owing [itemize by type of tax and taxing authority]				
(1) To the United States				$ . . . .
(2) To any state				$ . . . .
(3) To any other taxing authority				$ . . . .
Total				$ . . . .

FIGURE 8–10   Form 6

Schedule A-2.—Creditors holding security

(1) Name of creditor and complete mailing address including zip code	(2) Description of security and date when obtained by creditor	(3) Specify when claim was incurred and the consideration therefor; when claim is subject to setoff, evidenced by a judgment, negotiable instrument, or other writing, or incurred as partner or joint contractor, so indicate; specify name of any partner or joint contractor on any debt	(4) Indicate if claim is contingent, unliquidated, or disputed	(5) Market Value	(6) Amount of claim without deduction of value of security
		Total			$.....

Schedule A-3.—Creditors having unsecured claims without priority.

(1) Name of creditor [including last known holder of any negotiable instrument] and complete mailing address including zip code	(2) Specify when claim was incurred and the consideration therefor; when claim is contingent, unliquidated, disputed, subject to setoff, evidenced by a judgment, negotiable instrument, or other writing, or incurred as partner or joint contractor, so indicate; specify name of any partner or joint contractor on any debt	(3) Indicate if claim is contingent, unliquidated, or disputed	(4) Amount of claim
	Total		$.....

Schedule B—Statement of All Property of Debtor

Schedules B-1, B-2, B-3, and B-4 must include all property of the debtor as of the date of the filing of the petition by or against the debtor.

Schedule B-1.—Real Property

Description and location of all real property in which debtor has an interest [including equitable and future interests, interests in estates by the entirety, community property, life estates, leaseholds, and rights and powers exercisable for the debtor's own benefit]	Nature of interest [specify all deeds and written instruments relating thereto]	Market value of debtor's interest without deduction for secured claims listed in Schedule A-2 or exemptions claimed in Schedule B-4
	Total	$.....

FIGURE 8–10 Form 6 *(Continued)*

<u>Schedule B-2.—Personal Property</u>

Type of Property	Description and Location	Market value of debtor's interest without deduction for secured claims listed on Schedule A-2 or exemptions claimed in Schedule B-4
		Total $ . . . .
a. Cash on hand		$. . . . . .
b. Deposits of money with banking institutions, savings and loan associations, brokerage houses, credit unions, public utility companies, landlords and others		. . . . . .
c. Household goods, supplies and furnishings		. . . . . .
d. Books, pictures, and other art objects; stamp, coin and other collections		. . . . . .
e. Wearing apparel, jewelry, firearms, sports equipment and other personal possessions		. . . . . .
f. Automobiles, trucks, trailers and other vehicles		. . . . . .
g. Boats, motors and their accessories		. . . . . .
h. Livestock, poultry and other animals		. . . . . .
i. Farming equipment, supplies and implements		. . . . . .
j. Office equipment, furnishings and supplies		. . . . . .
k. Machinery, fixtures, equipment and supplies [other than those listed in Items j and l] used in business		. . . . . .
l. Inventory		. . . . . .
m. Tangible personal property of any other description		. . . . . .
n. Patents, copyrights, licenses, franchises and other general intangibles [specify all documents and writings relating thereto]		. . . . . .
o. Government and corporate bonds and other negotiable and nonnegotiable instruments		. . . . . .
p. Other liquidated debts owing debtor		. . . . . .
q. Contingent and unliquidated claims of every nature, including counterclaims of the debtor [give estimated value of each]		. . . .
r. Interests in insurance policies [name insurance company of each policy and itemize surrender or refund value of each]		. . . . . .
s. Annuities [itemize and name each issuer]		. . . . . .
t. Stock and interests in incorporated and unincorporated companies [itemize separately]		. . . . . .
u. Interests in partnerships		. . . . . .
v. Equitable and future interests, life estates, and right or powers exercisable for the benefit of the debtor (other than those listed in schedule B-1) [specify all written instruments relating thereto]		. . . . . .
	Total	$. . . . . .

FIGURE 8–10   Form 6 *(Continued)*

<u>Schedule B-3.—Property not otherwise scheduled</u>

Type of Property	Description and Location	Market value of debtor's interest without deduction for secured claims listed Schedule A-2 or exemption claimed in Schedule B-4
a. Property transferred under assignment for benefit of creditors, within 120 days prior to filing of petition [specify date of assignment, name and address of assignee, amount realized therefrom by the assignee, and disposition of proceeds so far as known to debtor]		$ . . . . . .
b. Property of any kind not otherwise scheduled		. . . . . .
	Total	$ . . . . . .

Debtor selects the following property as exempt pursuant to 11 U.S.C. § 522(d) *[or the laws of the State of . . . .]*

<u>Schedule B-4.—Property claimed as exempt</u>

Type of Property	Location, description, and so far as relevant to the claim of exemption, present use of property	Specify statute creating the exemption	Value claimed exempt
			$ . . . . . .
			. . . . . .
		Total	$ . . . . . .

<u>Summary of debts and property.</u>
[From the statements of the debtor in Schedules A and B]

Schedule		Total
	Debts	
A-1/a,b	Wages, etc. having priority	$ . . . . . .
A-1(c)	Deposits of money	. . . . . .
A-1/d(1)	Taxes owing United States	. . . . . .
A-1/d(2)	Taxes owing states	. . . . . .
A-1/d(3)	Taxes owing other taxing authorities	. . . . . .
A-2	Secured claims	. . . . . .
A-3	Unsecured claims without priority	. . . . . .
	Schedule A total	$ . . . . . .
	Property	
B-1	Real property [total value]	$ . . . . . .
B-2/a	Cash on hand	. . . . . .
B-2/b	Deposits	. . . . . .
B-2/c	Household goods	. . . . . .
B-2/d	Books, pictures, and collections	. . . . . .

FIGURE 8–10   Form 6 *(Continued)*

B-2/e	Wearing apparel and personal possessions	. . . .
B-2/f	Automobiles and other vehicles	. . . .
B-2/g	Boats, motors, and accessories	. . . .
B-2/h	Livestock and other animals	. . . .
B-2/i	Farming supplies and implements	. . . .
B-2/j	Office equipment and supplies	. . . .
B-2/k	Machinery, equipment, and supplies used in business	. . . .
B-2/l	Inventory	. . . .
B-2/m	Other tangible personal property	. . . .
B-2/n	Patents and other general intangibles	. . . .
B-2/o	Bonds and other instruments	. . . .
B-2/p	Other liquidated debts	. . . .
B-2/q	Contingent and unliquidated claims	. . . .
B-2/r	Interests in insurance policies	. . . .
B-2/s	Annuities	. . . .
B-2/t	Interests in corporations and unincorporated companies	. . . .
B-2/u	Interests in partnerships	. . . .
B-2/v	Equitable and future interests, rights, and powers in personalty	. . . .
B-3/a	Property assigned for benefit of creditors	. . . .
B-3/b	Property not otherwise scheduled	. . . .

Schedule B total $. . . . . . .

Unsworn Declaration under Penalty of Perjury
of Individual to Schedules A and B

I, ..., declare under penalty of perjury that I have read the foregoing schedules, consisting of . . . . sheets, and that they are true and correct to the best of my knowledge, information and belief. Executed on . . . .

Signature: . . . .

Unsworn Declaration under Penalty of Perjury
on Behalf of Corporation or Partnership
to Schedules A and B

I, ..., [the president *or other officer* or an authorized agent of the corporation] *[or* a member *or* an authorized agent of the partnership] named as debtor in this case, declare under penalty of perjury that I have read the foregoing schedules, consisting of . . . . sheets, and that they are true and correct to the best of my knowledge, information, and belief. Executed on . . . .

Signature: . . . .

Source: Schneeman, *Paralegals in American Law* (Delmar Publishers), pp. 676–80 (5 pages illustrated).

FIGURE 8–10   Form 6 *(Continued)*

The intention to declare bankruptcy is often known first to the debtor far in advance of the creditors' knowledge that the individual is unable to meet lawful financial obligations. At the time of declaration of bankruptcy, the most recent transactions of the bankrupt are subject to review because of the concern that debtors are tempted to confer fraudulent preferences or make fraudulent conveyances in the period immediately preceding the filing of the petition. Prior to discharge, the debtor is permitted to keep certain *exempt assets* defined under state and/or federal law. After filing a petition in bankruptcy, the debtor may not dispose of nonexempt assets without the court's permission.

Creditors' Claims

After satisfaction of the secured portion of secured creditors' claims and the liquidation of nonexempt assets, the estate is distributed to creditors according to claim priorities under the Bankruptcy Code, contrary to the popular belief of both debtors and creditors that earlier (older) claims have priority over newer ones. Figure 8–11 lists the creditors' claims and bankruptcy expenses that have priority.

Nondischargeable claims survive a bankruptcy. The debtor is responsible for them even after the discharge of the majority of creditors. Common nondischargeable debts include most debts incurred fraudulently or otherwise culpably, obligations toward dependents (alimony and child support), and some types of taxes.

Estates

Some estate record-keeping may be performed by the firm even if the lawyer is not a trustee of any property but is simply counseling executors in the discharge of their duties.

Case 8–10

Found: **Lawyer failed to supervise nonlawyer in record-keeping of estates.**

Ordered: Three-month suspension.

Many lay executors can handle most of the administration of small uncomplicated estates themselves and hire lawyers only to answer specific questions and review the final accounting, such as the Fiduciary's Account illustrated in Figure 8–12.

In the process of handling the estate, the executor must locate and notify all parties who may have an interest in the estate so that legitimate claims against the estate are registered.

FIGURE 8–11

Priority of Claims
under the
Bankruptcy Code

Creditors' Claims and Bankruptcy
Expenses That Have Priority

1. Administrative expenses allowed under § 503(b) of the Bankruptcy Code, and any fees and charges assessed against the bankruptcy estate under chapter 123 of title 28.
2. Unsecured claims allowed under § 502(f) of the Bankruptcy Code.
3. Certain allowed unsecured claims for wages, salaries, or commissions, including vacation, severance, and sick leave pay.
4. Certain allowed unsecured claims for contributions to an employee benefit plan.
5. Certain allowed unsecured claims of persons engaged in the production or raising grain, against a debtor who owns or operates a grain storage facility, or persons engaged as United States fishermen against a debtor who has acquired fish or fish produce from a fisherman through a sale or conversion, and who is engaged in operating a fish produce storage or processing facility. These claims have priority to the extent of $2,000 for each such individual.
6. Allowed unsecured claims of individuals, to the extent of $900 for each, arising from the deposit, before the commencement of the bankruptcy case, of money in connection with the purchase, lease, or rental of property, or the purchase of services, for the personal, family, or household use of such individuals, that were not delivered or provided.
7. Certain allowed unsecured claims of governmental units, to the extent that such claims are for:
   a. certain income taxes;
   b. certain property taxes;
   c. taxes required to be collected or withheld and for which the debtor is liable in whatever capacity;
   d. employment taxes;
   e. excise taxes; and
   f. customs duties arising out of the importation of merchandise, and penalties related to claims of a kind specified in this paragraph and in compensation for actual pecuniary loss.
8. Certain allowed unsecured claims based upon any commitment by the debtor to the Federal Deposit Insurance Corporation, the Resolution Trust Corporation, the Director of the Office of Thrift Supervision, the Comptroller of the Currency, or the Board of Governors of the Federal Reserve System, or their predecessors or successors to maintain the capital of an insured depository institution.

Source: Schneeman, *Paralegals in American Law* (Delmar Publishers), p. 681.

PROBATE COURT OF _____ COUNTY, OHIO

ESTATE OF _____, DECEASED

Case No. _____ Docket _____ Page _____

FIDUCIARY'S ACCOUNT

(For Executors and all Administrators)

The fiduciary offers an account of his trust, given below and on the attached itemized statement of receipts and disbursements, and accompanying vouchers. The fiduciary says that to his knowledge the account is correct, and asks that it be approved and settled.

[Check one of the following four paragraphs]

☐ This is a partial account. A statement of the assets remaining in the fiduciary's hands is attached.

☐ This is a final account. A statement of the assets remaining in the fiduciary's hands for distribution to the beneficiaries is attached.

☐ This is a distributive account, and the fiduciary asks to be discharged from his trust upon its approval and settlement.

☐ This is a final and distributive account, and the fiduciary asks to be discharged from his trust upon its approval and settlement.

[Complete if this is a partial account, or if one or more accounts have previously been filed in the estate]
The period of this account is from

_____ to _____

[Complete if applicable] Accounts previously filed in this estate, the accounting periods, and the fiduciary and attorney fees paid for each period, are as follows:

Date Filed	Accounting Period	Fiduciary Fees Paid	Attorney Fees Paid
		$	$

13.0 FIDUCIARY'S ACCOUNT

FIGURE 8–12   Fiduciary Account

This account is recaptivated as follows:

RECEIPTS

Personal property of decedent (not sold) . . . . $_____

Proceeds from sale of personal property . . . . _____

Real estate of decedent (not sold) . . . . _____

Proceeds from sale of real estate . . . . _____

Income . . . . _____

Other receipts . . . . _____

Total receipts . . . . $ _____

DISBURSEMENTS

Fiduciary fees [this accounting period] . . . . $_____

Attorney fees [this accounting period] . . . . _____

Other administration costs and expenses . . . . _____

Debts and Claims against estate . . . . _____

Ohio and federal estate taxes . . . . _____

Personal property distributed in kind . . . . _____

Real property transferred . . . . _____

Other distribution to beneficiaries . . . . _____

Total disbursements . . . . $ _____

BALANCE REMAINING IN FIDUCIARY'S HANDS . . . . $ _____

_____
Fiduciary

ENTRY SETTING HEARING AND ORDERING NOTICE

The Court sets _____ at _____ o'clock ____ .M. as the date and time for hearing the above account, and orders notice of the hearing to be given as provided by law and the Rules of Civil Procedure.

_____   _____
Date   Probate Judge

Source: Brown, *Administration of Wills, Trusts and Estates* (Delmar Publishers), Figure 12–18, pp. 312–13.

FIGURE 8–12   Fiduciary Account (*Continued*)

Case 8–11   Found: **Lawyer failed to determine existence of next of kin and transferred estate assets to spouse.**

Ordered: Indefinite suspension from the practice of law.

The executor manages the inventory records of the deceased's estate, including the description and location of all items of property, and dispositions where the proceeds go to the estate generally as opposed to going to a beneficiary in the original condition and form. Estates involving real property not held in joint tenancy and other valuable property not bequeathed directly to a beneficiary usually require an appraisal of all valuable property, with a supporting schedule of assets as illustrated in Figure 8–13.

Complicated estates subject to numerous and/or disputed claims require a schedule of claims as illustrated in Figure 8–14.

In insolvent estates, where the claims exceed the value of the property, claims are paid according to priorities defined in state probate codes.

Case 8–12   Found: **Lawyer, as executor, was incompetent in failing to discover estate assets that would satisfy county's claim against property for nonpayment of taxes.**

Ordered: Lawyer placed on probation.

Court-Awarded Costs

Courts award costs to successful parties to mitigate the expense of litigation. While firms may have claims on these costs through the client, the costs themselves belong to the client. The firm normally prepares the cost statement for the court's approval, receives the cost amount in trust, and disburses it to the client or applies it to the client's outstanding bills, already prepared according to the fee agreement.

Although the court may take the fee agreement into account in awarding costs, costs applied for do not have to relate to the fee agreement.

Case 8–13   Found: **Although not consistent with the fee agreement, costs claimed were not unreasonable by accepted standards.**

Ordered: Costs awarded on quantum meruit basis.

PROBATE COURT OF _____ COUNTY, OHIO

ESTATE OF _____, DECEASED

Case No. _____ Docket _____ Page

SCHEDULE OF ASSETS

[Attach to inventory and appraisal]

Page _____ of _____ pages.

[Insert a check in the column "Appraiser" opposite an item if it was valued by the appraiser. Leave blank if the readily ascertainable value was determined by Fiduciary]

Item	Appraiser	Value
		$

FORM 6.1 SCHEDULE OF ASSETS

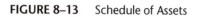

FIGURE 8–13   Schedule of Assets

Page _____ of _____ pages

Item	Appraiser	Value
		$

Fiduciary

Source: Brown, *Administration of Wills, Trusts and Estates* (Figure 12–16, pp. 305–306.)

FIGURE 8–13   Schedule of Assets (*Continued*)

Prob. 48

PROBATE COURT OF _____ COUNTY, OHIO

ESTATE OF _____, DECEASED

Case No. _____ Docket _____ Page

SCHEDULE OF CLAIMS
Revised Code Sec. 2117.16 to 2117.17, 2117.25

[Use extra sheets if necessary]

The fiduciary says that to his knowledge this schedule lists all claims against decedent or his estate. Such claims are recapitulated as follows:

Claims allowed . . . . $ _____

Claims rejected, contingent, or in suit . . . . $ _____

Total . . . . $ _____

[Check if applicable] ☐ The surviving spouse is the sole legatee and devisee under decedent's Will, and has not mainfested an intention to take against it. It is therefore unnecessary to cite the surviving spouse to make an election.

_____
Fiduciary

[Under "Footnotes" opposite an item requiring explanation, place the number of the appropriate footnote. Such notes should be included on the reverse to explain: any security for claims; maturity dates of claims not due; contingent claims; claims in suit; and dates of rejection of rejected claims]

Name and Address of Claimant	Amount Claimed	Payment Class	Date Presented	Date Allowed	Foot- Notes
	$				

Form 7.0 SCHEDULE OF CLAIMS

FIGURE 8–14 Schedule of Claims

Name and Address of Claimant	Amount Claimed	Payment Class	Date Presented	Date Allowed	Foot-Notes
	$				

FOOTNOTES

Source: Brown, *Administration of Wills, Trusts, and Estates* (Figure 12–17, pp. 307–308.)

FIGURE 8–14   Schedule of Claims

In a judgment or award, costs are added to the amount the client receives. In settlements, however, they are sometimes included with the accepted offer. If the firm is billing on a fixed fee or hourly rate basis, it simply collects its bill, often through a trust transfer, and the balance is remitted to the client. In a contingency fee situation, lawyers must be careful not to charge a percentage fee on amounts specifically agreed upon as costs.

Comprehensive Exercises

1. Using the information about the computer loan in Chapter 1, Exercise A(3), calculate the interest payments, paid at the end of each month, and show that the interest cost agrees with the Income Statement in Figure 1–2.

2. Design a checklist of personal income. Include unusual items that would be important to a person who derived income from them.

3. Design an assets checklist for a family law client. Separate the family from the personal assets.

APPENDIX A

ABA Rules

CLIENT-LAWYER RELATIONSHIP

RULE 1.5

Fees

(a) A lawyer's fee shall be reasonable. The factors to be considered in determining the reasonableness of a fee include the following:

(1) the time and labor required, the novelty and difficulty of the questions involved, and the skill requisite to perform the legal service properly;

(2) the likelihood, if apparent to the client, that the acceptance of the particular employment will preclude other employment by the lawyer;

(3) the fee customarily charged in the locality for similar legal services;

(4) the amount involved and the results obtained;

(5) the time limitations imposed by the client or by the circumstances;

(6) the nature and length of the professional relationship with the client;

(7) the experience, reputation, and ability of the lawyer or lawyers performing the services; and

(8) whether the fee is fixed or contingent.

(b) When the lawyer has not regularly represented the client, the basis or rate of the fee shall be communicated to the client, preferably in writing, before or within a reasonable time after commencing the representation.

(c) A fee may be contingent on the outcome of the matter for which the service is rendered, except in a matter in which a contingent fee is prohibited by paragraph (d) or other law. A contingent fee agreement shall be in writing and shall state the method by which the fee is to be determined, including the percentage or percentages that shall accrue to the lawyer in the event of settlement, trial or appeal, litigation and other expenses to be deducted from the recovery, and whether such expenses are to be deducted before or after the contingent fee is calculated. Upon conclusion of a contingent fee matter, the lawyer shall provide the client with a written statement stating the outcome of the matter and, if there is a recovery, showing the remittance to the client and the method of its determination.

(d) A lawyer shall not enter into an arrangement for, charge, or collect:

(1) any fee in a domestic relations matter, the payment or amount of which is contingent upon the securing of a divorce or upon the amount of alimony or support, or property settlement in lieu thereof; or

(2) a contingent fee for representing a defendant in a criminal case.

(e) A division of a fee between lawyers who are not in the same firm may be made only if:

(1) the division is in proportion to the services performed by each lawyer or, by written agreement with the client, each lawyer assumes joint responsibility for the representation;

(2) the client is advised of and does not object to the participation of all the lawyers involved; and

(3) the total fee is reasonable.

RULE 1.7

Conflict of Interest: General Rule

(a) A lawyer shall not represent a client if the representation of that client will be directly adverse to another client, unless:

(1) the lawyer reasonably believes the representation will not adversely affect the relationship with the other client; and

(2) each client consents after consultation.

(b) A lawyer shall not represent a client if the representation of that client may be materially limited by the lawyer's responsibilities to another client or to a third person, or by the lawyer's own interests, unless:

(1) the lawyer reasonably believes the representation will not be adversely affected; and

(2) the client consents after consultation. When representation of multiple clients in a single matter is undertaken, the consultation shall include explanation of the implications of the common representation and the advantages and risks involved.

RULE 1.15

Safekeeping Property

(a) A lawyer shall hold property of clients or third persons that is in a lawyer's possession in connection with a representation separate from the lawyer's own property. Funds shall be kept in a separate account maintained in the state where the lawyer's office is situated, or elsewhere with the consent of the client or third person. Other property shall be identified as such and appropriately safeguarded. Complete records of such account funds and other property shall be kept by the lawyer and shall be preserved for a period of (five years) after termination of the representation.

(b) Upon receiving funds or other property in which a client or third person has an interest, a lawyer shall promptly notify the client or third person. Except as stated in this rule or otherwise permitted by law or by agreement with the client, a lawyer shall promptly deliver to the client or third person any funds or other property that the client or third person is entitled to receive and, upon request by the client or third person, shall promptly render a full accounting regarding such property.

(c) When in the course of representation a lawyer is in possession of property in which both the lawyer and another person claim interests, the property shall be kept separate by the lawyer until there is an accounting and severance of their interests. If a dispute arises concerning their respective interests, the portion in dispute shall be kept separate by the lawyer until the dispute is resolved.

LAW FIRMS AND ASSOCIATIONS

RULE 5.1

Responsibilities of a Partner or Supervisory Lawyer

(a) A partner in a law firm shall make reasonable efforts to ensure that the firm has in effect measures giving reasonable assurance that all lawyers in the firm conform to the Rules of Professional Conduct.

(b) A lawyer having direct supervisory authority over another lawyer shall make reasonable efforts to ensure that the other lawyer conforms to the Rules of Professional Conduct.

(c) A lawyer shall be responsible for another lawyer's violation of the Rules of Professional Conduct if:

(1) the lawyer orders or, with knowledge of the specific conduct, ratifies the conduct involved; or

(2) the lawyer is a partner in the law firm in which the other lawyer practices, or has direct supervisory authority over the other lawyer, and knows of the conduct at a time when its consequences can be avoided or mitigated but fails to take reasonable remedial action.

RULE 5.3

Responsibilities Regarding Nonlawyer Assistants

With respect to a nonlawyer employed or retained by or associated with a lawyer:

(a) a partner in a law firm shall make reasonable efforts to ensure that the firm has in effect measures giving reasonable assurance that the person's conduct is compatible with the professional obligations of the lawyer;

(b) a lawyer having direct supervisory authority over the nonlawyer shall make reasonable efforts to ensure that the person's conduct is compatible with the professional obligations of the lawyer; and

(c) a lawyer shall be responsible for conduct of such a person that would be a violation of the Rules of Professional Conduct if engaged in by a lawyer if:

(1) the lawyer orders or, with the knowledge of the specific conduct, ratifies the conduct involved; or

(2) the lawyer is a partner in the law firm in which the person is employed, or has direct supervisory authority over the person, and knows of the conduct at a time when its consequences can be avoided or mitigated but fails to take reasonable remedial action.

RULE 5.4

Professional Independence of a Lawyer

(a) A lawyer or law firm shall not share legal fees with a non-lawyer, except that:

(1) an agreement by a lawyer with the lawyer's firm, partner, or associate may provide for the payment of money, over a reasonable period of time after the lawyer's death, to the lawyer's estate or to one or more specified persons;

(2) a lawyer who purchases the practice of a deceased, disabled or disappeared lawyer may, pursuant to the provisions of Rule 1.17, pay to the estate or other representative of that lawyer the agreed-upon purchase price; and

(3) a lawyer or law firm may include nonlawyer employees in a compensation or retirement plan, even though the plan is based in whole or in part on a profit-sharing arrangement.

(b) A lawyer shall not form a partnership with a nonlawyer if any of the activities of the partnership consist of the practice of law.

(c) A lawyer shall not permit a person who recommends, employs, or pays the lawyer to render legal services for another to direct or regulate the lawyer's professional judgment in rendering such legal services.

(d) A lawyer shall not practice with or in the form of a professional corporation or association authorized to practice law for a profit, if:

(1) a nonlawyer owns any interest therein, except that a fiduciary representative of the estate of a lawyer may hold the stock or interest of the lawyer for a reasonable time during administration;

(2) a nonlawyer is a corporate director or officer thereof; or

(3) a nonlawyer has the right to direct or control the professional judgment of a lawyer.

PUBLIC SERVICE

RULE 6.1

Voluntary Pro Bono Publico *Service*

A lawyer should aspire to render at least (50) hours of pro bono publico legal services per year. In fulfilling this responsibility, the lawyer should:

(a) provide a substantial majority of the (50) hours of legal services without fee or expectation of fee to:

(1) persons of limited means or

(2) charitable, religious, civic, community, governmental and educational organizations in matters which are designed primarily to address the needs of persons of limited means; and

(b) provide any additional services through:

(1) delivery of legal services at no fee or substantially reduced fee to individuals, groups or organizations seeking to secure or protect civil rights, civil liberties or public rights, or charitable, religious, civic, community, governmental and educational organizations in matters in furtherance of their organizational purposes, where the payment of standard legal fees would significantly deplete the organization's economic resources or would be otherwise inappropriate;

(2) delivery of legal services at a substantially reduced fee to persons of limited means; or

(3) participation in activities for improving the law, the legal system or the legal profession.

In addition, a lawyer should voluntarily contribute financial support to organizations that provide legal services to persons of limited means.

INFORMATION ABOUT LEGAL SERVICES

RULE 7.1

Communications Concerning a Lawyer's Services

A lawyer shall not make a false or misleading communication about the lawyer or the lawyer's services. A communication is false or misleading if it:

(a) contains a material misrepresentation of fact or law, or omits a fact necessary to make the statement considered as a whole not materially misleading;

(b) is likely to create an unjustified expectation about results the lawyer can achieve, or states or implies that the lawyer can achieve results by means that violate the Rules of Professional Conduct or other law; or

(c) compares the lawyer's services with other lawyers' services, unless the comparison can be factually substantiated.

RULE 7.2

Advertising

(a) Subject to the requirements of Rules 7.1 and 7.3, a lawyer may advertise services through public media, such as a telephone directory, legal directory, newspaper or other periodical, outdoor advertising, radio or television, or through written or recorded communication.

(b) A copy or recording of an advertisement or written communication shall be kept for two years after its last dissemination along with a record of when and where it was used.

(c) A lawyer shall not give anything of value to a person for recommending the lawyer's services, except that a lawyer may

(1) pay the reasonable costs of advertising or written communication permitted by this Rule;

(2) pay the usual charges of a not-for-profit lawyer referral service or legal service organization; and

(3) pay for a law practice in accordance with Rule 1.17.

(d) Any communication made pursuant to this rule shall include the name of at least one lawyer responsible for its content.

RULE 7.3

Direct Contact with Prospective Clients

(a) A lawyer shall not by in-person or live telephone contact solicit professional employment from a prospective client with whom the lawyer has no family or prior professional relationship when a significant motive for the lawyer's doing so is the lawyer's pecuniary gain.

(b) A lawyer shall not solicit professional employment from a prospective client by written or recorded communication or by in-person or telephone contact even when not otherwise prohibited by paragraph (a), if:

(1) the prospective client has made known to the lawyer a desire not to be solicited by the lawyer; or

(2) the solicitation involves coercion, duress or harassment.

(c) Every written or recorded communication from a lawyer soliciting professional employment from a prospective client known to be in need of legal services in a particular matter, and with whom the lawyer has no family or prior professional relationship, shall include the words "Advertising Material" on the outside envelope and at the beginning and ending of any recorded communication.

(d) Notwithstanding the prohibitions in paragraph (a), a lawyer may participate with a prepaid or group legal service plan operated by an organization not owned or directed by the lawyer which uses in-person or telephone contact to solicit memberships or subscriptions for the plan from persons who are not known to need legal services in a particular matter covered by the plan.

RULE 7.4

Communication of Fields of Practice

A lawyer may communicate the fact that the lawyer does or does not practice in particular fields of law. A lawyer shall not state or imply that the lawyer is a specialist except as follows:

(a) a lawyer admitted to engage in patent practice before the United States Patent and Trademark Office may use the designation "Patent Attorney" or a substantially similar designation;

(b) a lawyer engaged in Admiralty practice may use the designation "Admiralty," "Proctor in Admiralty" or a substantially similar designation; and

(c) [for jurisdictions where there is a regulatory authority granting certification or approving organizations that grant certification] a lawyer may communicate the fact that the lawyer has been certified as a specialist in a field of law by a named organization or authority but only if:

(1) such certification is granted by the appropriate regulatory authority or by an organization which has been approved by the appropriate regulatory authority to grant such certification; or

(2) such certification is granted by an organization that has not yet been approved by, or has been denied the approval available from, the appropriate regulatory authority, and the absence or denial of approval is clearly stated in the communication, and in any advertising subject to Rule 7.2, such statement appears in the same sentence that communicates the certification.

(c) [for jurisdictions where there is no procedure either for certification of specialties or for approval of organizations granting certification] a lawyer may communicate the fact that the lawyer has been certified as a specialist in a field of law by a named organization, provided that the communication clearly states that there is no procedure in this jurisdiction for approving certifying organizations.

RULE 7.5

Firm Names and Letterheads

(a) A lawyer shall not use a firm name, letterhead or other professional designation that violates Rule 7.1 A trade name may be used by a lawyer in private practice if it does not imply a connection with a government agency or with a public or charitable legal services organization and is not otherwise in violation of Rule 7.1.

(b) A law firm with offices in more than one jurisdiction may use the same name in each jurisdiction, but identification of the lawyers in an office of the firm shall indicate the jurisdictional limitations on those not licensed to practice in the jurisdiction where the office is located.

(c) The name of a lawyer holding a public office shall not be used in the name of a law firm, or in communications on its behalf, during any substantial period in which the lawyer is not actively and regularly practicing with the firm.

(d) Lawyers may state or imply that they practice in a partnership or other organization only when that is the fact.

IRS Form 8300

Form **8300**	**Report of Cash Payments Over $10,000**
(Rev. August 1994)	**Received in a Trade or Business**
Department of the Treasury Internal Revenue Service	▶ See instructions for definition of cash.
	Please type or print.

OMB No. 1545-0892

1 Check appropriate boxes if: **a** ☐ amends prior report; **b** ☐ suspicious transaction.

Part I   Identity of Individual From Whom the Cash Was Received

2 If more than one individual is involved, see instructions and check here . . . . ▶ ☐

3 Last name	**4** First name	**5** M.I.	**6** Social security number

7 Address (number, street, and apt. or suite no.)	**8** Date of birth (see instructions)

9 City	**10** State	**11** ZIP code	**12** Country (if not U.S.)	**13** Occupation, profession, or business

14 Method used to verify identity: **a** Describe identification ▶ ....

b Issued by ....   **c** Number ....

Part II   Person (See Definitions) on Whose Behalf This Transaction Was Conducted

15 If this transaction was conducted on behalf of more than one person, see instructions and check here . . . . . . ▶ ☐

16 Individual's last name or Organization's name	**17** First name	**18** M.I.	**19** Social security number

20 Doing business as (DBA) name (see instructions)	Employer identification number

21 Alien identification: **a** Describe identification ▶ ....

b Issued by ....   **c** Number ....

22 Address (number, street, and apt. or suite no.)	**23** Occupation, profession, or business

24 City	**25** State	**26** ZIP code	**27** Country (if not U.S.)

Part III   Description of Transaction and Method of Payment

28 Date cash received	**29** Total cash received $ .00	**30** If cash was received in more than one payment, check here . . . ▶ ☐	**31** Total price if different from item 29 $ .00

32 Amount of cash received (in U.S. dollar equivalent) (see instructions):

a U.S. currency $ _____ .00   (Amount in $100 bills or higher $ _____ .00)

b Foreign currency   _____ .00   (Country ▶ _____)

c Cashier's check(s)   _____ .00   Issuer's name(s) and serial number(s) of the monetary instrument(s) ▶ ....

d Money order(s)   _____ .00

e Bank draft(s)   _____ .00

f Traveler's check(s)   _____ .00

33 Type of transaction

a ☐ personal property purchased   **f** ☐ debt obligations paid
b ☐ real property purchased   **g** ☐ exchange of cash
c ☐ personal services provided   **h** ☐ escrow or trust funds
d ☐ business services provided   **i** ☐ other (specify) ▶
e ☐ intangible property purchased

34 Specific description of property or service shown in 33. (Give serial or registration number, address, etc.)

▶ ....

Part IV   Business That Received Cash

35 Name of business that received cash	**36** Employer identification number

37 Address (number, street, and apt. or suite no.)	Social security number

38 City	**39** State	**40** ZIP code	**41** Nature of your business

42 Under penalties of perjury, I declare that to the best of my knowledge the information I have furnished above is true, correct, and complete.

Sign Here

(Authorized signature of business that received cash)	(Title)	(Date signed)	( ) (Telephone number of business)

Cat. No. 62133S

Form **8300** (Rev. 8-94)

Form 8300 (Rev. 8-94)   Page **2**

Multiple Parties
(Complete applicable parts below if box 2 or 15 on page 1 is checked)

Part I   Continued—Complete if box 2 on page 1 is checked

3 Last name		**4** First name	**5** M.I.	**6** Social security number

7 Address (number, street, and apt. or suite no.)			**8** Date of birth (see instructions)

9 City	**10** State	**11** ZIP code	**12** Country (if not U.S.)	**13** Occupation, profession, or business

14 Method used to verify identity: **a** Describe identification ▶ ....

b Issued by ....   **c** Number

3 Last name		**4** First name	**5** M.I.	**6** Social security number

7 Address (number, street, and apt. or suite no.)			**8** Date of birth (see instructions)

9 City	**10** State	**11** ZIP code	**12** Country (if not U.S.)	**13** Occupation, profession, or business

14 Method used to verify identity: **a** Describe identification ▶ ....

b Issued by ....   **c** Number

Part II   Continued—Complete if box 15 on page 1 is checked

16 Individual's last name or Organization's name	**17** First name	**18** M.I.	**19** Social security number

20 Doing business as (DBA) name (see instructions)	Employer identification number

21 Alien identification: **a** Describe identification ▶ ....

b Issued by ....   **c** Number

22 Address (number, street, and apt. or suite no.)	**23** Occupation, profession, or business

24 City	**25** State	**26** ZIP code	**27** Country (if not U.S.)

16 Individual's last name or Organization's name	**17** First name	**18** M.I.	**19** Social security number

20 Doing business as (DBA) name (see instructions)	Employer identification number

21 Alien identification: **a** Describe identification ▶ ....

b Issued by ....   **c** Number

22 Address (number, street, and apt. or suite no.)	**23** Occupation, profession, or business

24 City	**25** State	**26** ZIP code	**27** Country (if not U.S.)

Item You Should Note

The term "cash" includes cashier's checks, bank drafts, traveler's checks, and money orders under certain circumstances. See the **Definitions** section of these instructions and Regulations section 1.6050I-1 for more details.

General Instructions

Who Must File.—Each person engaged in a trade or business who, during that trade or business, receives more than $10,000 in cash in one transaction or two or more related transactions, must file Form 8300. Any transactions conducted between a payer (or its agent) and the recipient in a 24-hour period are related transactions. Transactions are considered related even if they occur over a period of more than 24 hours if the recipient knows, or has reason to know, that each transaction is one of a series of connected transactions. This form may be filed voluntarily for any suspicious transaction (see **Definitions**), even if it does not exceed $10,000.

Exceptions.—Cash is not required to be reported if it is received:

● By a financial institution required to file **Form 4789**, Currency Transaction Report.

● By a casino required to file (or exempt from filing) **Form 8362**, Currency Transaction Report by Casinos, (except for cash received in nongaming businesses).

● By an agent who receives the cash from a principal, if the agent uses all of the cash within 15 days in a second transaction that is reportable on Form 8300 or on Form 4789, and discloses all the information necessary to complete Part II of Form 8300 or Form 4789 to the recipient of the cash in the second transaction.

● In a transaction that occurs entirely outside the United States. See **Pub. 1544**, Reporting Cash Payments Over $10,000 (Received in a Trade or Business), regarding transactions occurring in Puerto Rico, the Virgin Islands, and territories and possessions of the United States.

● In a transaction that is not in the course of a person's trade or business.

When and Where To File.—File Form 8300 by the 15th day after the date the cash was received. If that date falls on a Saturday, Sunday, or legal holiday, you may file the form on the next business day. File the form with the Internal Revenue Service, Detroit Computing Center, P.O. Box 32621, Detroit, MI 48232, or hand carry it to your local IRS office. Keep a copy of each Form 8300 for 5 years from the date you file it.

Statement To Be Provided.—You must provide a written statement to each person named in a required Form 8300 on or before January 31 of the year following the calendar year in which the cash is received. The statement must show the name and address of the business, the total amount of reportable cash received, and that the information was furnished to the IRS. Keep a copy of the statement for your records.

Multiple Payments.—If you receive more than one cash payment on a single transaction or on related transactions, you must report the multiple payments any time you receive a total amount in cash payments that exceeds $10,000 within any 12-month period. Report the amount received within 15 days of the date you receive the payment that causes the total amount to exceed $10,000. (If more than one report is required within 15 days, you may file a combined report. File the combined report no later than the date the earliest report, if filed separately, would be required to be filed.)

Taxpayer Identification Number (TIN).—You are required to furnish the correct TIN of the person or persons from whom you receive the cash and the person or persons on whose behalf the transaction is being conducted, if the transaction is being conducted on behalf of another person or persons. You may be subject to penalties for an incorrect or missing TIN. The TIN for an individual is the individual's social security number. For other persons, including corporations, partnerships, and estates, it is the employer identification number. (See Pub. 1544 regarding exceptions for furnishing TINs of certain nonresident alien individuals and foreign organizations.)

Penalties.—If you are required to file a return, you may be subject to penalties if you fail to file a correct and complete return on time and you cannot show that the failure was due to reasonable cause. You may also be subject to penalties if you fail to furnish a correct and complete statement to each person named in a required report on time. More severe penalties (minimum $25,000) may be imposed if the failure is due to an intentional disregard of the cash reporting requirements. In addition, penalties may be imposed for causing (or attempting to cause) a trade or business to fail to file a required report, for causing (or attempting to cause) a trade or business to file a required report containing a material omission or misstatement of fact, or for structuring (or attempting to structure) transactions to avoid the reporting requirements. These violations may also be subject to criminal prosecution which, upon conviction, may result in imprisonment (up to 5 years) or fines (up to $250,000 for individuals and $500,000 for corporations) or both.

Definitions

Cash.—The term "cash" means the following:

● U.S. and foreign coin and currency received in any transaction.

● A cashier's check, bank draft, traveler's check, or money order having a face amount of not more than $10,000 received in a **Designated Reporting Transaction** as defined below, or received in any transaction in which the recipient knows that such instrument is being used in an attempt to avoid the reporting of the transaction under section 6050I.

Note: *Cash does not include a check drawn on the payor's own account, such as a personal check, regardless of the amount.*

Designated Reporting Transaction.—A retail sale (or the receipt of funds by a broker or other intermediary in connection with a retail sale) of a consumer durable, a collectible, or a travel or entertainment activity.

*Retail sale.—*Any sale (whether or not the sale is for resale or for any other purpose) made in the course of a trade or business if that trade or business principally consists of making sales to ultimate consumers.

*Consumer durable.—*An item of tangible personal property of a type suitable under ordinary usage for personal consumption or use that can reasonably be expected to be useful for at least 1 year under ordinary usage, and that has a sales price of more than $10,000.

*Collectible.—*Any work of art, rug, antique, metal, gem, stamp, or coin.

*Travel or entertainment activity.—*An item of travel or entertainment that pertains to a single trip or event if the combined sales price of the item and all other items relating to the same trip or event that are sold in the same transaction (or related transactions) exceeds $10,000.

*Exceptions.—*A cashier's check, bank draft, traveler's check, or money order is not considered to be received in a designated reporting transaction if it constitutes the proceeds of a bank loan or if it is received as a payment on certain promissory notes, installment sales contracts, or down payment plans. See Pub. 1544 for more information.

Person.—Includes an individual, a corporation, a partnership, a trust, an estate, an association, or a company.

Recipient.—The person receiving the cash. Each branch or other unit of a person's trade or business is considered a separate recipient unless the branch receiving the cash (or a central office linking the branches) has reason to know the identity of payers making cash payments to other branches.

Transaction.—Includes the purchase of property or services, the payment of debt, the exchange of a negotiable instrument for cash, and the receipt of cash to be held in escrow or trust. A single transaction may not be broken into multiple transactions to avoid reporting.

Suspicious Transaction.—The term "suspicious transaction" means a transaction in which it appears that a person is attempting to cause Form 8300 not to be filed, or a false or incomplete form to be filed, or where there is an indication of possible illegal activity.

Specific Instructions

Complete all parts. Skip Part II if the individual in Part I is conducting the transaction on his or her behalf only.

Item 1.—If you are amending a prior report, check box 1a. Complete the appropriate items with the amended or correct information only. Complete all of Part IV. Staple a copy of the original report to the amended report.

To voluntarily report a suspicious transaction (see **Definitions**), check box 1b. For a suspicious transaction, you may also telephone the local IRS Criminal Investigation Division. If you do not know the number, please call toll-free 1-800-800-2877.

Part I

Item 2.—If two or more individuals conducted the transaction you are reporting, check the box and complete Part I on any one of the individuals. Provide the same information on the other individual(s) on the back of the form. If more than three individuals are involved, provide the same information on additional sheets of paper and attach them to this form.

Item 6.—Enter the social security number of the individual named. See **Taxpayer Identification Number (TIN)** above.

Item 8.—Enter six numerals for the date of birth of the individual named. For example, if the individual's birth date is July 6, 1960, enter 07 06 60.

Item 13.—Use fully descriptive terms such as plumber or attorney instead of nondescriptive terms such as merchant, businessman, or self-employed.

Item 14.—You must verify the name and address of the individual identified. Verification must be made by examination of a document normally accepted as a means of identification when cashing checks (for example, a driver's license, passport, or other official document). In item 14a, enter the type of document used to verify the identification. In item 14b, identify the issuer of that document. In item 14c, enter the document's number. For example, if the individual has a Utah driver's license, enter "driver's license" in item 14a, "Utah" in item 14b, and its number in item 14c.

Part II

Item 15.—If the transaction is being conducted on behalf of more than one person (for example, if the individual in Part I is buying a vehicle on behalf of two persons), check the box and complete Part II on any one of the persons. Provide the same information requested in Part II on the other person(s) on the back of the form. If more than three persons are involved, provide the same information on additional sheets of paper and attach them to this form.

Items 16 Through 19.—If the person on whose behalf the transaction was conducted is an individual, complete items 16, 17, and 18. Enter his or her social security number (SSN) in item 19. If the individual is a sole proprietor and has an employer identification number (EIN), enter both the SSN and EIN in item 19. If the person is an organization, put its name in item 16 and its EIN in item 19.

Item 20.—If a sole proprietor or other organization named in items 16 through 18 is doing business under a name other than that entered in items 16-18, enter the doing business as (DBA) name here.

Item 21.—If the person is not required to furnish a TIN (see **Taxpayer Identification Number (TIN)**), complete this item. Enter a general description of the type of official document issued to that person in item 21a (e.g., "passport"), the country that issued the document in item 21b, and the document's number in item 21c.

Part III

Item 28.—Enter the date you received the cash. If you received the cash in more than one payment, enter the date you received the payment that caused the combined amount to exceed $10,000. Also, see **Multiple Payments**.

Item 30.—Check the box if the amount shown in item 29 was received in more than one payment, e.g., as installment payments (see **Multiple Payments**) or payments on related transactions.

Item 31.—Enter the total price of the property, services, amount of cash exchanged, etc. (e.g., the total cost of a vehicle purchased, cost of catering service, exchange of currency) if the total price is different from the amount shown in item 29.

Item 32.—Enter the dollar amount of each form of cash received (see the definition of **Cash**). Show amount of foreign items in U.S. dollars. (For cashier's check, bank draft, traveler's check, and/or money order, provide the name of the issuer and the serial number of each instrument.) The sum of the amounts must equal item 29.

Item 33.—Check the appropriate box(es) that describe the transaction. If the transaction is not specified in boxes a–h, check box i and briefly describe it (e.g., car lease, boat lease, house lease, aircraft rental).

Part IV

Item 36.—Enter the EIN of your business. Enter your SSN only if your business has no EIN.

Item 41.—Describe the nature of your business. Use descriptive terms (attorney, auto dealer, jewelry dealer) rather than nondescriptive terms (business, store).

Paperwork Reduction Act Notice

The requested information is useful in criminal, tax, and regulatory investigations, for instance by directing the Federal Government's attention to unusual or questionable transactions. Trades or businesses are required to provide the information under 26 U.S.C. 6050I.

The time needed to complete this form will vary depending on individual circumstances. The estimated average time is 21 minutes. If you have comments concerning the accuracy of this time estimate or suggestions for making this form more simple, you can write to both the **Internal Revenue Service,** Attention: Reports Clearance Officer PC:FP, Washington, DC 20224; and the **Office of Management and Budget,** Paperwork Reduction Project (1545-0892), Washington, DC 20503. DO NOT send this form to either of these offices. Instead, see **When and Where To File** on page 3.

GLOSSARY

ABA Model Rules   Rules governing professional conduct promulgated by the American Bar Association and adopted to some degree in most states.

account   An economically significant component of the entity's operation.

account ledgers   A chronological listing of all transactions affecting an account; ledger.

accounting equation   Assets – liabilities = equity.

accounting principle   Rules and guidelines that promote accuracy and consistency of financial information.

accounting transaction   An economic event affecting the entity.

accounts receivable allowances   Amounts recorded as being possibly uncollectible, which are recorded only as a temporary amount and are not permanently removed from the accounts receivable balance.

accrual method   A system of preparing financial information that reflects all identifiable economic transactions as they occur.

accrued interest   Interest incurred but not yet paid at the effective date of the accrual.

accumulation account   An account reflecting only the totals of special journals, instead of each transaction.

allowance for doubtful accounts   The accepted account title for an accounts receivable allowance.

annuity   A series of equal periodic payments. In an ordinary annuity, payments are received at the end of the period; in an annuity due, the payments are received at the beginning of the period.

anticipated inflation   The expected rate of decrease in the value of money in the figure, usually expressed as an annual percentage.

asset   Tangible property and intangible rights to resources under the control of an entity, which arise from the economic activity of the entity and provide ultimate future benefits to owners.

associate (lawyer)   Lawyers who are employees of the firm and hold no equity.

associated counsel   Lawyer of counsel.

bad debts   Amounts billed that are considered to be uncollectible and are removed permanently from the accounts receivable balance.

balance sheet   A classified list of assets, liabilities, and equity showing the financial situation of an organization at a specified point in time.

balance sheet equation   Assets = liabilities + equity.

bill   A statement submitted to a client or other party detailing the obligation to the firm for services rendered and/or costs incurred in a legal representation.

billing amendment   A change or addition to a bill that has been issued.

billing rate   A value attached to lawyers' services, usually an hourly rate.

bonds   A written promise, secured by specific property, to pay a specified amount on a certain date, with or without interest payments before the due date.

bookkeeping   The accounting function concerned with establishing and maintaining economic records.

bring-forward   Record a future date for attention to a specific matter, usually a client-related matter; diarize.

capital gain†   Financial gain resulting from the sale or exchange of capital assets.

capital stock   An amount of equity an owner is required to maintain in a corporation to secure a specific portion of ownership.

cash method   A system of preparing financial information that reflects economic transactions only when there is an exchange of money.

chart of accounts   The complete listing of general ledger accounts and their corresponding numbers or abbreviations, if any.

check digit   A single digit added at the end of a numeric sequence to ensure that all numeric sequences are at least two digits different.

clearing account   A balance sheet account containing related transactions that regularly clear through another account.

client   A consumer of legal services provided by a law firm, whether or not compensated.

client accounts receivable ledger   A subsidiary ledger listing bills and payments on a client file.

client file   A specific matter undertaken by a lawyer on behalf of a client (not a file folder).

client trust ledger   A subsidiary ledger listing all trust transactions for a client's funds in a bank account.

client WIP disbursement ledger   A subsidiary ledger listing unbilled disbursements on a client file.

commingling†   The act of an agent, broker, attorney, or trustee in mingling his own property with that of his client, customer, or beneficiary.

common stock†   Ordinary capital stock in a corporation, the market value of which is based upon the worth of the corporation.

compound interest   Interest calculated on the assumption that unpaid interest becomes part of the principal for the next compounding period.

conflict of interest†   The existence of a variance between the interests of the parties in a fiduciary relationship.

conflict search   The investigation in a law firm's records to ensure that the interests of a client will not present a conflict of interest for the firm.

conservatism principle   Where there is a question of the true value, the value reflecting the lowest reasonable value for assets and income.

consistency principle   Congruity of accounting applications between accounting periods.

constructive trust†   A trust, created by operation of law, that is declared against a person who, by fraud, duress, or abuse of confidence, has obtained or holds legal title to property to which he or she has no moral or equitable right.

contingency fee   An amount payable (usually but not necessarily a percentage of an award or settlement) by a client subject to a desired outcome of a legal matter.

control account   A general ledger or memorandum account that controls transactions through its related subsidiary ledgers.

corporation†   An artificial person, existing only in the eyes of the law, to whom a state or the federal government has granted a charter to become a legal entity, separate from its shareholders, with a name of its own, under which its shareholders can act and contract and sue and be sued.

cost principle   The true value of financial transactions is reflected by the actual number of dollars exchanged in the transaction.

court-awarded fees   An amount awarded by a court to a prevailing party to be paid by the defeated party as a contribution toward the expense of litigation.

credit   An entry in double-entry bookkeeping that decreases assets and/or expenses, and/or increases liabilities, equity, and/or revenue.

debentures   Unsecured bonds.

debit   An entry in double-entry bookkeeping that increases assets and/or expenses, and/or decreases liabilities, equity, and/or revenue.

detail account   An account that always contains a record of each separate transaction affecting the account.

direct disbursement   Separate disbursements paid by individual check and often in advance of receiving the item or service.

disbursement   Payment for an item or service by the firm on behalf of the client.

dividend†   A payment made by a corporation to its stockholders, either in cash (a cash dividend), in stock (a stock dividend), or out of surplus earnings.

double-entry bookkeeping   A system of recording financial transactions in which each transaction has an equal and opposite effect in two or more accounts.

draw   A sum of money advanced to a proprietor or partner in anticipation of distribution of related net income.

earnings   An individual owner's share of net income.

economic entity   A separately identifiable unit of material activity and substance.

effective interest rate   The true interest rate in a compound interest calculation.

endorsement   A mark on the back of a check that signifies that the maker of the mark has received value for the check.

equitable title†   Title recognized as ownership in equity, even though it is not legal title or marketable title.

equity   The remaining value of an entity's assets after all obligations are met; net worth.

expense account   An approved reimbursement to personnel who purchase items and services on behalf of the firm from their own funds.

expenses   Decreases in assets incurred in supporting or incidental to normal business activity.

express trust†   A trust created by a direct or positive declaration of trust.

fee advance   An amount paid in advance to the firm and kept in its trust account for future expenses of the matter.

fee allocation   The apportionment of a firm's billed fees between its lawyers.

fiduciary relationship†   A relationship between two persons in which one is obligated to act with the utmost good faith, honesty, and loyalty on behalf of the other.

field of practice   A classification of an area of legal service.

financial information   Data related to the economic monetary events in an organization accumulated and classified to support decisions.

financial statement   A financial report in accepted form; balance sheet, income statement, statement of retained earnings, cash statement.

fiscal year   The period for which net income is distributed and taxed.

fixed fee   An agreement for a client to pay a determined amount for a specified legal service.

future value   The nominal value to which a series of payments will grow at a given interest rate.

gains   Nonrecurring and unanticipated value received in excess of the recorded value on the disposition of assets; increases in resources unrelated to the main activity of the firm.

general bank account   The firm's operating bank account.

general ledger (G/L)   The complete set of ledgers for financial accounts.

general partnership   A normal partnership.

general receipt   Payment for deposit into the firm's general account, usually payment for a client bill.

generally accepted accounting principles (GAAP)   The set of principles adopted by professional accounting bodies, industry, government, and educators providing guidelines for the preparation of financial information.

going-concern concept   The assumption that an entity will continue in its current enterprise into the indefinite future.

imputed interest rate   The rate of interest implicit in a calculation if all other variables are known.

income   The excess of total revenues over total expenses.

income statement   A classified list of revenues, direct costs against revenues, operating expenses, and gains and losses showing the financial activity during a specified period.

income statement equation   Revenue – expenses = income.

initial primary offering   The first primary offering of a public corporation.

interest   Amount charged by a lender to a borrower for the use of money.

interest rate   The percentage of the principal to be charged as interest, usually expressed on an annual basis.

interim bill   A bill rendered by the firm before the client's matter is concluded and the file closed.

internal controls   A comprehensive set of methods, procedures, forms, and approval requirements incorporated into the accounting system to safeguard assets, prevent and detect errors, ensure policies are followed, and ensure the accuracy and reliability of accounting data.

internal disbursements   Disbursements arising from a combination of goods and services that are generated within the firm on behalf of a client.

IOLTA   Interest on Lawyers' Trust Account; a program run by a state agency for collecting the interest from pooled trust accounts and directing the income toward publicly supported legal services.

joint venture†   Sometimes referred to as a joint adventure; the relationship created when two or more persons combine jointly in a business enterprise with the understanding that they will share in the profits or losses and that each will have a voice in its management.

journal   A complete record of a financial transaction; a collection of related journal entries.

journal entry   A complete record of a financial transaction.

laundering   The unlawful concealment of the source of illegally obtained funds to give an appearance of legitimacy.

lawyer of counsel   A lawyer who contracts services to a firm.

legal administrator   The senior staff member in a law firm who oversees organizational, personnel, accounting, and support matters; law office administrator.

lending terms   Conditions of the lending arrangement, including interest rate, basis of interest calculation, timing, and amount of payments.

liabilities   Obligations to pay a specific amount to a person or entity.

limitation date   A date that limits or restricts when an action can be taken—for example, the date by which a lawsuit must be initiated.

limited partnership   A limited partnership with (usually) one general partner who is responsible for the management of the enterprise and whose liability is not limited to its investment in the partnership. Limited partners usually do not become involved in management of the enterprise, and their liability is limited to the amount of their investments.

loss   Nonrecurring and unanticipated decrease in assets.

malpractice†   The failure of a professional person to act with reasonable care; misconduct by a professional person in the course of engaging in his profession.

management information   Data related to all economic events in an organization accumulated and classified to support decisions.

master profile   A standardized arrangement of conventions that regulate the recording of data.

matching principle   The recording of corresponding revenues and expenses in the same accounting period.

materiality principle   Disregarding negligible differences and transactions as being not worth recording.

memorandum ledger   A ledger that is not part of regular financial transactions, but provides information for anticipated or nonfinancial transactions; a list or schedule.

modified accrual method   A hybrid accounting method that recognizes revenue when it is billed, instead of when it is worked (full accrual) or collected (cash method).

mortgage†   A pledge of real property to secure a debt.

mortgagee†   The person to whom a mortgage is made; the lender.

mutual agency   The responsibilities and duties owed between partners.

net loss   Equivalent to negative net income.

nominal interest rate   Stated rate of interest for a lending arrangement. The nominal rate may or may not reflect the effective rate of borrowing.

objectivity principle   Dollars exchanged in a financial transaction is the best measurement of the value of the transaction.

partnership   An unincorporated unlimited-liability business organization whose purpose is to increase the wealth of two or more professional practitioner-owners through the provision of professional services to the public.

pegboard system   A manual accounting system using pressure-sensitive reproduction methods to record journals, ledgers, and subledgers concurrently.

periodicity   The somewhat arbitrary division of accounting information into periods.

personal service corporation   An incorporated limited-liability business organization whose purpose is to increase the wealth of its shareholders through the provision of professional services to the public.

petty cash   A small amount of currency and coin kept in the office to pay for items that can only reasonably be paid in cash.

pooled trust account   A bank account designed to hold the funds of more than one client.

postdated   A date on a check that is some time in the future.

posting   Recording a line from a journal in a ledger.

preferred stock†   Corporate stock that is entitled to a priority over other classes of stock, usually common stock, in distribution of the profits of the corporation (i.e., dividends) and in distribution of the assets of the corporation in the event of dissolution or liquidation.

present value   The dollar value of some amount(s) to be received in the future, as though the amounts were received today.

primary offering   The first presentation of a stock issue to the public.

prime rate   The rate charged by major financial institutions to their most creditworthy borrowers; the "risk-free" rate.

principal   Initial or capital sum.

private corporation†   A close corporation or other privately held corporation, as distinguished from a corporation whose stock is traded on a stock exchange.

profit   The excess of regular business revenues over their related costs.

proofing   Scrutinizing a check to ensure that all necessary elements are present and correct.

proprietorship   An unincorporated unlimited-liability business organization whose purpose is to increase the wealth of a sole professional practitioner-owner through the provision of professional services to the public.

public corporation†   A corporation whose stock is traded on a stock exchange, as opposed to a closely held corporation.

quantum   The amount of monetary compensation sought or awarded.

real interest   Basic cost of deferral of consumption.

realization rate   The percentage of time logged or billed in relation to the corresponding amount collected.

receipt allocation   The apportionment of a firm's collected fees between its lawyers.

recording errors   Errors in the recording of an otherwise correct and timely event.

responsible lawyer   The lawyer in a law firm who has primary contact with the client and primary responsibility for the conduct of a client's matter.

resulting trust†   A trust created by operation of law in circumstances where one person becomes vested with legal title but is obligated, as a matter of equity, to hold the title for the benefit of another person, even though there is no fraud and no declared intention to hold the property in trust.

retained earnings   The balance of income earned in all previous accounting periods that has not been distributed to owners as dividends.

retainer fees   An amount paid by a client to secure the availability of a lawyer, regardless of whether legal services are actually performed.

revenue   Increases in the assets of a business resulting from its normal operation and certain other sources.

revenue recognition principle   Revenue is recorded in the financial data when the transaction is complete, the value is determinable, and the related costs can be matched.

risk premium   Additional compensation required for a lender to advance funds to a particular borrower.

securities†   Certificates that represent a right to share in the profits of a company or in the distribution of its assets, or in a debt owed by a company or by the government.

separate trust account   A trust bank account designed to hold the funds of only one client, usually bearing interest that becomes part of the trust property.

settlor†   The creator of a trust; the person who conveys or transfers property to another (the trustee) to hold in trust for a third person (the beneficiary).

simple interest   Interest calculated as: principal × annual rate × years (or fractions of years)

source deductions   Amounts withheld from an employee's pay for remittance by the firm to a government agency.

source document   The first complete record of a transaction.

special journals   A collection of related journal entries used to simplify recording transactions in ledgers.

stable-dollar assumption   The assumption that the value of a dollar is constant over time.

stale-dated   A date on an uncertified check that is older than six months.

statement of cash flows   A financial statement showing the flow of cash within a business.

statement of retained earnings   A financial statement showing the activity of capital and retained earnings during a period.

stock market†   A market where securities are bought and sold.

stop payment   An order by a drawer to the drawee bank to refuse payment of a check when presented.

subsidiary ledger   One ledger in a set of related ledgers, which in aggregate correspond to a control account; subledger.

substantive errors   Incorrect or untimely accounting events.

summary invoice   An invoice from a supplier of client disbursements, normally listing disbursements for several files.

synoptic   A combination journal and ledger, usually for a bank or petty cash account.

term loan   A loan for a definite period, often specifying the frequency and amount of payments.

time data   Original records of time spent by lawyer and other timekeepers.

trial balance   A periodic list of the balances of all of the general ledger accounts, where the total of all debit balances is compared to the total of all credit balances; a list used in preparing financial statements.

trust†   A fiduciary relationship involving a trustee who holds trust property for the benefit or use of a beneficiary.

trust bank account ledgers   A ledger for an individual trust bank account.

trustee†   The person who holds the legal title to trust property for the benefit of the beneficiary of the trust, with such powers and subject to

such duties as are imposed by the terms of the trust and the law.

trust journal entry   A reassignment of trust property between two or more clients without a bank transaction.

trust receipt   Funds given to the firm for safekeeping.

trust transfer   Amounts transferred by the firm from a trust account to the firm's general account to pay a client's bill.

warrant†   A certificate issued by a corporation evidencing the right of its holder to receive a specified number of shares of stock in the corporation; i.e., a stock warrant or share warrant.

widely held corporation   A corporation with no clear majority or influential stockholders.

WIP disbursement deletion   Removal of an unbilled disbursement from the client disbursement ledger.

WIP time deletion   The removal of a time record from a client ledger before the record is billed.

WIP time ledgers   Subsidiary ledger for unbilled (WIP) time on a client file.

work-in-process (WIP)   Legal services already rendered, and disbursements already incurred by the firm, but not yet billed to the client.

ADDITIONAL MATERIALS AND RESOURCES

For many readers, this book will be the first complete introduction to the field of law office accounting, but it is far from the last word on the subject. Legislation and case law are always changing, and everyone working in a law office (lawyers, paralegals, and support staff) realizes that maintaining current information is a matter of survival. Further study and practical experience will expand the perspective of individual readers in different directions, and there is some excellent material available to them.

The following suggestions are by no means comprehensive, and inquisitive students of law office accounting will find many periodicals and reference lists in their local courthouse or university law library. The American Bar Association (ABA), state bars, and state bar associations regularly publish helpful material on a range of related subjects.

The Legal Profession

The legislation, rules, and regulations for all of the states in which a lawyer practices are essential in the law office. Most states promulgate rules that generally follow the model rules of the ABA, although many add particular wording to conform to other state legislation. Opinions published in law reviews and bar publications also clarify specific issues.

If the state bar or bar association does not publish notes to the state rules, the ABA publication *Annotated Model Rules of Professional Conduct* (ABA, 1992) contains a wealth of commentary on the practical usage and purpose of such rules.

The ABA distributes a wide variety of useful publications and can be contacted at:

Service Center, American Bar Association
750 North Lake Shore Drive
Chicago, IL 60611
(312) 988-6062

Other authoritative and comprehensive sources of practical guidance include:

Geoffrey C. Hazard, Jr. and W. William Hodes, *The Law of Lawyering* (Law & Business, Inc., New York, 1990)

Jonathan Lynton, Terri Mick Lyndall, *Legal Ethics and Professional Responsibility* (Delmar/LCP, 1994)

Accounting

Junior accounting staff should have access to a solid introductory accounting text for reference. Advanced staff with managerial responsibilities will find a management or cost accounting text useful as well. These are available at public libraries and college bookstores.

In locations where a user (sales) tax is imposed on legal services and disbursements, copies of the taxing authority's bulletins and regulations should be available to everyone in the office.

Trust rules of state bars often include periodic reporting standards on trust accounts. Sometimes only the required documents are specified, and the specific procedures must be inferred. All available guidelines should be kept on file for direction and reference.

The firm's CPA should be reminded to provide relevant changes and guidelines to the firm as they are adopted by the accounting profession.

Law Office Management

The Association of Legal Administrators (ALA) provides a bimonthly magazine and other reference materials to assist law office managers in specific areas such as office automation systems, human resources, and finance. Membership in the ALA is a benefit for all active firms. The ALA can be contacted at:

> The Association of Legal Administrators
> 175 East Hawthorne Parkway, Suite 325
> Vernon Hills, IL 60061
> (708) 816-1212

A useful guide to general law office management is:

> Jonathan Lynton, Donna Masinter, Terri Mick Lyndall, *Law Office Management for Paralegals* (Delmar/LCP, 1992)

Other Materials from This Author

The author is continually producing related works in this area including custom course design, workbooks, foreign supplements and annual updates, brief guides for special areas (such as law firm collections, selecting the best accounting software, and managing a bookkeeping practice for law firms), as well as management tools including a firm-specific operations manual. Contact the author through:

> LexSupport Publishing Inc.
> 2nd Floor, 827 West Pender Street
> Vancouver, B.C. V6C 3G8
> (604) 683-2584

INDEX

System Requirements

- IBM compatible with 386 processor or higher
- Windows 3.1 or higher with DOS 3.3 or higher
- 4 mbytes RAM
- One hard disk drive with at least 12 mbytes of disk space available (15 mbytes for full program)
- Monitors: Hercules, EGA, VGA, SVGA or higher
- Mouse required

Installation

Place disk 1 of the working model in your A or B drive. From the *Program Manager* within *Windows*, select *File* then *Run*.

TYPE: **A:INSTALL** *or* **B:INSTALL**

CLICK: ***OK***

Follow the on-screen instructions. When the installation is complete, a program group entitled *Timeslips Deluxe Working Model* will be created with icons entitled *TSReport, TSTimer* and *TSLayout*. Double-click on the icon entitled *TSReport*.

After you complete the Guided Tour and/or Tutorial, you are encouraged to explore parts of the program that are not covered. You can find out more about any feature by accessing the *Help* system that is provided with *Timeslips*. The *Help* system can be accessed by pressing **[F1]**, selecting the ***Help*** button, or choosing an item from the *Help* menu.

Starting *Timeslips*

TSReport, TSTimer, and *TSLayout* can be loaded from the *Program Manager* group independently. To begin, load *Windows* in the usual manner and display the *Timeslips Deluxe* program group. Run *TSReport*. When you first run the *Timeslips Deluxe Working Model*, the *Guided Tour Navigator* will be displayed. (If no *Navigator* is displayed, select *Navigator* from the *Help* menu.) To begin the Guided Tour or the Tutorial, select the button entitled **Learn Timeslips Deluxe**. You will be presented with five choices, described below.

DOUBLE CLICK:

The Overview

Select this option to take the Guided Tour, which will quickly show you the many features *Timeslips* has to offer, explaining exactly what each feature means to you. This process takes less than twenty minutes.

The Tutorial

The Tutorial is unique because it allows you to learn the program at your own pace, without holding a manual at your side. The exercises of the Tutorial will be displayed on your screen, providing you with information about each dialog's functions, and steps to perform to learn how to use the program.

Explore - Learning on your own

Some software users prefer to explore a new program on their own, without performing a set of Tutorial instructions. If you like, you may blaze your own trail, exploring the functions of the program using the Tutorial data we've prepared for you. Each time you select a button on the *Navigator*, additional information about that feature will be displayed along with the dialog opened by that button.

Whichever option you choose, you'll come away with a better understanding of *Timeslips*. These procedures may be used as often as you like, and are particularly useful in training new staff.

You may exit out of the *Overview* or *Tutorial* at any time by clicking on the *Script Control* icon located at the top right of the display, and selecting *Stop Script* (or just press **[Ctrl-Break]**).